THE
CELTIC
WORLD

BARRY CUNLIFFE

PROFESSOR OF EUROPEAN ARCHAEOLOGY, UNIVERSITY OF OXFORD

THE CELTIC WORLD

DESIGNED BY

EMIL M. BÜHRER

CONSTABLE

LONDON

Published in Great Britain 1992
by Constable and Company Ltd
3 The Lanchesters, 162 Fulham Palace Road
London W6 9ER
A Production of EMB-Service for Publishers
Copyright © 1990 by EMB-Service for Publishers
ISBN 0 09 471640 4
Printed in Singapore

CONTENTS

> *Physically the Celts are terrifying in appearance, with deep-sounding and very harsh voices. In conversation they use few words and speak in riddles, for the most part hinting at things and leaving a great deal to be understood. They frequently exaggerate with the aim of extolling themselves and diminishing the status of others. They are boasters and threateners and given to bombastic self-dramatization, and yet they are quick of mind and with good natural ability for learning. They have also lyric poets whom they call Bards. They sing to the accompaniment of instruments resembling lyres, sometimes a eulogy and sometimes a satire.*
>
> Diodorus Siculus, first century B.C.

At any time or place, you will find them

The Celts seen through Roman eyes were ferocious, flamboyant, and tensed with energy. This small bronze figure found near Rome and probably dating to the third century B.C. gives a brilliant impression of a Celt in battle wearing only his helmet, neck torque, and belt. Polybius describes how the *Gaesatae* fought in this manner, naked but for their torques.

A rather calmer impression is given by the warrior shown on the Gundestrup caldron *(right),* a large silver vessel of the second or first century B.C. found in a bog in Denmark. He marches to battle clothed in tight-fitting trousers, armed with shield, spear, and possibly a sword.

THE PORTRAIT
OF A CIVILIZATION

ready to face danger, even if they have nothing on their side but their own strength and courage. —Strabo

The Celts were the inhabitants of Europe in the pre-Roman period, occupying a vast territory stretching from the Pyrenees to the Rhine and from Ireland to Romania. They were barbarian in the classical sense of the word, energetic, quick-tempered, and "war-mad"; but their craftsmen created a brilliant art style and by the first century B.C. a truly urban society had begun to develop in many areas. It was against these people that the Roman armies moved in the first centuries B.C. and A.D., leaving only a Celtic fringe in Scotland, Ireland, Wales, and Brittany to survive unconquered. When the Roman world collapsed in the fifth century A.D., the Celts once more emerged from the obscurity of their windswept Atlantic regions. Populations moved from Ireland to Britain and from Cornwall to Brittany, while individuals—chiefly monks—carried the ideals of Irish monasticism deep into Europe. Politically and culturally the western Celts have been persecuted and subjugated; today their cry for the recognition of their separate identity is becoming louder... Our aim in this work is to follow the Celts throughout their entire history, beginning in the vague realms of European pre-history. But far more than a chronological account, the study of Celtic achievement in all its diversity acquaints us with a people too often dismissed as barbaric, too long neglected and misunderstood—a whole civilization, many-faceted but with an underlying unity.

Until just before 6000 B.C. most of Europe was still peopled with communities who subsisted by hunting wild animals and by collecting uncultivated fruits and plants. Yet a mere four thousand years later the first true European civilization had begun to emerge among the Mycenaean-Minoan cultures of the east Mediterranean. Thereafter, with minor setbacks, the Mediterranean became the forcing ground for the great civilizations of Greece and Rome while from the depths of temperate Europe the barbarian communities looked on, sometimes benefiting from lively trade and reciprocal exchange with their southern neighbors, sometimes moving against them

A PEOPLE WHOSE ROOTS LIE BURIED IN THE PAST

in violent onslaughts. Finally these barbarian communities were overcome and largely absorbed, as Rome perfected its military machine and employed it for colonialist expansion.

THE GREEK VIEW OF THE CELTS

One of the many cultural and intellectual advances which sprang from the civilization of Greece was the development of the scientific study of history and of geography. Curious about the barbarian peoples with whom they came into contact, and about whom they heard from travelers in distant lands, Greek writers became concerned to describe, in systematic fashion, the wider world and its populations. In the fourth century B.C. Ephorus claimed that there were four great barbarian peoples in the known world: the Libyans in Africa, the

Persians in the east, and in Europe the Scythians and the Celts.

The Celts (*Keltoi* in Greek) were, by then, well known to classical writers. The earliest reference to them was in an early sixth-century B.C. account of coastal travel from Cadiz and Marseilles. The original document has long since disappeared, but by a remarkable chance it is quoted in a Coastal Survey *(Ora Maritima)* compiled by Festus Rufus Avienus, Roman proconsul of Africa in A.D. 566. Though obscure in detail, it gives the clear impression that peoples, who could be classed together as Celts, lived close to the North Sea, in France, and in the southwest of Spain. This geographical spread is to some extent confirmed by Hecataeus of Miletus, who was writing about 500 B.C. He mentions two Celtic towns, Narbonne in southern France and Nyrax, probably in Carinthia, and in describing the Greek colony at Marseilles he notes that it lies close to the land of the Celts. Half a century or so later the great Greek historian Herodotus tells us that the Celts were living in the upper Danube valley, near the Pyrenees, and in Spain.

Tantalizing and imprecise though these scraps of evidence are, the general impression to be gained is that by about 600 B.C. most of western Europe from Austria to the Atlantic was occupied by tribes who were sufficiently similar to be thought of as culturally one people and who probably referred to themselves by a name which when translated into Greek sounded like *Keltoi.*

THE BEGINNINGS OF SETTLED LIFE IN EUROPE

How and when this cultural unity emerged can only be assessed by considering the archaeological evidence for man's development in Europe from the sixth to the first millennium B.C. Sometime within this span, so crucial to the history of the world, must lie the ethnogenesis of the Celts.

The spread of food production as a mode of subsistence, as opposed to food collection, was of vital significance in the development of European society. It freed man from the necessity to travel vast distances in seasonal pursuit of his food supply and allowed him, indeed forced him, to settle in hamlets and villages close

As time went by,
men began to build huts
and to use skins and fire.
Male and female
learnt to live together
in a stable union and
to watch over
their joint progeny.

Then it was
that humanity first
began to mellow.
Then neighbors began
to form mutual alliances,
wishing neither to do
nor to suffer violence
among themselves.

Lucretius, Book V

to his growing crops. A more sedentary way of life led to the creation of larger communities, to a growth in population, and to craft specialization, thus paving the way for the eventual emergence of civilization.

It was in the latter part of the seventh millennium B.C. that food-producing economies first appeared in southeastern Europe, in Crete, Greece, and Bulgaria, encouraged and no doubt directly inspired by the farming communities already established in nearby Anatolia.

Once established on the European mainland, food-producing economies spread rapidly. Within fifteen hundred years (by 4500 B.C.) there were farmers as far west as Holland; soon after 4000 B.C. southern and western France were colonized; by 3000 B.C. farming communities had sprung up over most of the British Isles; and within a few centuries food was being produced in Denmark. Thus it took only three and a half thousand years for communities extending over the whole of Mediterranean and temperate Europe to acquire the skills necessary to ensure a constant supply of food, controlled, albeit sometimes precariously, by their own skills and efforts.

In the initial zone of settlement, in Greece and the southern Balkans, permanent villages soon sprang up. Rectangular houses, built of packed mud or sun-dried bricks and roofed with steeply sloping gabled roofs of timber, were renewed many times on the same site, each one being erected on the debris of its predecessor. So intense was the activity that many of the villages created great mounds (or tells). At Karanovo in Bulgaria the Neolithic occupation gave rise to a mound twelve meters in height, while at Knossos, on Crete, below the latest palace, trial excavations have shown there to be seven meters of accumulated Neolithic debris.

As time went on, the Neolithic villages grew. At Knossos the earliest settlement covered half a hectare (nearly an acre), by the end of the Neolithic period it was nine times the size, while on the Greek mainland at Sesklo the settlement eventually reached ten hectares in extent.

This dramatic growth in the size of the population in southeastern Europe was matched by the speed with which farming communities spread across the rest of the continent. There were two main lines of

And this race of men from the plains
were all the harder, for hard land
had borne them; built on stronger
and firmer bones, and endowed with mighty
sinew, they were a race
undaunted by heat or cold, plague,
strange new foodstuffs. For many years,
among the beasts of the earth
they led their life. And none was yet
a driver of the curved plow,
none yet could turn the soil with iron blade,
nor bury a new shoot in the ground
nor prune the ripened branch from the tree.

Lucretius

advance: through temperate Europe along the easily worked loess soils which fringed the Danube and the Rhine, and around the northern shores of the Mediterranean.

The peasant communities who spread westward along the Danube soon adapted their way of life to suit their new environment. The most important difference was that since the area into which they moved was heavily forested, the most efficient agricultural regime involved a slash-and-burn economy. A community moving into an area of virgin forest would cut all easily

Until man could begin to control his principal food sources, he was dependent on the seasonal movement of the herds, on which he preyed, and on the collection of plant foodstuffs. But once animals had been domesticated and plants cultivated, the way was prepared for a more sedentary mode of life. The "Neolithic Revolution," as this complex of developments was once called, took

place in Anatolia and the Fertile Crescent (a wide zone of hilly land stretching from the Persian Gulf north to Syria and south again through the Lebanon) in the eighth and seventh millennia B.C. But as early as the ninth millennium, in a cave and village site at Zawi Chemi Shanidar, in modern Iraq, the first signs of the incipient domestication of sheep have been recognized. Among the early Neolithic communities sheep and goats were herded while two-rowed barley, emmer, spelt, and peas were cultivated. As the art of food production spread southward into the valleys of the Tigris and Euphrates, modes of production changed to suit the different environmental conditions and cattle became a significant element in the economy—as this seal stamp from Mesopotamia, dating to the end of the fifth millennium B.C., vividly demonstrates.

manageable undergrowth, reserving the best timber for building the great long houses in which they lived, and would burn the rest, the ash adding to the fertility of the soil. Amid the charred stumps the crops would be sown. After several seasons of cropping, soil fertility would begin to fail and the group would have to move on to a new territory. Some part of the population would perhaps return to old sites to begin again after the forest had regenerated, while other families would move off farther west to break new ground. In this way a vast territory from Romania to Holland was colonized in little more than seven hundred years.

By the third millennium it is possible to recognize significant changes. The cultural unity of the period of colonization was beginning to break down into distinct regional groups, while many of the settlements now show signs of defensive works. No doubt the phase of rapid movement

was over and people were beginning to settle down in defined territories as growth in population and the pressure on land forced them to protect their homes and their flocks.

While temperate Europe was in this way being opened up, other groups of farmers were working their way around the northern shores of the Mediterranean establishing coastal settlements in Italy, Sicily, southern France, and parts of Spain and Portugal. Once more the movement was rapid. Neolithic communities were established in Italy by 5600 and southern France by about 4000 B.C. The essentially coastal distribution of these early settlements strongly suggests that the colonists were sailors, probably fishermen as well as farmers, working their way from place to place and setting up new settlements wherever a suitable landfall was made.

In France the two streams of colonists met and merged and it was from here, sometime towards the middle of the fourth millennium, that boatloads of settlers, together with their seed, corn, and animals, began to cross the Channel to Britain and to brave the Celtic Sea to reach Ireland.

It is in these western regions, Iberia, France, and Britain, that the religious life of the Neolithic farmers reached its highest peak of elaboration, or more correctly, it is here that the most remarkable of their religious monuments survive. The dead were buried in collective tombs frequently built of large stone slabs set within mounds of soil and rubble. These megalithic tombs extend along the Atlantic seaboard from Spain to Denmark, and all seem to have been built in the comparatively short period between ca. 3500 and 2500 B.C.

Even more impressive are the sacred sites not apparently associated with burial: the finely built stone temples of Malta, the stone alignments of Brittany and Britain, and the circular henge monuments built of upright stones or timbers and often enclosed with banks and ditches which occur in some numbers in Britain and are most dramatically represented today by Avebury on Salisbury Plain in southern England. There is now little doubt that those responsible for their construction had a detailed knowledge of the movement of the sun and moon and were able to incorporate observations, made over many generations, into their planning and construction.

While these remarkable developments were taking place in the west, other parts of Europe, favored by their mineral wealth, were developing special skills in the mining of copper ores and the extraction of copper to make ornaments and weapons. The earliest exploitation of metal in Europe took place in the eastern Balkans as early as the fourth millennium, probably under influences from the east where copper working was by this time under way. Not long after, the east Alpine ores began to be worked as did those in Thuringia, and by 2400 B.C. the communities of Almeria, Algarve, and Alemtejo in Iberia were skillfully involved in extracting, alloying, and casting copper. Rich though these areas were in raw materials, they did not achieve the heights of civilization to which their more poorly endowed neighbors in Greece and the Aegean were soon to aspire.

MINOAN-MYCENAEAN CIVILIZATION

The rise of Minoan-Mycenaean civilization is one of the most dramatic events in European history, but to understand its basis it is necessary to look briefly at the situation in the area in the third millennium. During this period there developed in the Troad (in what is now western Turkey) a warlike society whose chieftains and their retainers lived in small defended settlements like the early "cities" on the site of Troy. There were a number of them, each commanding distinct territories and each supporting specialist smiths whose skills extended to alloying copper with tin to give greater strength to the weapons which they made. Tin was a rare commodity which had to be obtained by exchange via neighboring tribes. Thus there soon developed a complex network of reciprocal exchange involving the movement of tin and of other raw materials such as gold, silver, and lapis lazuli. As the Greek islands were drawn into the network, so the range of commodities was extended: silver from Siphnos, marble from Paros, and obsidian from Melos soon began to be exploited in the ever expanding system of exchange which linked Greece, Anatolia, and Crete. By the end of the third millennium one center, Crete, began to emerge above the rest. Its comparative fertility, long tradition

of settled economy, and large population, as well as its central position, were all factors favoring a quickening pace of development. By 2000–1900 B.C. there emerged on the island a palace-centered sociopolitical organization which can fairly be classed as a civilization. The island was divided into a number of distinct territories each dominated by a palace which would have served as the administrative and economic center of its region. The palaces were above all centers of redistribution where commodities were collected and stored prior to exchange and where manufactur-

The importance of cattle to the primitive Neolithic economy was considerable. Even a small cow would provide at least three times more meat than a sheep, but it was also the source of a wide range of other products: milk, leather, horn, bone, and blood. (Blood was an important source of salt among primitive agriculturists.) Moreover, the cow was a beast of burden.

This magnificent frieze, in bronze, stone, and bitumen, from the façade of a temple at Tell al'Ubaid in Mesopotamia, dating to the early third millennium, shows dairying activities in progress.
Although the forests of Europe supported wild oxen, domesticated cattle, together with sheep and goats, were introduced into southeast Europe from Anatolia by the earliest farmers.

ing industries were centered. Minoan culture flourished in a time of peace and stability, but two natural disasters, apparently earthquakes of some magnitude, intervened in about 1750 and 1500 B.C. It was after the latter, which must have shaken the strength of the community, that there is some evidence to suggest a takeover by a new hierarchy dominated by Greek speakers from the mainland Mycenaean culture.

The Mycenaean communities of mainland Greece were organized in small chiefdoms ruled by a prince or king called a *wanax* who, together with his retainers, lived in a fortified palace of the kind found at Mycenae, Tiryns, and Gla. Enormous energy was lavished on the tombs of the aristocracy, not only in the building of colossal structures like the so-called Treasury of Atreus at Mycenae (with its fine corbeled vault fifteen meters in height and diameter and its imposing entrance passage) but also

One of the greatest of Europe's religious monuments is Stonehenge on Salisbury Plain in southern England—a complex ritual site used and modified over many centuries. The earliest phase consisted of the outer bank and ditch with a circle of holes on the inside of the bank. Later a circle of blue stones, brought from Wales, was erected; and in its final stage (first half of second millennium B.C.) the great trilithons which now dominate the site were put up.

Pottery is a very important indicator of cultural differences and is much used by archaeologists to plot regional and chronological changes. Vessels like these two cremation urns of the Urnfield culture of southern Germany can readily be distinguished in form and decoration from this "bell beaker" from Britain, which is almost a thousand years older.

These six maps show, in very simplified diagrammatic form, significant successive stages in the development of European prehistoric culture. Although movements of people were involved, it is now clear that local inventiveness also played a role.

in providing the dead, buried in the somewhat earlier shaft graves at Mycenae, with quantities of gold, silver, ivory, and jewelry of a quality and variety never before seen in Europe.

It has been necessary to digress briefly to consider the Minoan-Mycenaean culture of the Aegean in the second millennium in order to understand something of the cultural influences which impinged upon central and western Europe at this time. Aegean civilization, with its complex network of exchange systems and its conspicuous consumption in beautifying the life and death of its leaders, made enormous demands on the raw material resources of Europe. Tin was acquired from northern Germany, Armorica, and Britain, gold from Ireland and Spain, amber from the Baltic,

and no doubt there was much more besides: rare woods, herbs, furs, and a host of other commodities no longer recognizable in the archaeological record.

The stimulus to production and exchange, which the Minoan-Mycenaean culture created, impinged upon much of Europe. In Armorica, Wessex, Germany, northern Italy, and Denmark flourishing cultures developed. All the while that the Minoan-Mycenaean world served as the pulse, the circulatory network of reciprocal exchange could invigorate far-flung parts of Europe.

The end came soon after 1200 B.C. The Hittite empire in Asia collapsed as the result of attacks by enemies from without, and rebellion within, while at the same time the Egyptian records talk of marauders

NEOLITHIC CULTURES

From the sixth to the third millennium, food-producing economies spread across Europe with astonishing speed, overland by way of the Danube, and by sea.

MEGALITHIC STRUCTURES

The third millennium saw the development, in western Europe, of a religious architecture which used large stone blocks to build tombs and temples.

BRONZE TECHNOLOGY

Knowledge of copper and bronze working developed in southeast Europe about 4000 B.C. and spread rapidly by the second millennium.

coming from the sea causing panic further heightened by invasions from Palestine. In this time of unrest the cultural and economic system of Aegean civilization broke down. Its structure had been complex and refined. Once the delicate balance had been upset by external troubles disturbing its essential systems of exchange and redistribution, the entire edifice tumbled and the Aegean plunged into a Dark Age from which, four centuries later, a greater civilization—that of Greece—was to emerge, rooted in the old.

URNFIELD CULTURE

With the loss of the stimulus provided by the Minoan-Mycenaean world, the pace of development in central and western Europe slackened: new centers of innovation and new axes of power emerged. This period, generally referred to in archaeological shorthand as the Urnfield period, is typified by the appearance of large cremation cemeteries, the ashes of the dead interred in urns. The tradition took form in Hungary sometime in the thirteenth century B.C. and was rapidly adopted farther west, in the area between the Elbe and Vistula, in southern Germany and the Alpine area, and in the Po Valley and the Italian peninsula. By the tenth century this entire region shared a similar culture, though regional differences in pottery styles and decorative techniques used on the now copious bronze work emphasize local differences. It is

difficult to resist the conclusion that, freed from their links with Aegean civilization, the communities of barbarian Europe established new and closer links of their own leading to a remarkable degree of convergent development.

Soon elements of the Urnfield culture penetrated the west, appearing in the Low Countries, France, Spain, and Britain. Whether to interpret this phenomenon in terms of a westward folk movement of Urnfield invaders, or to see it in terms of a gradual expansion of the exchange and redistribution system embracing the western communities, is a matter of debate. Probably we will never know the answer, but what is abundantly clear is that it was within this Late Bronze Age cultural complex of barbarian Europe that the Celts had their origins. The word *Celts* may have been the name of a particularly powerful tribe or even of a ruling household, or it may have been a generic term by which the disparate groups of central and western Europe distinguished themselves from their more distant neighbors. Once more we will never know. What is significant is that the whole region was bound by a common culture and that they spoke dialects of a branch of the Indo-European language group which linguists now recognize as sufficiently similar to be classed together and called Celtic. It was a realization of these things that allowed the early Greek geographers to generalize about the *Keltoi* of Europe—one of the four great peoples of the barbarian world.

Metal types also show marked regional and chronological variations. One region to support a highly developed bronze industry was Denmark (in spite of the fact that all the metal had to be imported). This elaborately decorated belt fitting of bronze, dating to about the fifteenth century B.C., from Langstrup, Zealand, indicates the skill of the Danish craftsmen. Belt plates of this kind have been found in a number of graves of females.

Throughout the Neolithic period and much of the Bronze Age, stone formed the principal material from which heavy-duty tools and weapons were made. Greater efficiency in making cutting edges was achieved by polishing the stone. Stone implements continued to be used throughout the Early Bronze Age, but it is frequently possible to see that they were being made in imitation of the more expensive bronze types. These stone axes of Neolithic date come from Switzerland.

THE BEAKER CULTURE

A mobile group, recognized largely from their distinctive pottery, can be traced in various parts of Europe in the early second millennium.

URNFIELD CULTURES

Following the breakdown of Aegean civilization, ca. 1200 B.C., central Europe developed a distinctive Late Bronze Age culture from which the Celts emerged.

HALLSTATT CULTURE

By about 700 B.C. the Hallstatt culture—the culture of the Celts—covered much of western Europe. It lasted into the fifth century B.C.

The expansion of the various cultures in Europe occurred in stages. Red shows the first phase; brown, the second; and yellow, the final stage.

15

HALLSTATT AND LA TÈNE CULTURES

rich by exchanging its salt for other commodities. It also occupied a significant position on the route along which Baltic amber passed to the Mediterranean.

Shown on these pages are typical objects of Hallstatt and La Tène culture. *From left to right:*

Horse rider used as decoration on a sixth-century bronze axe from Hallstatt.

Bronze pail, elaborately decorated in repoussé style. Sixth century, from Hallstatt.

When, in the early years of the nineteenth century, the great Danish archaeologist C.J. Thomsen was attempting to bring some order into the national archaeological collection in Copenhagen, he hit upon the scheme of dividing the prehistoric period in Europe into three ages—an age of Stone, an age of Bronze, and an age of Iron. This simple classification has remained a convenient shorthand ever since. But as the pace of discovery quickened during the nineteenth century, finer subdivisions were called for to contain the bewildering mass of new data that flooded into our museums and into private collections.

In 1846, on the shores of Lake Hallstatt in Austria, amid the magnificent mountain country of the Salzkammergut, Georg Ramsauer, director of the Hallstatt state mine, began to excavate the graves of a prehistoric cemetery where a flourishing community had buried their dead in the first half of the first millennium B.C. Between 1846 and 1862 he uncovered no less than 980 bodies. In 1876 the Vienna Academy of Sciences began to excavate

Small bronze figure, Hallstatt period, showing the dress of the period.

Human head detail from a fifth-century gold bracelet from a grave at Reinheim, Germany.

Iron spearhead of the third to second century B.C. from the site of La Tène, Switzerland.

Insular Celtic art on a cart handle found in the River Thames.

A brooch terminal of the fourth century from Oberwittighausen, Germany.

the nearby prehistoric salt mine. The finds were spectacular, not for their wealth but for the remarkable degree to which the salt-laden soil had preserved common things like the protective clothing of the prehistoric miners, the framed leather sacks which they had used to carry the rock salt, and their wooden implements.

Meanwhile in Switzerland other important discoveries were being made at La Tène, on the banks of Lake Neuchâtel. At the northeastern end, where the River Thielle flowed into the lake, a lowering of the water level in 1858 revealed lines of blackened timbers projecting from the mud. The discovery was immediately investigated by archaeologists sent from Zurich. The museum authorities were well prepared for such eventualities, for a few years before, when the waters of the Lake of Zurich were low, they had discovered the remains of several prehistoric settlements along the shore. At La Tène they were not disappointed; vast quantities of Iron Age metalwork were found: swords in their decorated sheaths, spears, shield bosses, horse gear, tools of all kinds to-

The discoveries at La Tène had provided a range of artifacts which could be compared with the finds from Hallstatt. They were clearly different and later. Thus when the Swedish archaeologist B.E. Hildebrand came to write of the Iron Age in 1872, he divided it into an earlier and a later phase named after the two great type sites of Hallstatt and La Tène. But archaeologists were not content with such a simple scheme: soon elaborations and subdivisions were introduced. The Hallstatt culture was divided into four phases called A, B, C, D, while the La Tène period was subdivided into three, I, II, and III. Although these terminologies are still in use, work in this century has focused on further refinements of phasing and of dating, each regional sequence producing idiosyncrasies of its own. As a working generalization, however, we can say that Hallstatt A and B phases belong to the Late Bronze Age and date roughly to the period 1100–700 B.C.; Hallstatt C (the first iron-using phase) falls within the seventh century; Hallstatt D spans the sixth and extends into the fifth. The La Tène phase begins in the second half of the fifth century and continues until the spread of Roman power swamps native culture, for which the dates differ across Europe.

Above all we must remember that the Hallstatt–La Tène terminology is simply a classificatory convenience imposed by archaeologists upon the changing cultures of late prehistoric Europe. The names do not imply different ethnic groups. Quite the contrary, it is highly probable that all communities which fall within this classification were Celts.

gether with ornaments, coins, and a host of other objects. For years it was conventional to regard the wealth of material recovered from La Tène as a votive deposit thrown into the lake to placate the gods. Recent scientific research has suggested, however, that it is more likely to have been a domestic and industrial settlement on dry land which was suddenly overwhelmed by a flood.

Above: Hallstatt occupies a spectacular location in the Austrian mountains on the side of a lake. The late nineteenth-century excavations of the salt mines and cemetery have made it one of the most famous prehistoric sites in Europe. Painting by Isidor Engl.

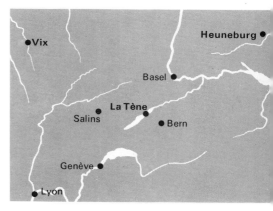

La Tène culture (fifth century onward): The type-site for the second stage of the European Iron Age is La Tène on the ancient course of the River Thielle, which flows into Lake Neuchâtel. Although producing a wide range of material, La Tène did not occupy the central position in the later Iron Age that Hallstatt did in the earlier.

THE EMERGENCE OF
THE CELTS

Celtic Europe in the Hallstatt period,
sixth and seventh centuries B.C., is
shown in brown shading on the map.
By the second century B.C. the Celts
reached their fullest expansion
(lighter shade).

White: Celtic agglomerations

Green: Celtic archaeological sites

Red: Important non-Celtic cities

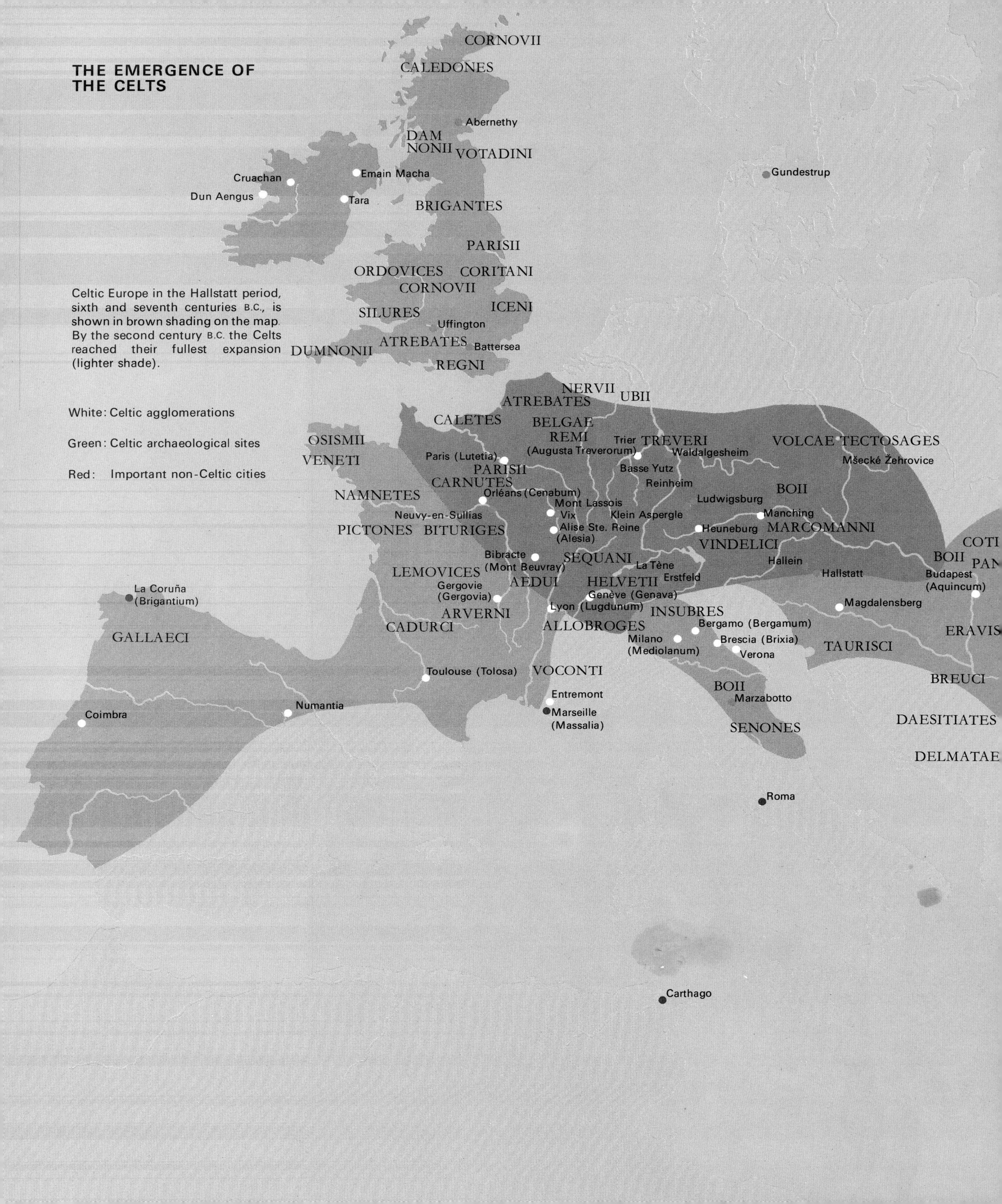

CORNOVII

CALEDONES

Abernethy

DAM
NONII VOTADINI

Cruachan

Dun Aengus

Emain Macha

Tara

BRIGANTES

Gundestrup

PARISII

ORDOVICES CORITANI

CORNOVII

SILURES   ICENI

Uffington

DUMNONII ATREBATES Battersea

REGNI

NERVII UBII
ATREBATES
CALETES   BELGAE
OSISMII   REMI
VENETI   Paris (Lutetia) (Augusta Treverorum) TREVERI   VOLCAE TECTOSAGES
                               Trier   Mšecké Žehrovice
                   PARISII   Basse Yutz
CARNUTES   Reinheim
NAMNETES   Orléans (Cenabum)   Ludwigsburg   BOII
          Neuvy-en-Sullias Mont Lassois   Manching
PICTONES BITURIGES Vix Klein Aspergle Heuneburg MARCOMANNI
                   Alise Ste. Reine   COTI
                   (Alesia)   VINDELICI   BOII PAN
          Bibracte   SEQUANI   La Tène   Hallein   Budapest
LEMOVICES (Mont Beuvray)   HELVETII Erstfeld   Hallstatt   (Aquincum)
          Gergovie   AEDUI   Genève (Genava)
          (Gergovia)   Magdalensberg
La Coruña   Lyon (Lugdunum)   INSUBRES   ERAVIS
(Brigantium)   ARVERNI   ALLOBROGES Bergamo (Bergamum)
GALLAECI   CADURCI   Milano   Brescia (Brixia) TAURISCI
                                            (Mediolanum) Verona
                        Toulouse (Tolosa) VOCONTI   BREUCI
                                    Entremont   BOII
Coimbra   Numantia   Marseille   Marzabotto   DAESITIATES
                                    (Massalia)
                                                  SENONES   DELMATAE

Roma

Carthago

TEVRISCI

NII

Olbia

ograd
ngidunum)

ORDISCI

DARDANI

TROCMI

Ankara
(Ancyra)

TECTOSAGES

TOLISTOBOGII

Pergamum

Delphi

The eighth century B.C. was a crucial time for the emergence of the Celtic peoples, a time of change and readjustment.

The Urnfield communities of central and western Europe—from about 1300 to 700—have left little evidence to suggest that there was any great disparity in wealth between the leaders and their subjects. Some burials have, admittedly, produced elaborate weapons or personal ornaments suggesting a certain level of wealth appropriate to a chieftain or warrior, but the stark differences of the preceding periods are unknown at this time—until the eighth century, when we begin to find hints of the emergence of a wealthy class. At Hart-an-der-Alz in Bavaria, for example, a cremation was found accompanied by a range of fine pottery together with three bronze vessels, representing the dead man's feast, his sword, and the bronze fittings from the wooden cart which would have conveyed him to the funeral pyre: here is a man above other men. It was at about this time too that evidence for horses, in the form of bridle fittings, increases; we are on the threshold of significant changes in the socio-political system.

Factors which may well have been instrumental in these social changes were the events now being played out in eastern Europe, the Pontic steppes, and beyond. We know that in this period the nomadic and semi-nomadic tribes whose traditional homeland lay in the steppe lands fringing the north shores of the Black Sea—peoples known to Greek writers as Cimmerians—were coming under increasing pressures from their easterly neighbors, Scythians. Eventually they decided to yield and move off. One branch penetrated Anatolia and throughout the seventh century served as a mercenary army in the battles between the kingdom of Uratu and the Assyrians, their name appearing many times in Assyrian documents of the period. Another group seems to have moved off westward into Europe, spreading along the Danube into Bulgaria and reaching as far west as the Great Hungarian Plain, where their burials, with echoes of their Pontic origins, have recently been recognized. It is possible that the appearance of these foreigners, bringing with them finely bred horses, may in some way have influenced the emerging aristocracy of the west.

19

Traces of the Celts can be found almost anywhere in temperate Europe. Their fortifications—hillforts and oppida—are to be seen spreading in a broad arc from Yugoslavia to the north of Scotland; the museums of Europe store thousands of objects recovered from the excavation of graves and of settlement sites or dredged from rivers and bogs; while many of our great cities, including Budapest, Paris, Belgrade, stand on Celtic foundations.

But the influence of the Celts is even more pervading: elements of the Celtic language survive in modern place names in many parts of Europe. The *dun* element in names

DISCOVERY OF THE CELTS

like London probably derives from the Celtic *dúnon* meaning a "fort" or "strong," while *vindos,* "white," and *maros,* "big," are name elements still recurring from place to place. Descriptive words like these, referring to natural landscape features, passed easily into everyday usage even though the area might be overrun by an alien culture with a language of its own. What makes the Celts live is that our knowledge of them does not depend solely upon dead scattered relics—archaeological and linguistic—but is greatly enlivened by descriptions of them as a people which come down to us from many classical authors. But even more remarkable is the survival of a considerable body of Celtic literature in the form of an oral tradition of heroic folktales which were eventually written down in Ireland in the latter part of the first millennium A.D. To read them today is to place oneself immediately in direct and startling communication with the world of the Celts, while to hear Gaelic, Welsh, or Irish spoken in the western fringes of Britain is to experience an eerie echo from the past.

The most dramatic surviving monuments left by the Celts are their hillforts—massively defended settlements which dominate the landscape. Old Oswestry, in the Welsh borderland, was used throughout the second half of the first millennium B.C. Its defenses, seen here from the air, incorporate many phases of rebuilding.

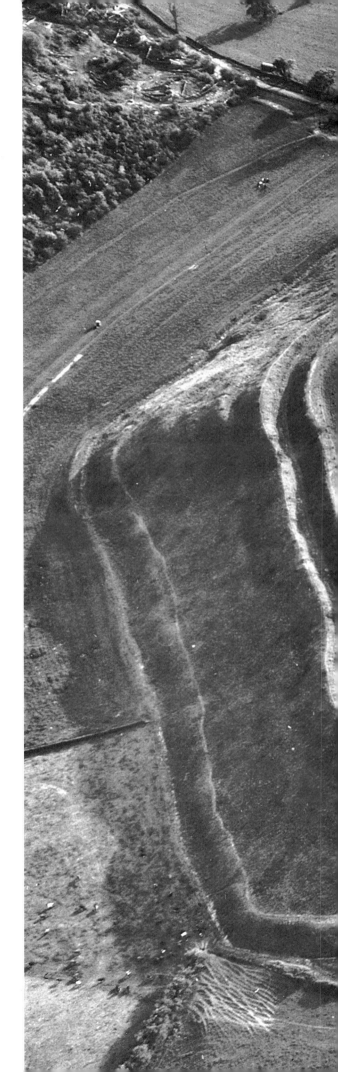

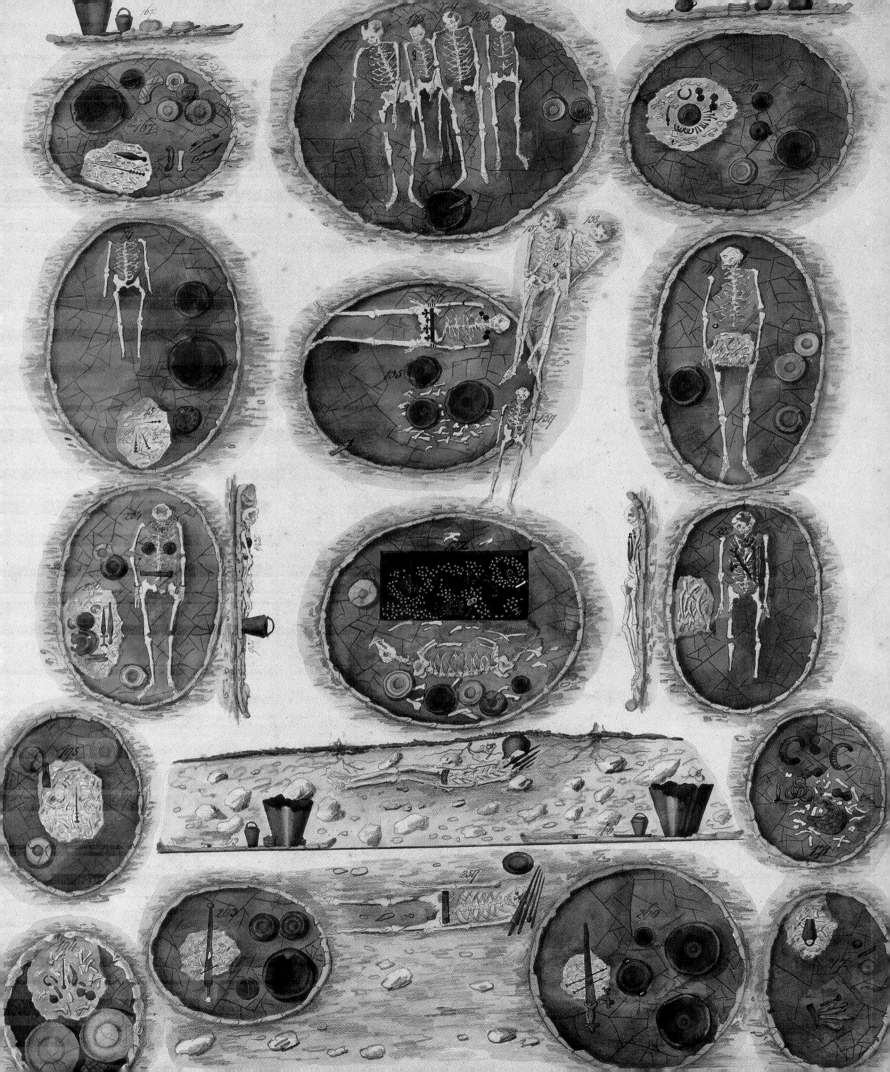

The most prolific source of archaeological material relevant to the Celts comes from the excavation of their cemeteries. Across the length and breadth of Europe tens of thousands of Hallstatt and La Tène graves have been excavated. Many, found in the last century, were grubbed out unceremoniously to satisfy the contemporary lust for collectable objects. Today cemeteries are excavated with minute care using a battery of scientific aids in an attempt to recover every last scrap of evidence.

The Celts, like most primitive peoples, believed in an afterlife; indeed one ancient writer tells us that so firm was their belief that they would even put off the settling of debts until they met again in the next world! Their attitude to the world to come is shown with great clarity by the way their graves were furnished with the equipment they would need—each according to his status. A wealthy female like the so-called princess buried at Vix in Burgundy was accompanied by all the equipment appropriate to the feast: a great krater or wine storage vessel, jugs, bowls, and cups, all imported from different parts of the classical world in the last decade of the sixth century. She also took with her her jewelry, including an enormous gold diadem, her amber necklace, and brooches. At the other end of the social scale, a poor woman

B.C. sees a leveling down with the development of large inhumation cemeteries, the individual graves showing little sign of widely differing status.

Although most of the objects buried with the dead were their personal ornaments and domestic equipment (like that accompanying the men and women from the Hallstatt cemetery shown opposite), occasionally one finds specialist equipment as well, like the collection from a second-century grave at Obermenzingen in southern Germany. Here, in addition to the usual sword, spear, and shield boss, were found three tools appropriate to a surgeon: a probe, retractor, and trephining saw.

The value of cemetery evidence to an archaeologist is considerable. Not only does it provide a wealth of domestic material reflecting on the life-styles of the

This page illustrates a selection of objects from Celtic graves. Shown above are four pottery vessels made by the La Tène communities living in the Marne region of France. The articles below are bronze personal ornaments from cremation graves of the Urnfield period in southern Germany.

might be lucky enough to possess a brooch or a cloak pin.

There was also a disparity in ritual, particularly evident in the early Hallstatt cemeteries. The poorer people tended still to cling to the old Urnfield cremation ritual, while the chieftains were usually inhumed in wooden chambers set within large barrows and were often accompanied by the funeral carts which took them to their graves and perhaps a joint of pork to sustain them on their journey. Later, in the La Tène period, although wealth differences are still evident at first, the third century

different communities but it enables the composition of populations to be assessed —physical types, nutrition, diseases, and death rates. Moreover, by observing their attitudes to death we can begin to come closer to the people themselves, to their fears, hopes, and aspirations. Writing of funerals in Gaul, Caesar says that everything the dead man was fond of, including his animals, was placed on his pyre and "slaves and retainers known to have been beloved by their masters were burned with them at the conclusion of the funeral rites." Celtic funerals were spectacular.

Opposite: Our knowledge of the famous cemetery of Hallstatt depends entirely on the meticulous records kept at the time, of which this painting by Austrian artist Isidor Engl is a superb example. It illustrates a wide range of burial practices.

THE LANGUAGE OF OBJECTS

The Celts were technically highly skilled. By the seventh century B.C. they had mastered all the techniques necessary to work bronze: It could be cast into elaborate forms for ornaments and tools or worked into sheets to make vessels which could be decorated in repoussé style by beating out designs from the back or enlivened with inscribed or chased decoration.

The extraction and forging of iron soon became widespread, iron by virtue of its strength being much favored for weapons and for tools. Raw materials were abun-

can offer fascinating insights into aspects of life undiscoverable by any other means. The three decorated items shown on this page give an incomparable impression of warriors, infantry and cavalry alike, progressing in orderly fashion to battle; but even more important they give precise details of clothing, a subject upon which classical writers are not particularly forthcoming, and since fabrics are seldom preserved in archaeological contexts, contemporary illustrations of this kind are our only source.

To an archaeologist, objects have an added interest. Man has always been prone to the dictates of fashion. Styles and forms change, sometimes rapidly, sometimes imperceptibly. A wealthy man would want the most up-to-date type of sword, while his wife would demand a fashionable brooch. Human pressures of this kind would ensure change, but change was not consistent. Once a satisfactory type of iron spearhead had evolved, there was little one could do to improve it and since spears were seldom decorated, all that the craftsman could do was to vary shape and weight slightly to better suit the object to its specific function as, for example, a lance for cavalry, or a throwing spear for infantry. Thus, although there was variation, there was little

In the valley of the River Po there developed a school of craftsmen whose particular skill lay in decorating bronze *situlae* (buckets probably for wine) in repoussé style. Ornamentation usually consisted of horizontal panels containing scenes from everyday life, or views of animals as in this detail from a fourth-century B.C. *situla* from the region of Este, northern Italy.

dant: iron was everywhere to be found; efficient copper and tin extraction had been organized for a thousand years; graphite and hematite to decorate pottery were being widely distributed; while materials like gold, silver, coral, amber, and glass, used to make luxury objects, were readily available for those who could afford them. In short, the surviving material remains of Celtic culture show that society was endowed with technology and the craft skills unsurpassed in Europe until the eighteenth century A.D.

Apart from providing evidence of a purely technological and functional kind, objects

significant evolution. Much the same could be said of swords. Once iron had replaced bronze for sword blades, the only significant factor affecting form was the nature of the warfare: a long slashing sword was ideal for cavalry tactics, but a short stabbing sword was much more efficient in close hand-to-hand fighting. While, therefore, the sword itself changed only within closely prescribed limits, its sheath, which was often decorated, could be subjected to the whims of fashion.

The study of changing styles, known to archaeologists as typology, is of considerable value in dating the graves or settle-

ments of the Celts. Typology works on the simple assumption that changes in style and form have a momentum and that the direction of change can be recognized, allowing objects to be arranged in a sequence which reflects their age. This is much the same kind of reasoning which would allow us, confronted with motor cars of different dates, to put them in a rough chronological order.

Brooches *(fibulae)* are particularly susceptible to change, not least because they are fashion objects, and thus provide a particularly valuable field for typological studies.

bows could be inscribed or inlaid, while their plates provided settings for coral or were worked into elaborate forms. Variations such as these allow regional styles to be defined and their distributions to be plotted.

The final stage in the typological study of objects is to assign absolute dates to the relative chronology of the sequence. For the Iron Age there are three principal methods: (1) by dating timbers through the study of tree rings (dendrochronology); (2) by association with datable imports from the classical world; and (3) by correlation with historical events.

The first of these methods has only recently been applied to Iron Age studies but is well developed in other fields of research. By establishing long sequences of tree ring variation for prehistoric Europe and linking them to sequences for the historic period, it will eventually be possible to date the cutting of any suitably preserved timber, for example in a burial chamber, to within a few years. More widely used at present is the second method. If in a

Far left: The famous silver caldron from Gundestrup in Denmark provides a marvelous range of detail about warrior equipment. Here we see a mounted warrior wearing a helmet with an animal crest.

Celtic weapons are frequently recovered not only from warrior graves but also from ritual deposits representing the spoils of war offered to the gods. The spears below, from La Tène (mid-third to second century B.C.), give some idea of the variation in type used. The bronze sword (third from top) is earlier; it also comes from Switzerland but dates to the eighth century B.C.

Below, center: The decorated bronze sheath for an iron sword found at Hallstatt (seen here in a redrawing) shows how much we can learn about a people who illustrate their own daily life. These military scenes depict wrestling (far left), foot soldiers and

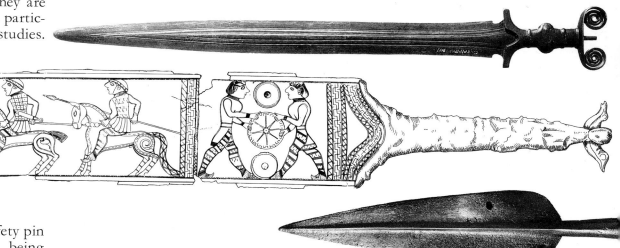

Technically these brooches are of safety pin type, the end of the spring pin being secured in a catch plate. Long unsupported catch plates of the type common in the Hallstatt period were "improved" in the early La Tène period by bending the end of the catch plate back towards the bow of the brooch to give added strength. In the middle La Tène period the ends of the plates were actually wrapped around the bow, and by the end of the period the resulting triangular-shaped plate was cast in one with the bow. This simple technological improvement was accompanied by a wide range of decorative variations—the

Celtic burial one finds Greek pottery vessels which are known to have been manufactured at a particular date, then the burial is likely to have taken place soon after that date (see pp. 36–37). Finally if objects can be shown to have been associated with an historical event, as for example the mass of coins and weapons buried at Mont Réa during the siege of Alesia in 52 B.C. (pp. 152–153), then one can assume that most of them were in current use at the time of the siege.

cavalrymen with typical weapons and gear, flanked by pairs of men who hold the circular symbol of warfare. The fourth-century B.C. sheath is about 70 centimeters (28 inches) long.

SCULPTURE AND COINS

The Celts of the Hallstatt period did not provide a great deal of visual evidence of their world and of themselves. Later, however, with growing contacts with the classical world and the introduction of coinage, representations become increasingly common and under Roman rule the Celtic population of countries like Gaul developed a vigorous style of representational art, in stone, bronze, and wood, largely ignoring the heavy hand of Roman classicism and allowing their inbred love of sinuous form to excel.

Celtic sculpture is generally very simple, the characteristics of the material used determining the form of the resulting creation. For example, the large pillar-like sculptures from Germany required the minimum of stone to be removed to produce the desired effect. It is, however, possible that these early works are rare copies, in stone, of subjects that were normally carved from tree trunks.

Metal, particularly bronze and gold, gave Celtic craftsmen greater scope, but throughout most of the La Tène period human and animal forms were subservient to the overall design. A human face might be incorporated, but it was simplified and broken down into its component parts according to the demands of the pattern. Only with the extension of Roman influence did the free human figure come into its own.

The classical cultures with which the Celts came into contact were by no means unprepared to depict these strange barbarians. King Attalus I of Pergamum was responsible for creating perhaps the most famous of all representations of a Celt in the bronze statue *The Dying Gaul* erected at Pergamum in the second century B.C. and widely copied elsewhere (for example, in marble in the Museo Capitolino, Rome). Pergamum also provides a vivid impression of Celtic armor in the famous reliefs, depicting spoils of war, which once decorated the Temple of Athene Nikepharos. Sculptures of this kind are an invaluable source of information for their realism and the accuracy of their representation.

In the late third century B.C. the Celts of central and western Europe began to adopt coinage inspired by the gold staters of the Macedonian kings and the silver of the western Greek colonies which had began to find their way into Celtic lands, possibly as pay or loot brought back by returning mercenaries. Once introduced, the art of coinage was widely adopted and spread rapidly, reaching the southeast of Britain by the beginning of the first century B.C. Coins soon became a medium for both artistic and political display. Celtic die engravers presented their motifs with great skill, interpreting conventional subjects like heads, horses, and chariots with typical Celtic vitality and love of flowing form, each tribe producing its own distinctive series which in later periods were frequently inscribed with the name of the ruler and sometimes his pedigree.

Celtic spirit pervaded the art of Roman Gaul. Some of the most beautiful representations of Gallo-Roman dress and manners come from this hybrid culture, by far the most outstanding being the three bronze figurines found at Neuvy-en-Sullias, and dating to the second or third century A.D.: a musician *(below)*; a figure believed to be a priest *(center)*; and a dancing girl *(far right)*.

Coins are a vital source of visual data, whether minted by the Celtic tribes themselves or by the classical societies with whom they came into contact.

Above, left to right: Southern Gaul; Redones tribe; Roman coin with Gallic trumpets and shields; Aulerci Cenomani.

Left: Carved stone pillar from Pfalz-feld, in the Rhineland, La Tène period, fifth—fourth century B.C. The design, with a head near the bottom, is repeated on all four sides of the column. Similarities in style have been pointed out with Etruscan Italy.

27

WRITTEN EVIDENCE

From ancient travelers' tales and traditions, or from their own experiences, Greek and Roman historians compiled descriptions of the Celts that we continue to rely on for information. Fifth-century B.C. historians like Herodotus (seen below right in a Roman bust of the second

century A.D. from Egypt) was heavily dependent on his informants, but his works stand at the head of the Greek historical tradition.

Most of the later accounts of the Celts depend directly or indirectly upon the lost works of Posidonius or on Caesar. This is particularly true of poets such as Lucan or Virgil, who refer romantically to Celts in much the same way as did the nineteenth-century poets.

Above: Virgil, seated between the Muses of Epic and Tragedy, in a mosaic from Tunisia.

Above right: Without the medieval scribes, who preserved and often re-copied ancient manuscripts, many Greek and Roman texts would never have survived. Monks also transcribed many Celtic folktales that had been passed down orally for centuries, particularly in Ireland. In this miniature painting from a medieval manuscript, a monastic copyist is shown at work.

The whole race, which is now called
Gallic or Galatic,
is madly fond of war, high-spirited
and quick to battle,
but otherwise straightforward
and not of evil character.
And so when they are stirred up
they assemble in their bands for battle,
quite openly and without forethought,
so that they are easily handled
by those who desire to outwit them;
for at any time or place
and on whatever pretext
you stir them up, you will have them
ready to face danger,
even if they have nothing on their side
but their own strength and courage.

Strabo

These are the researches of
Herodotus of Halicanarssus
which he publishes in the hope of
thereby preserving from decay
the remembrance of
what men have done,
and of preventing the great and
wonderful actions of the Greeks
and the Barbarians,
from losing their due meed
of glory.

Herodotus

Seen through the eyes of Greek and Roman writers, the Celts were barbarians—people who spoke no civilized language. Hecataeus, Herodotus, Xenophon, Aristotle, Hieronymus, Polybius, and Livy all have something to tell us of Celtic manners and of historical events involving Celtic invasions against the civilized world, but the amount of reliable ethnographic detail which they present is slight. The notable exception is Polybius, who, in describing the Celtic invasion of Italy, enlivens his story with fascinating asides on Celtic clothing, living conditions, and the selfless courage of the warriors.

It is, however, Posidonius, a Stoic philosopher who lived in the first century B.C., who provides the deepest insight into Celtic society. In Book 23 of his *History* he presented a detailed ethnographic account of the Celts as a prelude to discussing the first transalpine war, which took place in 125–131 B.C. Since it is known that he lived in southern Gaul for some while, we may reasonably suppose that he collected his material by firsthand observation. Unfortunately his "Celtic ethnography" no longer survives intact but comes down to us in extensive summaries provided by later Greek writers, Diodorus Siculus, Strabo, and Athenaeus. Although they naturally make modifications and additions of their own, their basic source is clearly Posidonius.

In addition we have the writings of Julius Caesar, general, politican, and polymath, who between 58 and 51 B.C. fought a series of bitter campaigns against the Celts of Gaul and Britain. Though not entirely unbiased, his accounts of Celtic society provide the last sight of the free Celts on the European mainland before their culture was subsumed by Rome, leaving only the Britons to carry on the Celtic traditions.

ARISTOTLE
The great Greek philosopher, writing about 330 B.C., uses the example of the Celts to discuss the nature of bravery.

POLYBIUS
Writing in the second century B.C., he gives a brilliant evocation of the relentless force of the Celts in his history of the third century B.C.—a time when the Celts were still a power to be reckoned with in Italy and when they were actually advancing into Greece and Asia Minor.

LIVY
In his great *History of Rome*, composed in the late first century B.C., Livy describes the Celtic attack on Rome in the early fourth century and its aftermath. He relied heavily on earlier sources including the writings of Posidonius.

STRABO
A Greek geographer who lived in Rome and Alexandria and traveled widely in the late first century B.C. and early first century A.D. His seventeen books on *Geography*, most of which survive, contain a valuable compilation of data from the Roman world and beyond. For his information on the Celts he used Posidonius as a primary source.

PLINY THE ELDER
Pliny (d. A.D. 79) composed a considerable work on *Natural History* in which he gives details of Druids and of Celtic medicine. His information comes from an unknown source.

JULIUS CAESAR
Caesar (d. 44 B.C.) came into close contact with the Celts when he conquered Gaul between the years 58 and 51 and led two expeditions to Britain. He had a unique opportunity to observe Celtic society firsthand, as recorded in his *Gallic Wars*.

CORNELIUS TACITUS
Tacitus (A.D. 56–ca. 120) was a famous historian whose *Annals* and *Histories* cover the period from the death of Augustus in A.D. 14 to the year 96. His earliest works, the *Agricola* and *Germania*, completed in 98, provide brilliantly observed accounts of the Britons and the Germans. The details of the Britons were probably obtained firsthand from his father-in-law, Julius Agricola, governor in Britain from A.D. 78 to 84.

We have no word for the man who is excessively fearless; perhaps one may call such a man mad or bereft of feeling, who fears nothing, neither earthquakes nor waves, as they say of the Celts. ...It is not bravery to withstand fearful things through ignorance, for example, if through madness one were to withstand the onset of thunderbolts, and again, even if one understands how great the danger is, it is not bravery to withstand it through high-spiritedness, as when the Celts take up arms to attack the waves; and in general the courage of barbarians is compounded with high-spiritedness.

Aristotle

Next in order is the Celtic country beyond the Alps. Its general shape and size have been previously described but now we must describe it in detail. Some authorities have divided the country into three parts, calling their inhabitants Aquitani, Belgae and Celtae, respectively. Of these they describe the Aquitani as completely different from the others, not alone in language but also in physical characteristics, being closer to the Iberians than to the Gauls. The rest of the population is Gaulish in physical appearance, but they do not all share the same language and furthermore, there exist slight differences in their respective ways of life and methods of government.

Strabo

Gaul comprises three areas, inhabited respectively by the Belgae, the Aquitani, and a people who call themselves Celts, though we call them Gauls. All of these have different languages, customs, and laws. The Celts are separated from the Aquitani by the river Garonne, from the Belgae by the Marne and Seine. The Belgae are the bravest of the three peoples, being farthest removed from the highly developed civilization of the Roman Province, least often visited by merchants with enervating luxuries for sale, and nearest to the Germans across the Rhine, with whom they are continually at war.

Caesar, *Gallic Wars*

The occupation of the Gauls by Roman generals and emperors was not prompted by self-interest, but happened at the invitation of the forefathers, whose quarrels had exhausted them to the point of collapse, while the Germans summoned to the rescue had imposed their yoke on friend and foe alike.

Tacitus, *Histories*

STRABO

JULIUS CAESAR

PLINY THE ELDER

POSIDONIUS

ANCIENT STORIES RETOLD

The Irish sagas, the heroic tales of the Celts, were first written down by Christian scribes in monasteries in the early eighth century. The monasteries were the foremost, and for some while the only, oases of literacy in an otherwise illiterate world. Here scribes had the leisure to produce masterpieces of calligraphy like the colophon to St. Matthew's Gospel from Durham, England, a detail of which is shown below.

The Roman invasion of Britain, in the years between A.D. 43 and 84, imposed upon much of the country a veneer of classical civilization which was abruptly dispelled in the fifth century A.D. by Germanic invasions. The result of these two cultural incursions was that Celtic tradition was all but destroyed in the area soon to become England. In the remoter parts of the west, however—in Cornwall, Wales, and Scotland—the Celtic language and elements of Celtic culture survived. But it was in Ireland, protected by the wild Irish Sea from the destructive effects of close contact with the European mainland, that the spirit of the Celts flourished and developed. While

Top: The Celts had transmitted their sagas in oral tradition from one generation to another. References to these stories turn up very occasionally in decorative form, as for example on the Gundestrup caldron, which was found in a bog in Denmark. It evidently illustrates a narrative involving supernatural beings: the grotesque female shown here may be Queen Medb, a character who appears in the Ulster Cycle.

Opposite: Typical of the monastic art of medieval Ireland, this brilliant illuminated manuscript painting from the seventh-century Book of Durrow shows Celtic influence. This small volume of the Gospels was once owned by the Columban monastery of Barrow, near Tullamore, County Offaly, Ireland.

the rest of Britain was governed by Rome, Ireland was experiencing the rule of a flamboyant aristocracy whose exploits were extolled in a series of ballads and poems which together form one of the great heroic traditions of European literature.

For centuries these tales would have been retold at communal gatherings. They became an essential element of the folk memory of the people and were learned by rote until sometime in the eighth century A.D., when they began to be written down by scribes in the early Irish monasteries. In later medieval copies of these first transcriptions they come down to us today. Amid the mass of miscellaneous literary fragments recorded in these medieval manuscripts there are four cycles of stories. The first are mythological stories about the "Tribes of the Goddess Danann" (*Tuatha*

Dé Danann), an ancient race of gods who inhabited Ireland in pre-Celtic times. Then comes the Ulster cycle, which describes the exploits of King Conchobar and his followers including the famous Cú Chulainn, the Hound of Ulster. Third is the Fenian cycle concerning the dealings of Finn mac Cumaill and his son Oisín. Fourth and finally, several stories are concerned with the kings who traditionally reigned in the period from the third century B.C. until the eighth century A.D.

Of these the most informative is the Ulster cycle, which contains one of the greatest prose sagas of the ancient world, "The Cattle-Raid of Cooley" (*Táin Bó Cualnge*). Although it did not take its final form until early in the eighth century, it is clear that it refers to a much earlier period and the storyteller has been at pains to retain the original flavor of the times. Ireland at this time was divided into four provinces *Ulaid* (Ulster), *Connachta* (Connacht), *Laigin* (Leinster), and *Mumu* (Munster). *Ulaid*, where the story is based, was ruled by a high king, Conchobar, whose court (*ráth*) was at Emain Macha near Armagh.

The society presented has remarkable similarities to Gaulish society at the time of Caesar and earlier. The methods of warfare, in particular, have an odd familiarity about them: the warriors are headstrong, courageous, and boastful. They fight in single combat or en masse, the noblemen in their chariots driven by charioteers; cattle raiding is a manly exploit, and head hunting an acceptable pursuit. There is much more besides. Noble women like Medb and Derdriu stand out as strong godlike personalities; the men are rounded individuals, fierce and brave at one moment, in fear and panic the next, while everywhere the gods are weaving a consistent skein of superstition throughout the narrative.

CELTIC SOCIETY

The prestige and wealth of the Celtic aristocratic class are evoked in this Gallo-Roman sculpture from the Paris area.

Opposite: Coin from the Danube region depicting a Celtic equestrian warrior. Ornate bronze sword handle from France, first century B.C.

They dine together in a circle,
with the most influential man in the center...
whether he surpass the others
in warlike skill, or nobility of family, or wealth.

Athenaeus

They terrified and fascinated their Greek and Roman neighbors, these "barbarian" inhabitants of the European heartland. They had no written history, not even a written language of their own, no dominant city-states to impose order and unity, no clear-cut boundaries. But as the shifting, roaming Celtic tribes began to settle, clustered here and there around a local chieftain in a natural hilltop defensive site, civilized life took shape. Their skills and resources were many: horsemanship, mastery of the wheel, mining, metalworking. This ingenuity gave them some control over a harsh environment and allowed for impressive cultural developments. They traded with the cultivated Mediterranean cities, accumulated surplus wealth, built stronger fortress-towns and ever more imposing tombs for their leaders.

Before this ancient Celtic world dispersed, to collide fatally with Rome, it enjoyed a brief flowering that has left enduring traces. Its tribes bequeathed a social structure across the centuries to the Irish Celts. Its hillforts were growing into cities and, by the time of the great collision, its craftsmen had become artists.

By the end of the eighth century the basis of Celtic society had been laid, and out of the amorphous shadowy background of the Urnfield cultures of the late Bronze Age there emerged a people whose life and aspirations can be seen with startling clarity.

Celtic society in its homeland of central and western Europe passed through three principal stages. At the beginning, ca. 700–400 B.C., its leaders were immensely rich. Into their hands passed societies' wealth gleaned from production and from the control of the networks of trade and exchange which developed in response to the demands of the classical world for raw materials. They lived in princely strongholds and were buried with their wealth in the traditional burial grounds of their dynasty. But all this was soon to pass: Towards the end of the fifth century a crisis arose as the result of which the old order collapsed and large sections of the population began to migrate southward to Italy and east to Greece and Anatolia. Soon after 200 B.C. the migrations were at an end and society gradually readjusted to a more organized and sedentary way of life, developing a thoroughly urban economy. In this section we start by looking at the flamboyant princely society of the early period known only through archaeological evidence, taking the story up to the moment when the great migrations get under way. The course of the invasions and the retrenchments and retreats which follow are the subject of another chapter (pp. 126–159). Here we must pause to look at the Celts in detail, their physical appearance, dress, their weapons and warfare, and the organization of their society. It is probably true that no barbarian people in the prehistory of the Old World has been so fully described. They were a menace to Greece and Rome—a people to be feared but also respected. In a world growing increasingly enervated by luxury, the Celts were a people to whom the classical writers could look in wistful envy. In consequence they were frequently presented as the "noble savage" contrasting with the decadence of the times. Such an approach necessarily colored objectivity, yet if we carefully skim off the polemic and reassemble the fragments, the Celts emerge resplendent in their energy, fearfully courageous, and yet doomed to failure.

33

The three centuries from about 700 to 400 B.C. saw the emergence and the fall of a rich aristocratic culture in the very heart of the Celtic world occupying a zone stretching from Bohemia to Burgundy. While the peasant population were, for the most part, still being buried in simple cremation graves in the old Urnfield tradition, their leaders were being carried to their tombs on beautifully carpentered funerary carts drawn by two horses, and inhumed in timber-built graves beneath great barrows, together with their luxurious possessions.

There are striking similarities between the burial of the rich Hallstatt chieftains and the old established rituals long practiced farther east in the area of the Pontic steppes: Inhumation, wooden vehicles, horses, rich grave goods, plank-built grave

but they represent only one element in a rapidly changing society. Alongside them, often in the same cemeteries but in much larger numbers, are the graves of warriors, each man buried with his long sword of bronze or iron. Some were otherwise unaccompanied or were perhaps provided with a joint of pork and a knife to eat it with; others would have in addition an array of vessels in pottery and bronze; while the richer graves would contain the harness of the dead man's horse. In other words, within the material derived from the many hundreds of graves of this period excavated in Czechoslovakia and southern Germany, it is possible to detect a closely stratified society based on the prowess of the warrior and ruled by a hierarchy whose social position provided the power which enabled them to grow rich.

THE EARLY CHIEFTAINS

chambers, and large barrows are all characteristics which can be found among the Scythians of the period. So impressive are the parallels that some archaeologists have been led to believe that the Hallstatt chieftains were actually a dynasty of Pontic horsemen who traveled westward and set themselves up as overlords. But when one looks closely at late Urnfield society, all the significant elements can already be distinguished—the increasing use of horses, burial carts, and a growing disparity between the rich and poor. The emergence of the Hallstatt chieftains is, then, the culmination of a process of socio-political change which had its roots in the past. What is new is the greatly increased differential in wealth and the desire to demonstrate, even to monumentalize, this. The rich burials of this early Hallstatt period (Hallstatt C) are concentrated in the east of the region, in Bohemia and Bavaria,

The sixth century saw a distinct shift in the focus of the rich aristocratic burials farther west to the zone between Stuttgart and Zurich, the Jura, and the Côte d'Or (Burgundy). One reason for this change in the center of wealth probably lies in the foundation of the Greek trading port of Massilia (Marseilles) close to the mouth of the Rhone. The port would have provided the principal funnel by which trade and reciprocal exchange was facilitated between the civilized Mediterranean world and the Celtic, barbarian, hinterland (see pp. 38–39). Those barbarian communities, by virtue of their positions on trade routes or because of the commodities and mineral wealth which they could command, were able to engage in this lucrative contact and to accumulate wealth which, because of their social structure, soon became concentrated in the hands of the aristocracy.

By the middle of the fifth century another shift of focus north and west can be detected: the richer aristocratic graves are now concentrated on the Middle Rhine and in the Marne area of northern France. Why this movement should have taken place is not immediately apparent, but it may in part have resulted from a reorientation of trade routes which came about in the early fifth century when the Etruscans extended their power across the Apennines into the Po valley and began to trade directly with the Celts through the Alpine passes. From the distribution of imported Etruscan wine flagons among the barbarians it would seem that the new trade routes bypassed Burgundy, Jura, and the upper Danube and dealt directly with the new power complexes on the Middle Rhine and the Marne. While a shift in power may have been affect-

ed by developing Etruscan trading patterns, there may well have been other more direct causes which we can no longer isolate—perhaps land exhaustion and increasing population led to a migration, or maybe there was a change in political power brought about by some internal struggle. We are unlikely ever to know for certain. The fact, however, remains that in these fifth-century centers of power and wealth

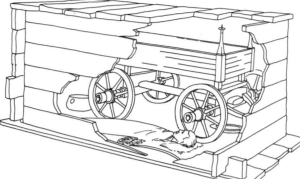

Burial chamber of a wealthy Celtic warrior, laid to rest beside his funerary cart, his archer's equipment, and other possessions. This reconstruction sketch depicts one of the many wooden graves in the great aristocratic burial mound of Hohmichele in the Heuneburg region of southern Germany, dating to the sixth century B.C.

Below left: An elaborately decorated dagger from a chieftain's grave at Magdalenberg.

The focus of the rich aristocratic burials of the seventh to fifth century changed with time: there seems to have been a consistent move to the west and north away from the original center in Bohemia and the Upper Danube. The map emphasizes how small was the territory within the total Celtic area which was dominated by the wealthy aristocracy. Elsewhere there were many hundreds, even thousands, of burials, but none with the range of luxury objects found in the central region.

HALLSTATT CULTURE

Hohen Asperg
Vix
Heuneburg
Camp du Château
SCYTHIANS

CELTIBERIANS

ETRUSCANS
ILLYRIANS

GREECE

on the Rhine and the Marne we see the last and most brilliant flowering of early Celtic aristocratic culture. No longer were imported luxuries—the Etruscan wine-drinking equipment and Greek red-figured vases—considered sufficient in their own right, but in addition there developed, in the courts of the rich, an entirely new lively art style.

Opposite page:
A variety of opulent goods from the Greek world found their way into the courts and the graves of the Celtic chieftains. The bronze hydria, a water or wine vessel some 60 centimeters (24 inches) high, from Grächwil, Switzerland, shows Greek-style decoration; early sixth century B.C.
The small Scythian horseman is a fourth-century gold collar ornament from Kul Oba.

WEALTH AND POWER

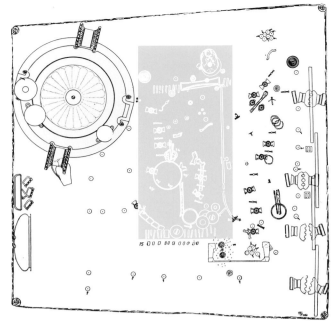

Of the centers of wealth and power in the Hallstatt and early La Tène world, two stand out above all others: Mont Lassois in the upper valley of the Seine, and the Heuneburg on the edge of the Swabian Alb overlooking the upper Danube. Both commanded important trade routes and both developed during the sixth century as the centers of wealthy aristocratic chiefdoms. About the site of Mont Lassois comparatively little is known because large-scale excavations have not yet been undertaken. Today the site stands out as an isolated hill dominating the route leading from the Rhone valley to the Seine. It is enclosed by defensive earthworks within which trial excavations have produced ample evidence of the wealth of the community: hundreds

The huge bronze krater, 1.64 meters in height, found in the Vix burial chamber (see plan above). This wine vessel was so large that it had to be transported from the Mediterranean in sections and assembled on site. It is even possible that the Greek master craftsman traveled with his creation and put it together himself. Only one other vessel of this kind has been found, again in a barbarian grave, at Trebeniste in Yugoslavia. Both were probably made specifically for export. They were diplomatic gifts to satisfy barbarian taste.

Above right: Detail from the neck of the Vix krater.

of brooches, ornate locally made pottery, and a range of exotic imports including shards of Greek black-figured pottery and fragments of amphorae in which the Mediterranean wine was imported. There can be little doubt that the occupants enjoyed a level of luxury denied to the rest of the population.

Within sight of Mont Lassois, near the village of Vix, French archaeologists uncovered what must rank as one of the greatest archaeological discoveries in barbarian Europe—the tomb of a woman, quite possibly a member of the ruling hierarchy, filled with objects of outstanding value dating to the end of the sixth century. The burial was housed in a timber chamber beneath a vast barrow 42 meters in diameter and more than 6 meters high. The female, judged to have been about 35 years old, lay in the center of the chamber decked

out in her finery. The date of the burial is indicated by the objects found in it: one of the bronze basins was very similar to one found in a tomb in Tarquinia dated 520 B.C.; of the Greek cups one was made between 530 and 520, the other between 520 and 515. Thus it is probable that the woman was buried sometime within the last twenty years or so of the sixth century. The lavish care with which the "princess" of Vix was buried is a reminder of the high regard with which women could be held in Celtic society. Much the same impression is gained from the great burial mound of Hochmichele, near Hundersingen close to the stronghold of Heuneburg. Here excavations were able to show that the principal burial, though robbed in antiquity, had once housed the body of a woman wearing amber and glass beads. She had been accompanied by her funeral

Floor plan of the magnificent tomb uncovered at Vix, near Châtillon-sur-Seine, France, in 1953.

The sixth-century Vix burial chamber contained, in the center, the skeleton of a woman who had died at the age of thirty to thirty-five years. Her remains were surrounded by considerable quantities of jewelry, including bracelets, torques, brooches, a necklace, and a golden diadem.

At the upper left of the chamber were the large krater (see photograph opposite) and several cups.

The area at the right contained the four detached wheels of the funerary cart. The skeleton, at center, lay on the chassis of this cart.

another as the courts of the local aristocracy, but our knowledge is restricted to the former where an extensive program of large-scale excavation has recently been completed. It was to the late Hallstatt (Hallstatt D) period that the principal occupation belongs. The most remarkable aspect of the settlement was that in one phase (Heuneburg IV) the fortifications were rebuilt in a style totally alien to barbarian Europe: A stone foundation 3 meters broad was laid to support a wall of sun-dried mud bricks, some 4 meters in height, and along one side it was protected at regular intervals by forward-projecting rectangular bastions. Every detail has a foreign appearance, and we can only assume that the entire work was erected under the direction

The Heuneburg, in southern Germany overlooking the Danube, became the strongly defended seat of a noble Celtic family in the late sixth and early fifth centuries. Exotic imports such as wine and fine pottery were acquired from the Mediterranean, while the local craftsmen produced a range of jewelry and high-quality pottery of native inspiration. The site had been defended in the Bronze Age and was fortified again later in the Middle Ages.

cart and the chamber had been decked out with finely woven fabrics. Nearby and undisturbed was a smaller chamber in which a man and woman had been interred on an ox hide, the man accompanied by his bow and quiver of arrows (pp. 34–35). In an adjacent chamber was another man, this time with a spear. In all, a total of thirteen burials were discovered in the mound. The elaboration of this tomb, carrying with it the possibility that some of the bodies found were those of servants or retainers ritually slaughtered to accompany the dead leader to the grave, gives an impression of the pomp and ritual which must have attended the burials of the Celtic aristocracy.

The Hochmichele cemetery is close to two strongly defended hillforts, the Little Heuneburg and the Great Heuneburg. Both are likely to have served at one time or

of a man thoroughly conversant with Greek building techniques. That mud-brick architecture proved totally unsuitable in a north European climate is shown by the fact that the defenses were soon rebuilt as timber-laced earthworks in traditional Celtic manner.

Inside the stronghold excavations have shown the interior to have been densely built up with large timber houses and workshops replaced by new structures at frequent intervals. The occupants clearly enjoyed a standard of luxury comparable to that of the lords of Mont Lassois: Locally made jewelry was plentiful, wine and Greek painted pottery were imported, while local potters copied Etruscan black (bucchero) vessels and made elegant red, black, and white painted vessels of their own. The dynasty was short-lived, but must have been a source of wonder to the peasants.

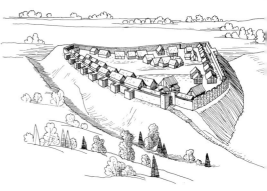

An overlay on the photograph of the Heuneburg, above, indicates the fortifications of this site in the Hallstatt period. The sketch (directly above) gives some idea of the unusual Greek-style mud brick wall, some four meters high, with projecting bastions.

Throughout the eighth, seventh, and sixth centuries B.C. the Greek cities of mainland Greece and of western Anatolia were busy establishing colonies around the shores of the Mediterranean and the Black Sea. By 700 B.C. Sicily, southern Italy, and the Bay of Naples had been reached; by 600 B.C. colonists had extended to the western shores of the Black Sea and to the southern coast of France. By 480 B.C. the Black Sea was encircled, while in the Mediterranean colonies spread westward along the Mediterranean coast of Iberia.

The expansion and consolidation of Greek trading interests soon began to impinge upon those of their rivals, the Estruscans. For the Etruscans the situation was made worse by the growing power of the Carthaginians in the western Mediterranean and by the emerging Roman state much nearer

And since the qualities
of the climate
are spoiled by the excess of cold,
the land bears
neither wine nor oil, and
therefore the Gauls,
being deprived of these fruits,
concoct a drink out of barley
called zythos (beer),
and they wash honeycombs
and use the washings as a drink.
They are
exeedingly fond of wine and
sate themselves
with the unmixed wine imported
by merchants;
their desire
makes them drink it greedily
and when they become drunk
they fall into a stupor or into
a maniacal disposition.
And therefore
many Italian merchants
with their usual love of lucre
look on the Gallic love of wine
as their treasure trove.
They transport the wine by boat
on the navigable rivers
and by wagon through the plains
and receive
in return for it
an incredibly large price;
for one jar of wine
they receive in return a slave,
a servant
in exchange for the drink.

Diodorus Siculus

Wine, imported from the Mediterranean lands, was consumed in quantity in the Celtic world. "Many Italian merchants, with their usual desire for easy money, look on the Gallic love of wine as their treasure trove," said the historian Diodorus

Siculus. He describes (see full quotation at right) the transport of wine by boat or wagon. This Gallo-Roman relief shows a river barge laden with wine casks. From Cabrières-d'Aygues, Vaucluse, in France.

to home. The crisis came to a head at the beginning of the fifth century, when the Strait of Messina between Sicily and Italy was closed to Etruscan shipping and, after the resounding defeats of two military expeditions, at Himera and Cumae (474), the cities of Etruria began to reorganize their trading patterns, reaching northward across the Po valley and through the Alps to the rich barbarian lands beyond.

Barbarian Europe had much to offer the cities of the Mediterranean. Of prime importance were rare metals like tin which could be got from Cornwall, Britanny, and northwest Iberia by means of a complex network of coastal and riverine routes.

Given the importance of tin (an essential component in bronze), it is easy to understand the prominence accorded to their western trade routes by the early Greek writers. Gold, silver, and bronze were to be had more widely. Amber from the Baltic which the Celts made jewelry, and of course Mediterranean wine in quantity.

It would be wrong to think of the exchange of these commodities taking place according to modern methods of buying and selling. While there were undoubtedly reg-

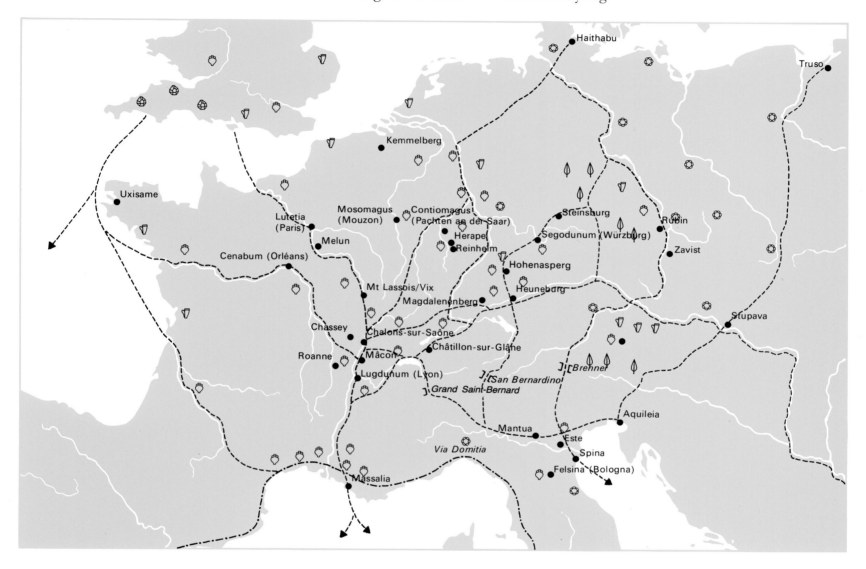

shores was a highly desirable commodity. There was also salt to be acquired from the salt deposits of Austria and Germany or from the western coastal salt works.

In addition to mineral extraction there were also items which leave less tangible remains in archeological terms: corn from the Scythian steppe lands, furs from the European forests, and no doubt a wide range of plant products. Nor should we forget that Strabo listed among the exports from Britain hunting dogs and slaves.

In return the classical world could offer manufactured goods like the bronze vessels and Attic pottery mentioned above as well as materials such as glass and coral, from

ular trading expeditions, like those which set out to acquire Cornish tin by barter from the natives, the process would generally have been more complex, involving reciprocal exchanges of various kinds between the Celtic tribesmen—exchanges determined by social mechanisms such as bride-price, gift exchange, and the payment of tithes. No doubt diplomatic gifts and payments made to secure rights of passage were another mechanism by which such exotic items as the Vix krater could enter the barbarian world.

◊ Iron

⊕ Tin

◈ Amphorae (proving trade with Greeks)

◎ Amber

▽ Salt production

Map showing the principal trade routes used by the Celts, as well as the Celtic commercial centers, in the eighth to sixth century B.C. Commodities and products are designated by symbols, as explained in the key.

REVOLUTION AND MIGRATION

During the fifth century B.C. the political and social organization which supported the princely aristocracy of Germany and France began to break down. Wide disparities in wealth lessen considerably, many of the old strongholds go out of use (Heuneburg was burned), and there is increasing evidence of unrest and movement culminating, in the fourth and third centuries, in vast migrations which brought the Celts into conflict with the Romans, Greeks, and the Hellenistic rulers of Asia Minor.

To classical historians like Livy the migration of the Celtic peoples could be explained in simple terms (quotation at far right)—"excess of population" and "adventurous young men" were sufficient to provide both the cause and the means. But we must remember that Livy was attempting to explain to this audience a dimly remembered episode in terms which they would easily understand—not dissimilar to those used by historians to account for the Greek colonization of the Mediterranean. He was not presenting a reasoned socio-economic analysis; nor are we now in a position to do so. At best we can attempt to isolate some of the potentially relevant factors. At a simple economic level, we have seen that exchange mechanisms involving the Greeks via Massilia and later the Etruscans through the Alpine passes were responsible for providing the physical trappings of wealth. It is possible that the growing threat of Roman expansion through Etruria had a sufficiently disruptive effect on the Etruscan economy to deflect them from their northern markets. Rome, with the whole of the Mediterranean at its disposal, had little need of these markets. If this is so, it will have contributed to the changes now under way in barbarian Europe.

The society of the early chieftains was a society based on conspicuous consumption. Vast quantities of wine and no doubt food were dissipated at feasts, and each luxury object used must have represented a colossal expenditure of society's surplus consolidated in the hands of the aristocracy. If this surplus had been constantly redistributed (as it would appear to have been in, say, Minoan society), little problem would have arisen; instead it was ritually destroyed by being buried with the dead aristocrat. The amount of gold alone which was confined to the soil in two centuries or

so was staggering. It is highly unlikely that a primitive economy rooted to one location could have sustained such a level of consumption for long. But throughout the period of the early chieftains (700–400 B.C.) there was a constant shift of location which might, in part, have resulted from the over-exploitation of the environment and the search for new productive land.

Another factor, clearly reflected in Livy's account, is population. Throughout the Late Bronze Age and into the Hallstatt period there is a considerable body of archaeological evidence to suggest an increase in population—the land is packed with settlement. In theory all the time that the carrying capacity of the environment can support the population there is little tension, but as soon as saturation point is reached and population approaches carrying capacity, society will begin to take preventive measures. The appearance of well-defined territories is one such measure, so clearly demonstrated in the archaeology of the chieftain settlements. Another procedure commonly adopted is for surplus population to be sent from the parent territory to colonize new areas. This is precisely what Livy believed to have happened with the Celts. His description perfectly fits the demographic model.

Inevitably, at a time of population increase, there was stress. That the Heuneburg was burned on several occasions is witness to the fact. The flagrant disparity in wealth, so evident in the archaeology of the period, cannot have failed to contribute to the tensions which built up in society. Ambitious younger sons of the aristocracy, had they wished to maintain their status, had no option but to gather a band of followers and move off to seek their fortunes, leaving the homeland in the hands of old men clinging to traditional ideals.

The picture of these times is far too complex for us ever to be able to reconstruct it in great detail.

The Celts are now on the threshold of history, but before we can follow them farther we must pause to discover, in the pages that follow, with what manner of men we are dealing.

Hemmed in by the great forests of the European plain to the north, the Atlantic to the west, and the Scythian settlement to the east, the Celts could migrate in only one direction: south through the Alpine passes into Italy and southeast through the territory of the Illyrians (Yugoslavia) to Greece and Anatolia. The Alpine passes like the St. Gotthard, Switzerland (shown here), were well known to them: Luxury goods of Mediterranean manufacture had long been imported over these mountain routes.

Contemporary descriptions supplemented by archaeological detail provide us with an intimate and fascinating picture of the Celts. We know not only what they produced, but how they lived.

Central to Celtic life was the feast. It was above all a time when the community could come together to reaffirm its oneness. The people could relive the glories of the past, display their hierarchies and loyalties, and communally enjoy the largess redistributed by their chieftains.

PROFILE OF THE CELTS

The caldron and the hearth formed the focal point of the feast. Bronze caldrons and iron caldron chains, together with flesh hooks for lifting the joint out of the stew, have been found on a number of archaeological sites. The reconstruction shown here from the museum of Asparn, near Vienna, is based on precise archaeological detail.

The classical writers are quite specific about Celtic feasts. It was the responsibility of kings to provide lavishly for their people. Posidonius (quoted by Athenaeus) tells us of the Gaulish king Louernius, who built a vast square enclosure within which "he filled vats with expensive liquor and prepared so great a quantity of food that for many days all who wished could enter and enjoy the feast prepared, being served without break by the attendants." How common such a display was in the Celtic world it is difficult to say, but for the most part feasts appear to have been more intimate and held indoors.

Drink was all important. "The drink of the wealthy class is wine imported from Italy or from the territory of Massilia. This is unadulterated, but sometimes a little water is added. The lower classes drink wheaten beer prepared with honey, but most people drink it without: it is called *cornia*" (Posidonius/Athenaeus). The communal nature of the gathering was further emphasized by drinking from a common cup carried from one person to another by a slave. "The slave serves the cup towards the right not towards the left"; they drink "a little at a time, not more than a mouthful—but they do it rather frequently!" Polybius too was impressed by Celtic capacity for alcohol.

Various foods would have been served. Strabo, writing of the Belgae, says, "They have large quantities of food together with all kinds of meat especially fresh and salt pork." The importance of pork to the diet is amply demonstrated by the evidence from graves, in many of which the dead man was provided with a joint of pork or even a whole pig for his first feast in the afterworld.

The scene inside the house is brilliantly set by Diodorus Siculus. Describing the participants, he goes on to say that "beside them are hearths blazing with fire, with caldrons and spits containing large pieces of meat. Brave warriors they honor with the finest portions of meat." This last point is amplified by Athenaeus, who says, "And in former times when the hindquarters were served up, the bravest hero took the thigh piece, and if another man claimed it they stood up and fought in single combat to death." Expanding upon the matter of single combat at feasts, he adds, "Assembling in arms they engage in mock battle-drill and mutual thrust and parry. But sometimes wounds are inflicted and the irritation caused by this may lead even to the slaying of the opponent unless bystanders hold them back."

Now this is a particularly fascinating series of observations. Athenaeus, or more correctly Posidonius from whom he was quoting, was interested only to record curiosities of behavior, but behind these comments it is possible to see something of the mechanisms of social order at work. First of all the person who considered himself the bravest hero took, or expected to be given, a particular cut of meat which demonstrated his assumed status to the assembled company. If the action passed without comment, his status was thus confirmed in the eyes of all, but if another man aspired to this position he could dispute the apportionment. Simulated combat might decide the issue, but the dispute could easily escalate and bloodshed ensue. In this simple ritual, then, we can recognize one of the procedures by which social status was acquired and confirmed.

The later Irish literature adds striking confirmation. In the story of *Bricriu's Feast (Fled Bricrenn)* the chief character Cú Chulainn has to contend with two other warriors for the "hero's portion." The same theme is reiterated in *The Story of Mac-*

Dathó's Pig (Scéla Mucce Meic Dathó). Here, amid showers of abuse and boasting one warrior after another claimed his right to carve the pig until Conall, having speared his rival in the chest "so that blood flowed from his mouth," took up his position with the carving knife. By keeping the best part for himself and giving only the forelegs to the Connacht men present, he insulted them sufficiently to provoke a fight. The result of the evening's entertainment was a pile of corpses on the floor and blood flowing through the doorway. In this particular tale the feast provides the vehicle for the aggression between the two groups (the men of Connacht and the Ulster-men) to be played out ritually. Although there is violence, it is at least contained.

They also invite strangers
to their banquets,
and only after the meal
do they ask who they are
and of what they stand in need.
At dinner they are wont to be moved
by chance remarks to wordy disputes,
and to fight in single combat,
regarding their lives as naught.

Diodorus Siculus

An important social event like a feast was circumscribed by formality. Athenaeus (quoting Posidonius) provides the details: "When a large number dine together they sit around in a circle with the most influential man in the center, like the leader of a chorus.... Beside him sits the host and next, on either side, the others in order of distinction. Their shieldsmen stand behind them while their spearmen are seated in a circle on the opposite side and feast in common like their lords." Clearly the seating plan was of great import if delicate susceptibilities were not to be upset.

The feast was also an occasion when the community could reminisce about the past —about its history and the exploits of its heroes—and could plan its future. It was no doubt on an occasion such as this that the professional bards would sing or recite the oral traditions of the tribe contained in the great sagas of the kind which survive in the Irish literature—partisan works lavishing praise upon the ancestors of the

audience. Diodorus Siculus tells us of these men. "They have lyric poets," he says, "whom they call Bards. They sing to the accompaniment of instruments resembling lyres, sometimes an eulogy and sometimes a satire." But the bards are not to be confused with men whose task it was to proclaim the praise of those present: "The Celts have in their company ... companions whom they call parasites. These men pronounce their praises before the whole

assembly and before each of the chieftains in turn" (Athenaeus).

So something of the flavor of the Celtic feast emerges: noisy, drunken, bombastic, resounding with exaggerated boasting, redolent with threats, and often very dangerous. Yet it was an essential mechanism to hold society in check, an institution vital to the ordered functioning of the community.

The Celtic feast was a raucous, boastful affair. From the classical writers we learn that the Celts sat on the floor on skins or dried grass but had their food served on low wooden tables. A great deal of wine was consumed. The reconstruction above is by the Swiss painter, Mark Adrian.

PHYSICAL APPEARANCE

Above right: Celtic heads forming a decorative motif: their ferocious look, consistent with Greek and Roman descriptions of the Celts, is mitigated by the rather abstract treatment. Silver disk from Manerbio, northern Italy, third—second century B.C., probably a horse harness fitting.

Physical likenesses of the Celts, in various degrees of stylization, are found frequently throughout the Celtic world. This stone sculpture of a woman, a work of the first century B.C. or A.D. found in France, is sufficiently realistic and individualized to be a portrait study.

Opposite: Altogether different from the works shown above, this magnificent bronze of a young man is the work of an artist thoroughly schooled in Roman techniques. Yet his treatment of the hair, and the way the sideburns form flowing scrolls, show the Celtic spirit. This first-century A.D. work, found at Prilly, Switzerland, no doubt gives a faithful likeness.

The classical writers were all agreed that the Celts were a dramatic looking people, quite distinctive in their appearance. A miscellany of contemporary opinions will serve to set the scene:

"Almost all the Gauls are of tall stature, fair and ruddy, terrible for the fierceness of their eyes, fond of quarreling and of overbearing insolence" (Ammianus Marcellinus).

"Physically the Gauls are terrifying in appearance, with deep sounding and very harsh voices. The Gallic women are not only equal to their husbands in stature but rival them in strength as well" (Diodorus Siculus).

Queen Boudicca "was huge of frame and terrifying of aspect with a harsh voice. A great mass of bright red hair fell to her knees" (Dio Cassius).

To a dweller in the Mediterranean, then, these northern barbarians were tall, fair, well built, and with raucous sounding voices, but like all ethnic descriptions these generalizations must obscure the great underlying variety. Tacitus, a more perceptive observer, distinguished several types among the Britons: the inhabitants of Scotland with reddish hair and large limbs, the southern Welsh with swarthy faces and curly hair, and those occupying the southeast of the country who most resembled the Gauls. Here is a firm reminder that, while the Celts as a whole may have differed from the Mediterranean races in the lightness of their pigmentation and their greater bulk, there were many outlying groups who had developed distinctive characteristics sufficient to distinguish them from the generalized norm.

The classical observers were particularly interested in the Celts' treatment of their hair. There was evidently some variation. Diodorus Siculus says that some Celtic men wore short beards while others did not. He adds "the nobles shave the cheeks but let the moustache grow freely so that it covers the mouth." Writing of the Britons, however, Caesar tells us that "they wear their hair long and shave the whole of their bodies except the head and the upper lip." Strabo provides a particularly interesting detail: "Their hair is not only naturally blond, but they also use artificial means to increase this natural quality of color. For they continually wash their hair with limewash and draw it back from the forehead to the crown and to the nape of the neck, with the result that their appearance resembles that of Satyrs or of Pans, for their hair is so thickened by this treatment that it differs in no way from a horse's mane."

To confront in battle a tall, heavy-limbed Celt with his hair standing out in a spiky mass must have been, to say the least, intimidating. (The Roman name for Gaul, Gallia Comata, meant the shaggy-haired Gauls!)

Personal appearance was clearly a matter of some concern to the Celt. Strabo mentions that to be fat was socially unacceptable, while the archaeological evidence shows that women used mirrors as well as tweezers, presumably for plucking hair. That they also used makeup is mentioned indirectly by the Roman poet Propertius who chides his mistress for painting herself like a Celt. The decoration of the body, though for more warlike pursuits, is also mentioned by Caesar in his famous account of the Britons, who dyed their bodies with woad which produced a blue color and made them appear more terrifying in battle. These varied accounts, borne out many times over by representations of the Celts in bronze and stone, endow the bones of the archaeological evidence with flesh and blood.

DRESS AND ARMS

The Celtic chieftain who dominates this page has been pieced together from a wide range of archaeological and literary evidence. Every significant detail in the reconstruction can be supported. Most of the evidence for ornaments and weapons comes from the excavation of graves and settlement sites. For details of clothing we have to rely largely on the accounts of the ancient historians, supported by the occasional sculptural representation.

Few pieces of Celtic art portray the people as vividly as this small bronze face mask *(above right),* with its swept-back hair and drooping mustache, from a late first-century B.C. grave at Welwyn in southern Britain.

Below: An elaborately decorated bronze clasp from a leather belt, dating to the early fourth century B.C., from Hölzelsau in Austria. Belts were almost always worn by men; women sometimes wore girdle chains composed entirely of bronze links.

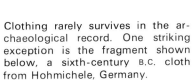

Clothing rarely survives in the archaeological record. One striking exception is the fragment shown below, a sixth-century B.C. cloth from Hohmichele, Germany.

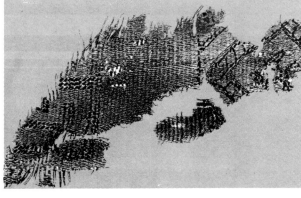

Far right: Neck torques had a magical significance. Sometimes the Celt would go into battle naked but for his neck torque, which he believed would protect him from danger. The great silver torque from Trichtingen, Germany, dating to the second century B.C., may have been made for a cult figure. It was probably too heavy to wear.

Above and at right: Gold bracelets or arm rings were popular among the aristocracy. They were usually elaborately decorated by Celtic craftsmen working in the courts of the aristocracy. The example shown above is from the rich grave of Waldalgesheim, Germany. At right, gold bracelets from a hoard discovered at Erstfeld, Switzerland. All three are from the fourth century B.C.

Above: Brooches *(fibulae)* were used to fasten cloaks at the breast or on the shoulder. They were often worn in pairs joined by a chain. The left-hand example, in silver, comes from Switzerland. The other two, in bronze, are German.

Comparatively little is known of clothing from archaeological evidence, but the classical writers refer to Celtic trousers, tunics, and cloaks and tell us that they were often brightly colored. It is possible that the tartans of the Scottish clans continue the Celtic tradition.

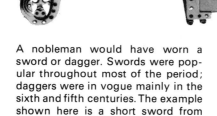
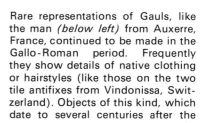

A nobleman would have worn a sword or dagger. Swords were popular throughout most of the period; daggers were in vogue mainly in the sixth and fifth centuries. The example shown here is a short sword from Hallstatt.

Rare representations of Gauls, like the man *(below left)* from Auxerre, France, continued to be made in the Gallo-Roman period. Frequently they show details of native clothing or hairstyles (like those on the two tile antifixes from Vindonissa, Switzerland). Objects of this kind, which date to several centuries after the

end of Gaulish independence, demonstrate the tenacity of Celtic culture.

Those tribes
which are regarded
as enjoying good government
have a solemn ordinance
that any rumor
or news of state interest
which comes
from a neighboring tribe,
must be brought
to a magistrate
and shared
with no one else.

Caesar

Caesar clearly recognized the difference between the noble class, which included the men of learning, and the rest, but he was not specific about the important distinction between the free and unfree, which must surely have existed. His reticence may be explained by the fact that neither of these classes would have been of any significance to him in his wars.

The one important point of difference between Irish and Gallic society is that among some of the more civilized Celtic tribes the institution of kingship had been abandoned by Caesar's time, the leadership of the community now being placed in the hands of an annually elected chief magistrate *(vergobret)*.

Caesar's comment quoted above makes reference to clients and dependents. This institution was of crucial importance to Celtic society. In essence, a commoner attached himself voluntarily to a nobleman,

Tribal or family life is seldom depicted in Celtic or Gallo-Roman art. The heads which appeared on coinage, like the stater of the Andecavi *(above)*, are intended to represent the kings though usually they are very stylized

Motherhood is occasionally represented in religious sculpture. The delicate relief of the "Three Mothers," a commonly recurring triad of deities, from the town of Vertillum, in Burgundy *(top, and detail at right)*, provides a Gallo-Roman version.

Opposite page: The three cloaked figures, from the Roman fort of Housteads on Hadrian's Wall in northern Britain, are probably also a triad of local deities. The recurrence of the group of three reflects Celtic belief in strength in numbers.

providing armed attendance when demanded in return for protection. But the relationship also had an economic significance. The lord (who did not himself engage in food production) owned cattle which he would grant on loan to his clients in return for a fixed rent in kind and in service. In Irish law, for example, the annual rent for six cows was a calf, a salted pig, three sacks of malt, half a sack of wheat, and a handful of rush candles. In this way the food produced by the free commoners was redistributed to the nonproductive aristocrats, cattle forming the medium by which the process was carried out. As Caesar was at pains to point out, the rank of a nobleman was directly related to his following of clients. A man with many clients who all owed him allegiance could field a large force when it came to organizing a raid. And since a successful raid would bring a man more cattle, which could be invested in additional clients, society provided the mechanism by which the aristocracy could maintain its hold and increase its power.

The Irish literature provides an intimate picture of the intricacies of Celtic tribal organization in the first millennium A.D. The tribe *(túath)* was ruled by a king *(rí)* through a general assembly of the people *(óenach)* which usually met once a year in the open countryside often amid the ancestral tombs. Society was rigidly divided into three classes: the Nobles, the Free-commoners, and the Unfree; and within each class there were grades of status which were formalized by each free man having a carefully defined *honor price*. This formed the basis of any assessment for compensation which might, for example, have to be paid to him or his family in the event of insult, injury, or death.

Within the Noble class were placed, in addition to the warriors, the specialists and master craftsmen *(oesdána)*, the jurists, the doctors, the carpenters, the metal workers, and the men of learning—the bards and the priests. The Freecommoners comprised the peasant farmers and the craftsmen of lesser ability. Together they formed the productive level of society providing the surplus upon which the aristocrats, and those serving their needs, could be maintained. Finally there was the amorphous mass of the Unfree, the families who had been degraded, subjugated communities, and slaves. These groups provided the bulk of the labor.

This outline of Irish society seems to be very similar to the situation in Gaul which Caesar describes, with one notable exception which will be considered later. "Throughout Gaul," he says, "there are two classes of men of some dignity and

importance. The common people are nearly regarded as slaves; they possess no initiative and their views are never invited on any question." He goes on to discuss the two upper classes, the Druids (the learned men whom we will consider in detail later, pp. 106ff) and the Knights who "all take part in war whenever there is need and war is declared. The greater their rank and resources, the more dependents and clients do they possess. This is their only source of influence and power."

THE FAMILY

The tribe was composed of a number of kins or families, which in Irish and Welsh law were considered to extend to four generations. The basic family unit for practical purposes consisted of the man and his wife or wives, along with their children with their wives and any children (and possibly also grandchildren): the grouping known as the *gelfine* (see chart at right). The family or kin could also be defined much more broadly, to include all the members of older generations and their descendants (as in the other groupings in the chart). The most frequent grouping for legal matters was the four-generation *derbfine*: the descendants of a common great-grandfather.

Land was held in common by the kin and distributed for use among the individual families, and when there were goods to be inherited or fines to be paid, all members of the *derbfine* were expected to share.

Kingship was based on a similar social unit: any male member of the royal family was eligible to succeed. Marriages usually took place outside the *derbfine*, and in the case of the royal household they were probably contracted outside the *túath*. An institution of great importance was that of fosterage. Children (both sexes) were placed in the care of foster parents whose responsibility it was to train the children in adult skills. In Irish law a boy would return home at seventeen, a girl at fourteen. The ties made during this period, especially between foster brothers, were particularly binding.

GELFINE

Man (A) and wife

This basic family group includes a man and wife *(above)*, plus the generations of their direct descendants *(below)*. Thus the row of four

couples here symbolizes the son, grandson, great-grandson, and great-great-grandson (with their wives) of the man A and his wife.

Broader groups can be associated with the basic line of the *gelfine*. The *derbfine*, for example, includes the *gelfine*, but starts one generation

DERBFINE

earlier with the father of the man A, plus the brothers of A and each brother's direct descendants for two more generations.

IARFINE

Extending the family still wider, the *iarfine* begins with the grandfather of A, to include the two groups shown above, plus another direct line descending from the grandfather of A for four generations.

INDFINE

The largest grouping includes the groups shown above, plus the great-grandfather of A and three generations of his direct descendants.

For their journeys and
in battle
they use two-horse chariots,
the chariot carrying
both charioteer and chieftain.
When they meet with
cavalry in the battle
they cast their javelins
at the enemy
and then descending
from the chariot
join battle with their swords.

Diodorus Siculus

A NATION OF HORSEMEN

Surely the most brilliant representation of the spirit of the horse: a design carved through the turf to the underlying chalk on a hillside near the fort of Uffington in southern Britain. The White Horse, some 110

The horse was essential to the Celts, both in war and in peace. The Greek and Roman historians naturally emphasized its military aspects, but this gives a very one-sided impression. When we look at other kinds of evidence, we find the horse everywhere present: in the graves and in the farmstead, on coins, and in one unique and resplendent example (shown on this page), on the British chalk hill at Uffington, carved into the landscape itself. We must weigh all the evidence if we are to understand how the horse could emerge so dramatically into the military arena, to terrify the armies of Caesar.

There is little doubt that the domesticated horse had been introduced into Europe before the emergence of the Celts (and it has been suggested that the horse may have been harnessed as far back as Upper Paleolithic times). In the Later Bronze Age of central Europe, horses would have been

700 B.C. The fact that much of the horse gear of this period bears strong similarities to that in use among the horse-riding communities occupying the Pontic steppes—the natural home of the horse—suggests that there may well have been a sudden influx of eastern horses, complete with gear, into central and western Europe at this time. There is no need to explain this phenomenon as an actual invasion. On present evidence it is more likely to result from a new pattern of reciprocal exchange, following the movement of people from the Pontic steppes into the Great Hungarian Plain. For the Celtic aristocracy the horse became a symbol of prestige and was eagerly acquired.

In many of the rich Hallstatt and early La Tène graves, as we have seen, the funeral cart which carried the dead aristocrat to the tomb was interred with him; so too were the harnesses of the horses that were yoked to the vehicle—but not the horses themselves. Either the horse was too valuable a commodity to be killed or, more likely, the ritual precluded horse burial. This is in striking contrast to the burials of the horse-riding communities who now inhabited the eastern parts of Hungary.

A number of the Hallstatt graves have produced three sets of harness fittings; two

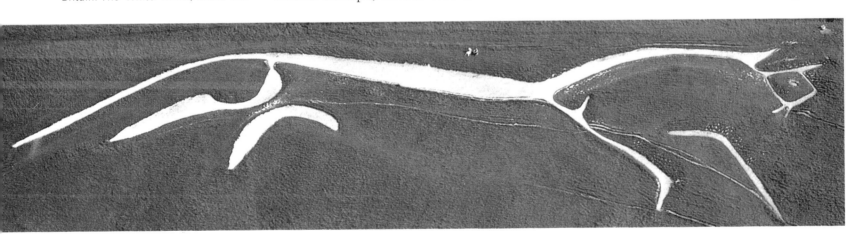

meters long, probably dates to the first century B.C. The scouring of the white horse was carried out annually by the local population until comparatively recently.

Opposite: This Gallo-Roman sculpture from Portieux, Vosges, France, though of native workmanship, attempts a realistic representation of the horse. The group symbolizes the victory of heavenly powers over the underworld.

extensively used for traction, harnessed in yokes with bridles of leather and mouthpieces probably of leather, and with side pieces of wood or occasionally bone. Towards the end of the Urnfield period bronze harness fittings start to become more common, and with the beginning of the Hallstatt C period, Europe is swamped in bronze horse gear.

All this would seem to imply that horses suddenly came more widely into use about

were for the draught animals, and the third presumably for the chieftain's riding horse. Although horse riding is sporadically attested heretofore in central and western Europe, this is the first clear evidence that it has now become widespread. The long slashing sword which at this time became popular—a type particularly suitable for fighting from horseback—is an added reminder that cavalry now played an important part in Celtic warfare. The scene of

Horses are sometimes depicted as the bearers of deities. The goddess Epona *(right)* is shown riding side-saddle, on this Gallo-Roman relief from Altbachtal (Rheinland). The unknown rider god *(far right)*, probably of Thracian origin, was found at Whitcombe in Dorset, England.

A lively trade in horses must have developed in Celtic Europe. This Gallo-Roman relief from Dijon, France, shows a cloaked horse trader at work. Many beasts were probably obtained through exchange mecha-

nisms from the steppes via eastern Europe, but horse breeding must have been carried out by most communities, so that the breaking of young horses was a common scene.

Below: Two beautiful Gallo-Roman bronzes of spirited young foals: from Châlon-sur-Marne, France, and *(at right)* from Aventicum, in Switzerland.

the four horsemen on the scabbard from Hallstatt (pp. 24–25) shows that the lance was also a favored cavalry weapon.

By the end of the seventh century, then, we can be tolerably certain that fighting from horseback was a significant element in Celtic life. The horse was also used to pull war chariots, but this, as part of the battle, will be considered in more detail below (pp. 54–55). In the works of the classical writers, charioteering greatly overshadowed fighting from horseback. While this may reflect merely the novelty of chariot warfare in classical eyes, it may well imply that in the third and second centuries B.C. cavalry played only a subservient part in warfare. An interesting Celtic institution is, however, referred to by Pausanius when he writes of the *trimarcisia*—a unit of three riders consisting of a nobleman and two attendants, much like the knight and squire of the Middle Ages. The function of these attendants was to look after their lord and provide him with a new horse if necessary. It is possible that a similar institution was in force among the Brigantes of Yorkshire in the first century A.D. We hear that Queen Cartimandua insulted her husband Venutius by running off with his armor bearer.

If this man had been a member of Venutius's *trimarcisia*, then by seducing him Cartimandua had greatly weakened her ex-husband's fighting efficiency.

By the time that Caesar was fighting his way through Gaul, chariot warfare was a thing of the past: he encountered only infrantry and cavalry. As the Celts came increasingly into contact with the classical world, so their fighting methods were modified. The importance of cavalry is many times emphasized by Caesar. Of King Dumnorix, Caesar says, "He maintained at his own expense a considerable force of cavalry which he kept in attendance upon him"—a nobleman with a personal squadron of well-trained horsemen would have been a formidable foe. Of cavalry tactics we learn a little from Caesar's battle against the Nervii in 57 B.C. Although we are told that the Nervii had practically no cavalry, the few they deployed were put to good use against the Romans. "Our cavalry [i.e., the Romans] crossed the river with the slingers and archers and engaged the enemy's horsemen. These kept retiring into the wood where their comrades were and then reappearing to charge our troops who dared not pursue them beyond the end of

the open ground." Here the horsemen were used as an irritant to distract the Romans before the battle proper ensued. They could, however, be used more aggressively to break their opponents' ranks.

As the result of a rabble-rousing speech given by the Celtic war leader Vercingetorix, as a prelude to a set piece engagement with Caesar, his horsemen cried that they would swear a solemn oath not to allow any man who had not ridden twice through the enemy's column to enter his home again or to see his relatives. In the event, the onslaught failed and the cavalry fled, afraid of being surrounded, only to be hacked down all over the field.

A motif much favored on Celtic coins: Ultimately the inspiration came from Hellenistic prototypes, but Celtic die cutters interpreted the horse in their own style, sometimes reducing it to its constituent elements in a pleasing abstract design. Shown here are coins from different tribes of the Celtic world: the Unelli *(left)*, Parisii *(above)*, and coins from the Atrebates, the Jura area, and *(bottom)* Romania.

The Celtiberians of western Spain, renowned for their horsemanship, were readily employed by the Romans as cavalry auxiliaries. This small cult wagon in bronze comes from Mérida in Spain, second—first century B.C.

The classical writers were particularly impressed by the effectiveness of the Celtic chariot in warfare. Chariots were not new to Europe at this time; examples have been found in Sweden depicted on tombs of the tenth century B.C., and were well known to the Mycenaean Greeks. In the hands of the Celts of the third and second centuries the chariot came into its own as a formidable and highly effective item of military equipment. By the middle of the first century B.C., however, when Caesar was making his way through Gaul, new methods of cavalry fighting had replaced the old and not until he set foot on the remote and backward island of Britain did he encounter chariots, apparently for the first time. His shrewd military assessment of them cannot be bettered. He starts by describing how in chariot warfare the Britons begin by driving all over the field hurling javelins and causing as much pandemonium as possible. "Then after making their way between the squadrons of their own cavalry, they jump down from

check and return them in a moment. They can run along the chariot pole, stand on the yoke, and get back into the chariot as quick as lightning." When it is remembered that Cassivellaunus, the local resistance leader, was able to command four thousand

Chariot warfare earned the Celts a particularly terrifying reputation, and inspired a great diversity of artistic representations. This clay model of a horse-drawn chariot is among the earliest portrayals of a horse-drawn vehicle found in Europe. From Grosseto province, central Italy, possibly as early as the ninth century B.C.

the chariots and fight on foot. In the meantime their charioteers retire a short distance from the battle and place the chariots in such a position that their masters, if hard pressed by numbers, have an easy means of retreat to their own lines." Thus, he concludes, with a soldier's admiration, "they combine the mobility of cavalry with the staying power of infantry."

The immense skill of the charioteers evidently made a deep impression on him. He describes how by daily training and practice they became so proficient that "even on a steep incline they are able to control the horses at full gallop and to

chariots, the nature of Caesar's difficulties can more easily be appreciated.

Chariots were used in all the subsequent major battles between the Romans and the Britons and as late as A.D. 84, when Agricola was fighting in the north of Scotland, we still read of the noise of the maneuvering chariots in the field between the two armies drawn up in readiness for the battle. Agricola's cavalry squadrons easily routed the war chariots and one of the last vignettes we are given is of the runaway chariots and the riderless horses of the cavalry wheeling about in their terror and plunging head-on into the ranks of the infantry.

The literary evidence, with all its vivid detail, is supported by other types of data. Chariots driven by wild-haired Celts are a favorite motif for the reverses of Celtic coins, while pieces of chariots, invariably the bronze and iron fittings, have been recovered from a variety of contexts ranging from burial chambers to ritual deposits in bogs. From all these scraps it is possible to build up a detailed picture of the Celtic chariot. Two-wheeled, strong in structure, pared down to the minimum, it was, in trained hands, quite lethal.

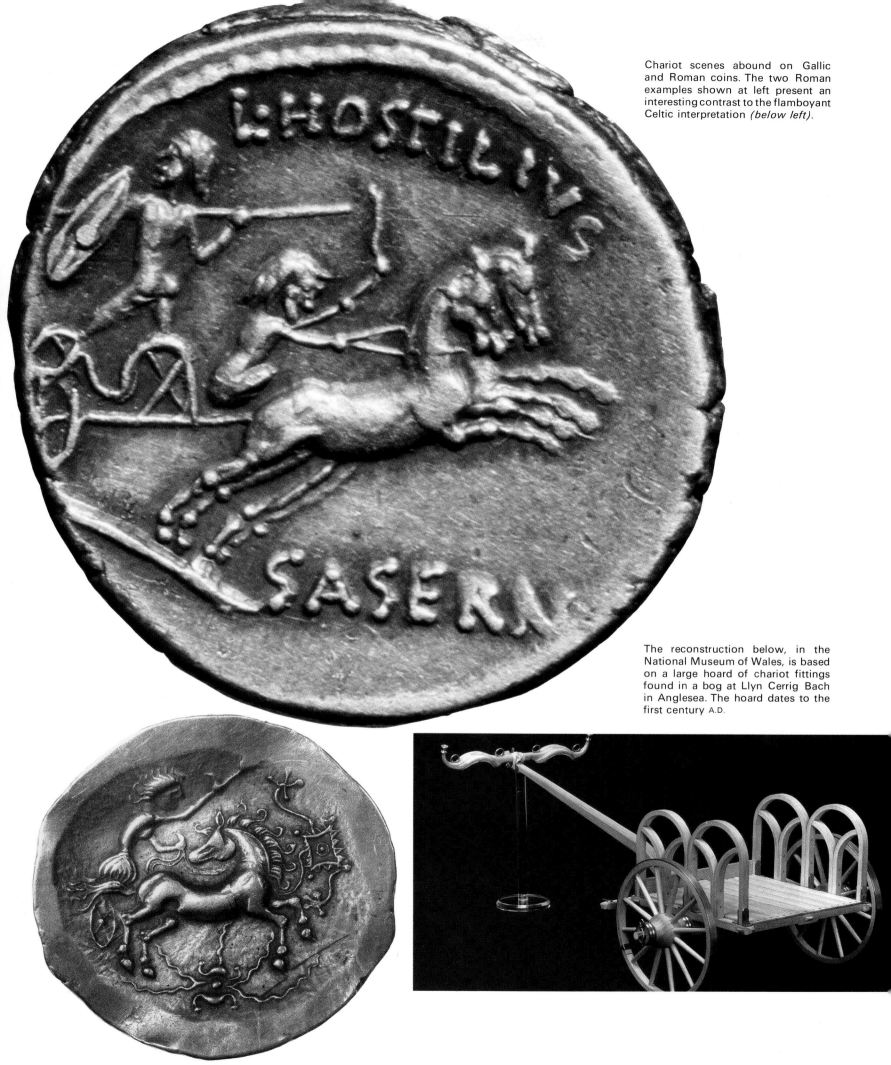

Chariot scenes abound on Gallic and Roman coins. The two Roman examples shown at left present an interesting contrast to the flamboyant Celtic interpretation *(below left)*.

The reconstruction below, in the National Museum of Wales, is based on a large hoard of chariot fittings found in a bog at Llyn Cerrig Bach in Anglesea. The hoard dates to the first century A.D.

Celtic warfare changed dramatically over the centuries. The violent and ill-organized onslaughts of the fourth and third centuries have little in common with the carefully planned campaigns fought by the Gauls against Caesar in the first century. Such a change was the inevitable result of the contact between the two peoples. Here we will be concerned with the more archaic form of Celtic warfare viewed through the eyes of men writing of events on the Italian peninsula from the third to the first century. Strabo, with evident fascination, describes

ARMS, ARMOR AND WARFARE

the armor of a typical Celt. He carries, he says, "a long sword fastened on the right side and a long shield, and spears of like dimension, and the *madaris* which is a kind of javelin. There is also a wooden weapon resembling a 'grosphus' which is thrown by hand... with a range greater than that of an arrow." He also mentions the use of bows and slings but implies that they were of only limited importance.

Swords and spears of various types are well attested in the archaeological record. We learn from Diodorus Siculus something of the subtlety of the Celtic spear. Some of the javelins, he says, were forged with a straight head while some are twisted with breaks throughout the entire length so that the blow not only cuts but also tears the flesh—the recovery of the weapon ripping open the wound.

For protection the warrior carried an oval-shaped shield in his left hand of sufficient size to cover most of the body. The majority of them were made of wickerwork or of two planks joined together. They may also have been covered with leather to give added strength or, more rarely, with bronze, but shields of this kind were designed for display rather than active fight-

ing. Helmets were also worn, the majority of them probably being of leather.

The more wealthy warriors could have afforded to adorn themselves with bronze helmets of the kind which Diodorus Siculus so vividly describes: "On their heads they wear bronze helmets which possess projecting figures lending the appearance of enormous stature to the wearer. In some cases horns form one piece with the helmet while in other cases it is the relief figures or the fore parts of birds or quadrupeds." Helmets of this kind have been found from time to time (p. 59) and are shown worn by the riders depicted on the Gunderstrup caldron (p. 25)—a very satisfying example of how literary, archaeological, and illustrative evidence come together in mutual support.

Celtic warfare was not complete without noise—noise from the yelling warriors, from the beating of the sides of their carts and wagons, and from their war trumpets. "Their trumpets," says Diodorus, "are of a peculiar barbaric kind. They blow into them and produce a harsh sound which suits the tumult of war." Trumpets of this kind, the carynx, are beautifully illustrated on the Gundestrup caldron (p. 56) as well as on coins, and actual examples have been found in Britain.

The Celt is now ready for battle—hot-headed, excitable, but totally without co-ordination. "The whole race is war-mad, high-spirited and quick to battle," writes Strabo.

And when they are stirred up they assemble in their bands for battle quite openly and without forethought, and so they are easily handled by those who desire to outwit them. For at any time or place, and on whatever pretext you stir them up, you will have them ready to face danger, even if they have nothing on their side but their own strength and courage.

The easily provoked Celt, however brave, was no match for a cold, calculating Roman commander.

We have already seen that the feast provided the institution by which disputes within the tribe could be settled or at least contained. At a different level the battle, in early Celtic warfare, allowed intertribal differences to be displayed and resolved, sometimes without much bloodshed. A most interesting description of Celtic battle procedure, which allows us to consider these matters more fully, is given by Dio-

dorus Siculus and deserves to be quoted *in extensio*.

Diodorus begins by describing the general preparations, the cavalry and chariots and the overall lineup with the nobles and their supporters: "They bring into battle as their attendants free men, chosen from among the poorer class, whom they use as char-

ioteers and shield-bearers in battle." He proceeds to describe the opening movements of the battle:

When the armies are drawn up in battle array they are wont to advance before the battle-line and to challenge the bravest of their opponents to single combat, at the same time brandishing before them their arms so as to terrify their foe. And when someone accepts their challenge to battle, they loudly recite the deeds of valor of their ancestors and proclaim their own valorous quality, at the same time abusing and making little of their opponent and generally attempting to rob him beforehand of his fighting spirit.

In another passage Diodorus talks of the power of the Druids in time of battle.

The Celtic shield of wood or leather, sometimes covered in bronze, protected the whole body from the knees to the shoulders, as in the Gallo-Roman sculpture of a Celt *(left)*, from Mondragon, France. Above *(left to right)* are shields from Witham, northern England, and Horath, Germany (reconstructions), and the Battersea shield from the River Thames.

Opposite page: The harsh-sounding Celtic war trumpets with their frightening animal-head terminals are shown in operation on the Gundestrup caldron found in Denmark.

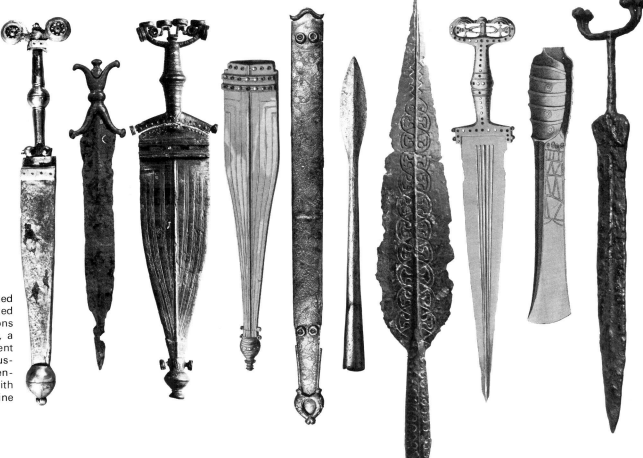

The Celt at war, so fully described by classical writers, is also illustrated by a wide range of Celtic weapons found in archaeological contexts, a selection of which, from different parts of western Europe, are illustrated here. Of the body armor mentioned in the texts little survives with the exception of a number of fine bronze helmets.

In addition to the weapons themselves, and the occasional representation of warriors on repoussé or inscribed metalwork (pp. 24–25), models of warriors have been found. The horseman above dates to the seventh century B.C. and comes with others from a cult chariot found at Strettweg in Austria.

For often as armies approach each other in line of battle with their swords drawn and their spears raised for the charge, these men come forth before them and stop the conflict, as though they had spellbound some kind of wild animals. He adds the moral rationalization, "Thus even among the most savage barbarians anger yields to wisdom."

Here is a brilliant evocation of early Celtic warfare, the very essence of which is the institution of single combat—conflicts between tribes could be, and probably usually were, resolved by a display of arms followed by individual contests between warriors. This is precisely the kind of warfare which is found in Homer and which is reflected in the biblical story of David and Goliath. Only if spirits ran high would general battle ensue, and then if such a situation threatened, the priests could intervene. In other words, we are dealing with ritualized warfare sparing of manpower. Contact with the Romans, of course, changed all this. The Roman mentality required the pitched battle with a clear-cut result. The Celts had to adapt. In one of the finest battle descriptions available to us, the historian Polybius describes the confrontation between the Romans and the Celts at Telamon, in Tuscany, in 225 B.C. To begin with, the battle was confined to

the hill and opened with a cavalry engagement, the rest of the two armies looking on, but the Romans, having caught the Celts between two forces, closed in on them.

They were terrified by the fine order of the Celtic host, and the dreadful din, for there were innumerable horn blowers and trumpeters, and the whole army was shouting their war cries at the same time: there was such a tumult of sound that it seemed that ... all the country round had got a voice and caught up the cry. Very terrifying too were the appearance and gestures of the naked warriors in front, all in the prime of life and finely built men, and all in the leading companies richly adorned with gold torques and armlets.

Eventually Roman discipline prevailed and the Celts were routed.

Some of them, in their impotent rage rushed wildly on the enemy and sacrificed their lives, while others, retreating step by step on the ranks of their comrades, threw them into disorder by their display of faint-heartedness.

The Celtic mentality could not cope with the relentless Roman military machine; once the fortunes of battle had turned, their resolve crumbled and they went berserk or panicked.

More than three hundred years later in the north of Scotland a similar scene was played

They have bronze helmets with tall crests, which give their wearers
the appearance of enormous height.

Diodorus Siculus

out following the battle of Mons Graupius (p. 154)—after a crushing defeat the Britons fled, "the men and women wailing together... many left their homes and in their rage set fire to them... they would try to concert plans, then suddenly break off. Sometimes the sight of their dead ones broke their hearts—more often it goaded them to fury—some of them laid violent hands on their wives and children in a kind of pity" (Tacitus). This terrible collapse of morale and reason was the fatal flaw in the Celtic mentality.

The selection of arms and helmets illustrated here come from northern Italy, France, and Switzerland and date from the fourth to the second century B.C.

The typical Celtic helmet had a narrow projecting neck guard (which might otherwise be mistaken for a peak) and was often provided with hinged ear flaps. Occasionally they supported the horns and other protuberances which Posidonius noted.

This magnificent helmet was found in a third-century B.C. Celtic grave at Ciumesti in Romania. The bronze bird of prey which perches on the crest had eyes of colored glass and its wings are articulated.

A stone-built house at Vaucluse, France. Of uncertain date but built in native style.

FROM HAMLETS TO CITIES

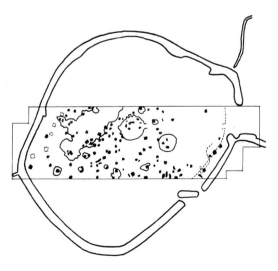

The roundhouse occurs in western Celtic regions, particularly in Britain. The plan above shows a typical Iron Age farmstead excavated at Little Woodbury in southern Britain. The two timber-built roundhouses were of different dates. The enclosure contains the storage pits, granaries, and working areas of the farm.

Celtic settlement pattern was diverse: each region had its own vernacular architecture, determined to some extent by the raw materials available, and settlements ranged in size and complexity depending upon the organization of the community represented. In the Hallstatt period the two extremes are defined by peasant farms, on the one hand, and princely strongholds, such as Heuneburg, on the other. Later, in the first century B.C., urban centers of enormous size developed to serve the increasingly complex needs of society.

Throughout the whole of the Hallstatt and La Tène periods, whatever the nature of the large nucleated settlement, the basic settlement unit was the isolated farm or small hamlet—a cluster of simple houses integrated into an agricultural landscape.

Houses were well built and usually of sufficient size to accommodate the extended family. An interesting divergence in tradition can readily be recognized between the circular houses, which are found in all parts of the British Isles, and rectangular buildings prevalent in continental Europe: the British house-type harks back to an older, Atlantic tradition of building. Among the rectangular houses there is a considerable variation in size and style, from the little one-roomed log cabins recently found at Most-na-Soci in Slovenia to the great aisled halls of the Low Countries.

Sometimes, particularly in Britain, a few houses were grouped together in an enclosure, the total complex representing the installations necessary for a single family. In mainland Europe the hamlet or the village appears to have been the more usual unit of settlement, but once more the diversity of the pattern should be emphasized.

The house (or family complex) was for the most part a self-contained unit wherein many of the basic necessities of life could be manufactured. Corn brought in from the fields was threshed and stored, either long-term in below-ground silos, or for immediate use in small granaries raised above ground to keep the corn away from damp and from rodents. Milling to make flour would have been a regular activity for the womenfolk, while most houses were provided with their own bread ovens.

Clothing would have been made in the home. There is ample evidence from settlement sites of spinning and of weaving on large upright looms, while finer weaving to make braid and a form of tablet weaving are also attested. Carpentry, not only of the basic kind necessary for house building and repairs, was highly advanced, as our discussions below (pp. 124–125) will serve to demonstrate, and knowledge of timber, coppicing, and other forms of forest management was commonplace. It is likely that, for much of the period, pottery making was carried out in the village, but later, with the development of urban centers, commercial production soon got under way.

The extent to which iron and bronze working were home industries is debatable. Most communities would have had their own blacksmith and the manufacture of small bronze trinkets is a comparatively simple task, but the knowledge and skills required to extract the metals in the first place and, in the case of bronze, to produce a suitable alloy, were most likely in the hands of specialists. We must suppose, then, that some communities, probably working full time, like the copper miners in the Tyrol (pp. 114–115), made their living producing ingots of metal which could then enter the exchange network and eventually end up in the farms and hamlets.

The house plan typical of most of Europe was rectangular, but the superstructures were built in a variety of techniques. At the open air museum of Asparn near Vienna, reconstructions of all the major types have been attempted, based on a careful consideration of the archaeological evidence.

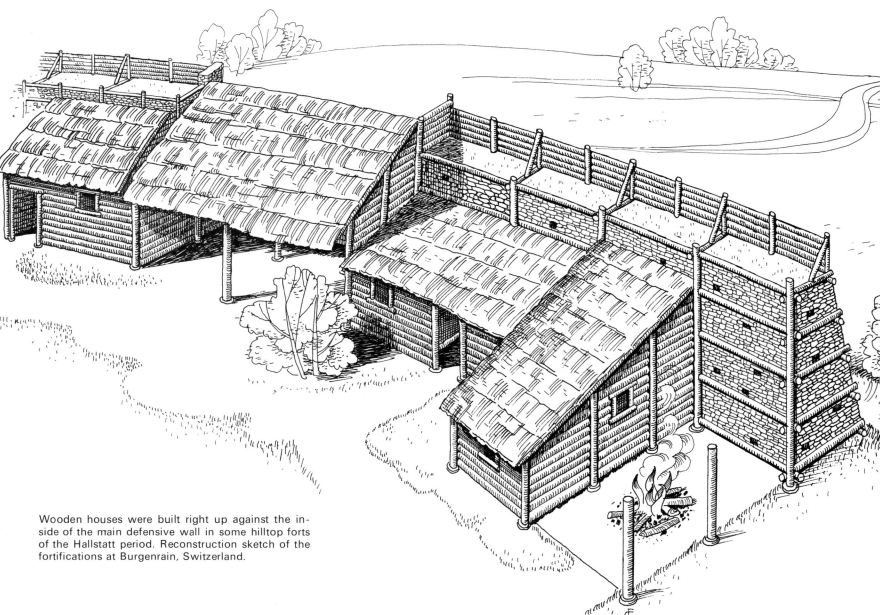

Wooden houses were built right up against the inside of the main defensive wall in some hilltop forts of the Hallstatt period. Reconstruction sketch of the fortifications at Burgenrain, Switzerland.

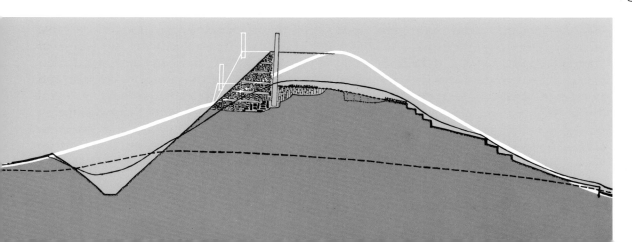

The defenses of Wittnauer Horn in Switzerland were massive. The Hallstatt period rampart, built of timbers and stone (and fronted by a ditch 3 meters deep), was set into the front of an earlier, more massive rampart of the Late Bronze Age.

61

HILLFORTS

At times of stress, Celtic communities throughout Europe built defended enclosures, usually on well-protected hilltop sites. These hillforts performed a variety of functions, but for the most part they were communal structures built by the inhabitants of the surrounding countryside for the use of the clan. Some show signs of having performed functions of an urban kind.

The tradition of defending a hilltop with an earthwork or a palisade was long established in Europe, and indeed can be traced back to Neolithic times, but it was not until the Urnfield period that hillforts became at all common in Europe. One of the most impressive of these early forts is the Wittnauer Horn in the Jura, a settlement spectacularly perched on a steep-sided ridge and defended by a single massive bank cutting off the approach. The bank, 40 meters in width, is composed of a loose framework of horizontal timbers packed with stone and soil. On one estimate the bank contains no less than 24,000 cubic meters of timber all of which would have had to be cut, trimmed, and hauled into position. Quite clearly, to build even a modest-sized fort of this kind would have involved a colossal expenditure of energy and must imply organized communal effort of a grand scale.

The explanation for the early hillforts must be sought in the increasingly aggressive nature of society—defenses on this scale are a sure sign that the people were in a state of sustained stress, and the fact that over much of Celtic Europe forts continued to be built throughout most of the first half of the first millennium B.C. is an indication of how long this situation lasted.

Although these early hillforts have a superficial resemblance to each other, there is no need to suppose that all performed the same functions. In Britain, where the archaeological evidence is at its best, many of the early forts were only very lightly occupied and it may be that they were inhabited only in times of stress or perhaps were used as communal storage areas for grain or animals frequented at certain times during the year. Wittnauer Horn, however, with its rows of well-constructed houses, gives the appearance of more permanent occupation, but there are no signs that any member of the community possessed exceptional wealth. In the sixth century, on the other hand, hillforts were being built, or renovated, by the aristocracy as we have seen at Mont Lassois and Heuneburg.

It seems, then, as though the technique of hilltop defense was being employed to serve a multitude of functions, the common factors being the need for defense and the

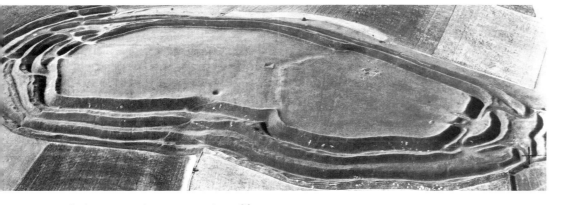

Maiden Castle, in Dorset, England, is one of Britain's largest and strongest hillforts. The central plateau, measuring some 18 hectares (about 35 acres) in area, was occupied from the fourth century to A.D. 70. The multiple ditches, sometimes more than 20 meters deep, and the ramparts between, supplementing the natural slope, stand out as shadows in this aerial photograph. The fort was attacked by the Roman general Vespasian in A.D. 43. The cemetery of the defenders was found at the entrance.

The sites chosen for hillforts usually had strong natural defenses which could be enhanced by walls or banks and ditches. The desire for protection is dramatically illustrated by the fort of Dún Aengusa on the island of Aran off the Irish coast.

The entrance was potentially the weakest point of most hillforts. Accordingly entrances were often protected by additional earthworks designed to confuse the attacker and protect the main gate. At the south-

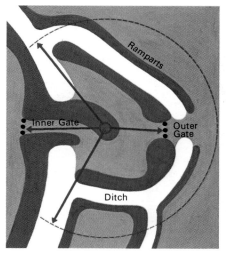

ern British hillfort of Danebury there were two gates at the main entrance with a flat topped earthwork between providing a command post from which the occupants, armed with slings, could protect the gates and command the approach.

ability of the community to work together to satisfy that need.

With the social upheaval which began in the fifth century B.C. the majority of the hillforts in Europe show signs of abandonment. One explanation for this might be that the massive folk movements which ensued relieved much of the pressure on land and thus reduced stress in the central areas, but the full story is likely to be far more complex and can only begin to be understood when we know more of the settlement type of the fourth and third centuries.

There are several exceptions to this generalization, of which Britain provides one of the best-known examples. Here, in a wide arc of land stretching from north Wales southward and eastward towards Kent, hillforts continued to be built, and were increasingly strongly defended, from the fifth to the first century. Each fort now seemed to dominate a well-defined territory within which it now played an important central function providing its hinterland with many benefits of an urban kind: facilities for trade and exchange; a religious center; defense when needed; a resident population, some of whom were engaged in manufacturing pursuits; and presumably administrative control of the community. Hillforts were still being built in the first century B.C. in France against Caesar's advance, and almost a hundred years later, a Roman general had to hack his way through more than twenty forts before he could claim to have conquered the southwest of Britain. In the Celtic fringes of Britain some forts were still occupied well into the Roman period.

THE FIRST CITIES

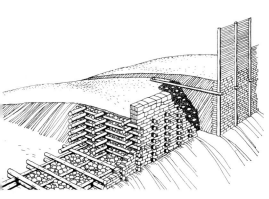

Towards the end of the second century B.C. barbarian Europe began to develop a range of new settlements, large enough and sufficiently complex in their functions to be called cities. The cause of this significant cultural advance is probably two-fold. Society had now, after centuries of unrest, stabilized and became more sedentary; moreover, transalpine Europe had been exposed to influence from the urban world of the Mediterranean for four hundred years. Trade between them was vigorous and it is easy to understand how southern ways will have been absorbed and emulated. This is not to say that the creation of cities was superficial, quite the contrary; the emergence of urban life reflects deep-rooted changes in Celtic society.

government was an important step towards civilization.

Another factor of significance was the widespread acceptance of coinage as a form of exchange. Gold and silver coins minted by the different tribes came into general use in central and western Europe from the third century B.C. onward, based on Macedonian and Greek prototypes. Mercenaries or raiders returning from expeditions in Mediterranean lands would have become conversant with such curiosities. To begin with, coins (imported and local) would have functioned largely in gift exchange, but by the end of the second century smaller denominations were in use, demonstrating the existence of a full money economy with coins being used in market

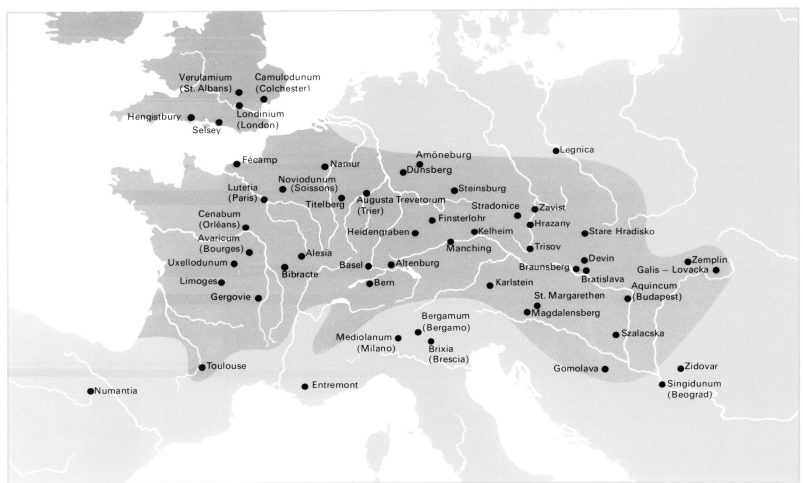

Top: The Murus Gallicus, which so impressed Caesar, was composed of timbers faced with stone and embedded in earth.

Urban centers (or oppida), as the map shows, sprang up all over Celtic Europe in the first century B.C. and spread to Britain by the early first century A.D.

In the central area from Bohemia to central France the old Celtic aristocracy was a thing of the past. Caesar tells us how in many tribes the head of state was now an annually elected magistrate and to aspire to kingship was an offense punishable by death. The emergence of an oligarchic

exchange. Such a system would have greatly facilitated trade with the classical world as well as between neighboring tribes.

To gain some idea of how these sites functioned, we must consider the urban center at Manching, close to the Danube in upper Bavaria. At its greatest extent the ramparts of Manching, 7 kilometers in length, enclosed some 375 hectares (or 700 acres). Although the built-up area was substantially less, it was still a very large settlement by any standards (compare, for example, the Iron Age town with its modern successor: this page left). Within the built-up area it is possible to recognize well-laid-out streets with orderly arrangements of timber buildings erected alongside. Iron working was carried out on a very large scale, use being made of the nearby deposits of bog iron. (It is estimated that the nails holding the timbers in the rampart together would alone have weighed 300 tons.) Other industrial activities included the working of copper and bronze to make brooches and cart fittings (stone molds for the castings were found), the minting of coins (represented by a number of fragments of clay molds for making the coin blanks before striking), the manufacture of glass beads and bracelets, and a pottery industry which was producing high-class wares for distribution over a very considerable area.

The great rampart erected to protect the community incorporated a type of construction which Julius Caesar saw and described in France, calling it a *murus Gallicus* (Gallic wall). The technique involved was to build up an open-box structure with a crisscross of timbers laid horizontally. These were nailed firmly together and a vertical stone wall was built in front with the ends of the cross timbers poking through. Behind the wall and within and behind the timber framework, soil and rubble were piled. Caesar was impressed with the solidity of construction, noting that the stonework protected it from fire while the timber structure gave a resilience which it was impossible for a battering ram to breach. The *murus Gallicus* style of building was widely adopted in Europe in the first century B.C., but it clearly develops from a tradition of rampart construction which goes back to the Urnfield period. Manching was the chief town of a tribe called the *Vindelici*, and according to the evidence of the objects found, it was in use throughout the first century B.C., ending its life in destruction some time towards the end of the century. One possibility is that it was destroyed by the Romans, who campaigned through the area in 15 B.C.

Each of the more advanced of the central

group of tribes will have had one or more towns of this type. Caesar encountered a number as he campaigned through Gaul, perhaps the most famous being Bibracte (Mont Beuvray), the capital of the pro-Roman tribe called the Aedui. The formidable hilltop is enclosed by 5 kilometers of defenses estimated to have stood 5 meters in height. Within, roads meandered from one quarter to another without evidence of rigid planning except that certain areas were set aside for different functions. The iron workers, for example, tended to occupy the slopes of the hill, while jewelers and the enamelers had their workshops close together along one of the main streets. The excavators also identified a consecrated place, a market area, and

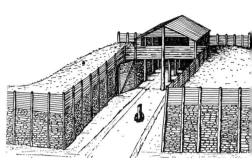

Reconstruction of one of the main entrances of the oppidum at Manching, with its gate set back between the inturned ends of the rampart to give added protection.

what they believed to be an aristocratic quarter.

Bibracte continued to thrive well after Caesar's conquest and remained in use up to about 5 B.C., by which time the urban life of the region had begun to focus on the new Roman foundation at Autun in the valley some kilometers away to the east.

The Celtic urban center (oppidum) at Manching is one of the best known in Europe as the result of meticulous excavations carried out between 1953 and 1967. The defensive circuit (in white) makes use of the River Paar, a tributary of the Danube.

THE SHIFTING TRIBES

The god of the hunt, a favorite deity among so many of the diverse Celtic tribes. Hunting was very popular with the Celts, as so much evidence attests, although they were also an agrarian people whose frequent migrations were often motivated by the exhaustion of old farmland and the quest for new. This statue is one of the few Celtic artworks that show the typical coat worn by the people.

The tribal situation was always fluid. At the height of the migrations whole tribes or parts of tribes would move across vast territories settling temporarily and then moving on again. Even as late as the first century B.C., when the main phase of migration was at an end, we learn from Caesar how the Helvetii of Switzerland, considering that they had outgrown their territory, burned their homes and moved west en masse only to be intercepted, defeated in battle, and sent back by Caesar.

Another factor affecting the tribal map was the changing fortunes, of the individual tribes—a tribe, powerful at one moment with many lesser tribes dependent upon it, might suddenly lose prestige and sink into oblivion. The situation in Gaul in the middle of the first century B.C. provides an insight into these matters. There were two principal factions headed, respectively, by the Aedui and the Sequani. Caesar sums up the situation: "As the Aedui had long enjoyed very great prestige and had many satellite tribes, the Sequani were the weaker of the two since they depended on their own resources." It would seem then that a system of clientage existed at tribal level, the principal tribes receiving tribute from their satellites, presumably in return for protection. However, as the result of battles, in which the Aeduian aristocracy was wiped out, the Sequani demonstrated their superiority, and many of the tribes previously dependent on the Aedui went over to them. To counter this the Aedui solicited, and eventually obtained, the patronage of Rome, as a result of which dependent tribes flocked back to them, leaving the Sequani isolated. Those lesser tribes who for reasons of ancient feuds and rivalries could not bring themselves to be clients of the Aedui chose instead the Remi as protector who, as Caesar says, "by taking good care of them, were able to maintain the unaccustomed power they had suddenly acquired."

The example typifies the fickle nature of tribal allegiances; it also demonstrates with great clarity how important Roman patronage had now become in upsetting and readjusting the balance of power. Yet in spite of all this the tribal pattern was sufficiently well established for tribal units to form a basis of the administrative structure under Roman rule when one by one the Celtic territories were subsumed.

BOII

The Boii were one of the more mobile of the Celtic tribes. In the fifth century a substantial number migrated from north of the Alps and settled in the Po valley, the rest staying in the traditional territories in Bohemia. The north Italian group suffered under the Roman advance, while those in Bohemia later migrated westward into France, forced out by the Cimbri and Teutones.

HELVETII

A tribe occupying much of modern Switzerland. In the first century A.D., as the result of population growth and pressure from tribes to the north, they decided to migrate westward into Gaul. In 58 B.C. Caesar halted their migration and defeated them, forcing the remnants to return home.

AEDUI

Paramount tribe in central France occupying the territory around Autun. By virtue of their position close to the Rhône trade route, they adopted elements of classical culture. By Caesar's time, because of intertribal fighting, their position of supremacy was in decline, but by aligning themselves with Rome they soon restored their former importance.

ARVERNI

Powerful tribe occupying the Massif Central in Caesar's time. They were violently opposed to Rome.

VENETII

Maritime tribe living in the southwest of the Armorican peninsula. They were traders and acted as middlemen in shipping goods from Britain to the south. In 56 B.C. they rebelled against Caesar but were soundly beaten in a sea battle at Quiberon, and as a result all the leading men were executed and the rest sold as slaves.

NERVII

One of the Belgic tribes of northern Gaul living in central Belgium, east of the Scheldt. They put up powerful resistance to Caesar and were virtually annihilated by him.

SCORDISCI

After the migration into Greece had failed, many thousands of Celts poured back into central Europe to find land to settle. One group, the Scordisci, led by Bathanatos settled between the rivers Drava and Sava with an oppidum on the site of Beograd. They were a powerful force in the subsequent settlement in the rest of Transdanubia.

DUROTRIGES

Powerful but politically backward tribe occupying Dorset in southern Britain. Vespasian, then a legionary commander, had to destroy more than twenty native hillforts, including Maiden Castle, before the tribe would submit.

ICENI

British tribe occupying Norfolk and Suffolk. They allied themselves to Rome after the invasion of Claudius and were ruled by a client king, Prasutagus. When he died, there was trouble resulting in a widespread uprising led by Queen Boudicca. The rebellion was ill-prepared and soon failed.

whom settled in southern Gaul while the other moved into Anatolia. The Gaulish group possessed a vast treasure of gold and silver which was pillaged by the Romans in 106 B.C.

ERAVISCI

Tribe occupying much of Transdanubia (in modern Hungary) with one of their principal settlements on the Danube at Budapest. It is possible that they moved into the region from the north in the first century A.D. Eraviscan culture remained strong throughout the early part of the Roman occupation: Celtic dress and jewelry continued to be worn even by the rich families as is witnessed by tombstone reliefs.

They are wont
to change their abode
on slight provocation,
migrating in bands
with all their battle-array,
or rather setting out
with their households
when displaced
by a stronger enemy.

Strabo

TRINOVANTES

Occupied part of eastern England just north of the Thames. In Caesar's time they were in conflict with their neighbors the Catuvellauni. They became allies of Rome and their chieftains grew rich on trade with the Roman world, acquiring luxury objects and wine.

VOLCAE

The Volcae were originally neighbors of the Boii in central Europe. An offshoot of the tribe probably contributed to the Volcae Tectosages, one branch of

BRIGANTES

Large confederacy stretching across northern England from the Irish Sea to the North Sea. In the first century A.D. it seems to have been allied to Rome, but jealousies broke out between Queen Cartimandua and her husband Venutius and eventually Roman troops had to intercede on the queen's behalf. Venutius was later beaten in a pitched battle.

PARISII

A tribe living in the region of modern Paris. Their chief city, Lutetia, was the predecessor of Paris.

La Tène—site of fifth to second-century Celtic settlements on the shores of Lake Neuchâtel in Switzerland. This name, associated with a site that now lies submerged, has come to designate a period in time rather than a place.

RELIGION AND MYSTERY

The Gallo-Roman relief of mother goddesses, from Alesia, typifies the Celtic tradition of sacred triads. The horned Cernunnos, god of the underworld, inspired statues throughout the Celtic world (opposite, a German example).

As a nation the Gauls are extremely superstitious;
and so persons suffering from
serious diseases, as well as those who are exposed
to the perils of battle, offer human sacrifices.

Caesar

Skulls that gaze out from stone temple walls...statues of animals, horned figures, men-beasts...and everywhere triple groupings of gods, priests, heads. Such evidence leaves no doubt that the Celts carried on an active spiritual life, marked by apparitions, cults, talismans, and supernatural symbolism. Roman witnesses, some sympathetic and some contemptuous, have added their words to the record, giving us accounts of coldblooded human sacrifices and superstitious taboos, while explaining the priestly role of the druidic elite. The shadow-world of the Celtic supernatural is filled with landmarks. What our guides do not provide—for no doubt it did not exist—is a master-plan, a world-system, a hierarchy like that of the Greek and Roman pantheon. Moreover, the deeper significance of so many Celtic religious symbols eludes us as it did the Romans, since the druids imparted their teaching only by word of mouth, in woodland clearings, by sacred springs, or in temple sanctuaries closed to any outsider. And thus we find ourselves with more questions than answers concerning the religion—or religions—of the Celts.

The Celts were a superstitious people. The supernatural pervaded every aspect of life —the spirits were everywhere: in ancient trees, weird rocks, and in the rivers and bogs. No part of the daily routine could be carried out without some reminder of the gods. They were responsible for the seasons and they controlled the natural world of which man was a part: they therefore had to be placated through intermediaries—the druids—who knew the ancient wisdom and could ensure that the correct procedures were at all times followed.

The Celts believed that if a human life was at risk through serious disease or because of exposure to danger, it was because the gods were wrathful. The only way to placate their antagonisms, and to save the endangered life, was therefore to offer another life in its place. Criminals were preferred as sacrifices, but if the supply of criminals was insufficient, numbers could be made up by substituting innocent men. The method of sacrifice varied, but the most dramatic of the practices described by the ancient writers comes once more from the pen of Caesar. "Some tribes," he says, "have colossal images made of wickerwork, the limbs of which they fill with living men: they are then set on fire, and the victims are burned to death."

Caesar may well have overemphasized human sacrifice, at which he professed horror, in order to justify in the minds of his readers his brutal campaigns against the Celts in Gaul. But that it formed a part of Celtic ritual there can be no doubt.

The evidence concerning Celtic religion is particularly rich. The classical writers provide tantalizing insights into the nature of offerings, of beliefs, and, in particular, about the priestly class, the druids (pp. 106–111). It is possible to extend this picture, with data derived from archaeological excavations, to throw more light on the location and arrangement of ritual sites. To this we may add interpretations based on the enormous range of iconographic data which survives, including religious sculpture and dedications, much of it created by Celtic populations under Roman domination. Finally there is available the wealth of detail, often obscure and difficult to use, which escaped the censorship of the Christian scribes who committed the sagas of the pagan Irish to writing.

A PAGAN TRINITY

Three was a sacred or auspicious number in the ancient world. It is hardly surprising therefore that triplism recurs, to some extent, as an element in the Celtic supernatural. Less mystical than the Christian trinity, this Celtic theme simply implied an added strength or potency because it is more than one. We have already mentioned the fighting unit, the *trimarcisia*, which comprised the nobleman and his two supporters—a somewhat secular and more practical expression of the same concept. Allusions to triplism occur in the Irish literature. The three mother goddesses of war, Mórrígan, Macha, and Bodb, are known collectively as Mórrígna (the great queens).

"I swear," said Cú Chulainn, "by the gods by whom Ultonians swear, that I will bruise you against a green stone of the ford."
"I will become a gray wolf for you," said the Mórrígan, "and take the flesh from your right hand as far as to your left arm."
"I will encounter you with my spear," he said, "until your left or right eye is forced out."
"I will become a white red-eared cow," she said, "and I will go into the pond beside the ford in which you are in combat, with a hundred white red-eared cows behind me. And I and all behind me will rush into the ford, and the Fair Play of Men that day shall be brought to a test, and your head shall be cut off from you."
"Your right or your left leg," he said, "I will break with a cast of my sling, and you shall never have any help from me, if you leave me not."
Thereupon the Mórrígan departed into the Fairy Hill of Cruachan in Connacht, and Cú Chulainn returned to his bed.

The *Taín*

Because the number three represents strength, many deities were depicted in triple from. The style of representation varies considerably, from very crude engravings like the "three mothers" *(above)* from Burgundy dating to the third century A.D., to such sophisticated Gallo-Roman renderings as the three-headed god molded on the side of a terracotta vase from Bavay, France, second century B.C. *(opposite)*.

The goddess Brigit also has three aspects. The male gods show the tendency less clearly, though Lugh appears with two brothers and Dagdá is sometimes associated with two other names.

In Celtic and Romano-Celtic iconography triplism is amply represented, in particular in the reliefs of the "Three Mothers" which recur in virtually every part of the Celtic world. They are usually depicted as seated deities accompanied by attributes of fertility such as fruit, cornucopias, and occasionally infants. See, for example, the fine relief from Vertillum in the Côte d'Or (page 48). Triads of this kind, which are particularly common in this area of Burgundy, must

represent the aspects of a popular local deity. A similar concentration occurs in the Cotswolds in southern England. Male triads have been found there as well, but less frequently (p. 49, above).

Another form in which triplism can manifest itself is in the tricephalos—the three-faced head. This might take the form of a simple boulder carved with three faces: a well-known example was found at Corleck, Cavan, in Ireland, and another has turned up more recently in Wiltshire. A more sophisticated representation is shown opposite.

Finally we might mention the triskele—a simple decorative motif consisting of three elements which appear to move in the same direction about a single central point. Triskeles, quite commonly used in Celtic art, must ultimately have derived from a solar symbol to which, of course, connotations of strength are attached. It is possibly significant that the triskele was the motif used to decorate the boss of a shield found at Llyn Cerrig in Anglesey. Could it be that by decorating the shield in this way, the craftsman sought to give his patron more than just physical protection?

"Dark one are you restless
do you guess they gather
to certain slaughter the wise raven
groans aloud
that enemies infest
the fair fields
ravaging in packs
learn I discern rich plains
softly wavelike
baring their necks
greenness of grass
beauty of blossoms
on the plains war
grinding heroic
hosts to dust
cattle groans the Badb
the raven ravenous
among corpses of men
affliction and outcry
and war everlasting
raging over Cuailnge death of sons
death of kinsmen
death death!"

The Mórrígan in the *Taín*

EARTH MOTHER AND TRIBAL FATHER

Beneath the confusing mass of detail about the Celtic supernatural which survives in the Irish literature and is reflected in the iconography remaining from the Roman period, a simple underlying theme emerges: The female deities are all in some way reflections of an earth mother-goddess, while the male gods, whatever their specific attributes, all have abilities appropriate to the tribal god. We can perhaps see in this apparent simplicity the foundation stone of Celtic religion.

The Irish literature helps us to endow these shadowy concepts with a certain substance. The great male god—the god on whom the tribal deities were based—was the Dagdá, a name which means "The Good God." The Irish story of the "battle of

I am she
that is the natural
mother of all things,
mistress and governess
of all the elements,
the initial progeny of worlds,
chief of the powers divine,
queen of all that are in hell,
the principal of them
that dwell in heaven,
manifested alone
and under one form
of all the gods and goddesses.

Lucius Apuleius

Moytura" explains the meaning of the epithet. In the council of war before the battle, each god declares his qualifications. When it comes to the Dagdá's turn, he simply says, "All that you promise to do I will do myself alone," to which the others reply, "It is you who are the *good god*." Clearly then, "good" in this context has no moral implication, it means the "all-competent"—"the good-at-everything." The Dagdá, thus endowed, is the basis for all other personifications of the deity.

His female counterpart, in the Irish literature, was the Mórrígan—the "great queen." She appears in many guises as Panic, the Raven of Battle, and in triple form with Macha and Bodb. She is essentially a mother-goddess—a goddess of fertility—but more than that, she is the introducer of fear and irrationality, who can undermine men in times of crisis and sometimes delights in doing so.

In the relationship between the two, the male Dagdá (the tribal personification of all skills), and the female Mórrígan (the earth, fertility, and uncertainty), everything can be explained: good and evil, rational and irrational, bravery and fear. Life results from the interplay of these opposing elements.

In the Celtic world of Ireland these two aspects were annually united for the common good at the festival of *Samhain* celebrated on the first of November. During Samhain, the limbo period between the ending of one year and the beginning of the next, the spirits were loosed and the world was in chaos. The word appears to mean a coming together; on these occasions the whole tribe presumably assembled for feasting and to ensure, through sacrifice, the continued fertility of the crops and herds. In Celtic mythology Samhain was the time of reconciliation between the tribal god and the earth-mother in her tribal guise, when they came together for intercourse—the act ensuring that the balance of the forces had been restored and that the fertility of the land and of the people was renewed.

In these pages we endeavor to reduce the plethora of Celtic myths and deities to their essentials. What emerges is clearly the survival of a very ancient pan-European belief, which the Celts in their different territories and at different times embroidered, to provide a fabric of great intricacy.

Northern Irish sculpture of a radiating god.

The belief in a goddess of creation and destruction is very deep-rooted, and in spite of a veneer of Christianity, it can be traced throughout medieval Europe. The sculpture *(right)* of a Sheela-na-gig—evidently a fertility deity—is on a corbel in the medieval church at Kilpeck in Herefordshire. It is one of the few that survived destruction in a spate of nineteenth-century puritanism.

The tribal god could take on many guises, but one of the most popular was that of a hunter. Here we see him, resplendent in his antler crown and holding a magical torque, on the first-century B.C. Gundestrup caldron, found in Denmark.

The good god, Dagda, in the Irish literature, is represented as a figure of great strength. He carries a massive club and a magic caldron which is inexhaustible and possesses the power to inspire and rejuvenate. In this Gallo-Roman bronze from Prémeaux, in France, he is depicted as the Dis Pater—a version of the Roman Jupiter.

The rich iconography of Celtic Europe presents us with a bewildering variety of deities. In all, more than four hundred names are recorded, but three-quarters of these occur only once, leaving little doubt that each locality probably supported its own versions of the pan-Celtic tribal and nature gods.

Caesar, evidently not concerned to discuss the variety of Celtic deities in any detail, merely reports the diversity and interprets it in terms which his Roman readers could understand: If a Celtic god, no matter what he was called, had the same characteristics as a Roman god, then surely they must be the same.

The other classical authors are no more helpful. However, Lucan, a Greek poet who wrote in the second century A.D. after traveling in Gaul, mentions three Celtic gods by name—Esus, Taranis, and Teutates —who clearly have their counterparts in Ireland and Wales. Taranis comes from the same word as the Welsh *taran* and Irish *torann*, meaning "thunder," while the name Teutates is the same root as *tuáth*, "tribe" in Irish. Why Lucan should have given special preference to these three is not immediately apparent; they occur but rarely in the archaeological record. In all probability he simply enlarged on some scrap of inconsequential data with a poet's license. It would be wrong to think of the Celtic gods arrayed in a *pantheon* as were the more ordered deities of the Greeks and Romans. The Celtic supernatural beings were more shadowy figures whose relationships and hierarchies are ill-defined, but there are vague hints in the Irish literature that the gods were conceived of in rather the same way as the tribe was organized. At the head was the tribal god and his consort, the earth mother (as we have already seen, p. 72–73), but above them there is the vague concept of the "mother of the gods"—an upper echelon from whom the tribal gods were descended. Thus, in this very ill-defined area, it would seem that the tribal gods related to some higher deities in the same way as the tribal chief was descended from the tribal gods. The parallel might be extended down to the next level. Just as the skilled class in the tribe was divided into craftsmen, healers, and men of learning, so there is evidence among the deities of these same specializations, although how these craftsmen-gods related to the tribal, all-

competent deity is obscure. These matters were probably equally vague even in the minds of the Celts.

The problem of whether or not there was a defined hierarchy among the Celtic gods is further complicated by the Irish *Tuatha Dé Dannan*, "the peoples of the Goddess Dann"—a confederation composed of a number of deities. While this may dimly reflect the notion of a family of gods, it could equally well be explained in terms of clientage and the dominance of one tribal god over those of subservient tribes.

When we consider the individual gods, one stands out above the myriad of minor immortals by virtue of his extensive distribution—the god Lug. In Ireland his special day, *Lugnasadh* (the first of August), was one of the four great festivals in the Irish calendar (pp. 110–111), while at Lugdunum (Lyons) in Gaul the feast of the divine emperor Augustus was celebrated on the same day—an interesting example of how the Romans adapted native religious susceptibilities to their own official uses. The god's name survives as an element in Celtic place names throughout Europe, while dedications to the deity have been found as far apart as Switzerland and Spain. In another guise, that of Find—"the Fair-haired One"—his name survives in the Roman

Right: Riding gods were popular throughout the Celtic world. They represented the tribal god as a warrior. This Romano-British example comes from Willingham Fen near Cambridge.

Taranis, Celtic god associated with thunder, was conflated in the Roman mind with Jupiter. In the Gallo-Roman period he was therefore often depicted with such attributes of Jupiter as the thunder bolt. In this bronze statuette from France he is also shown with a wheel in his left hand.

The Gauls all assert their descent
from Dis pater
and say that it is the Druidic belief.
For this reason they count periods of time
not by the number of days
but by the number of nights;
and in reckoning birthdays
and the new moon and new year
their unit of reckoning is
the night followed by the day.

Caesar

names of *Vindobona* (Vienna), and *Vindonissa* in Switzerland. So widespread, and no doubt powerful, a deity must have had a deep-seated appeal to the Celts. His association with the August festival—an important date in the agrarian calendar—suggests that he may have been a fertility god.

A recurring theme in Celtic iconography is the horned god of which two main types may be distinguished: the antler horned god, Cernunnos, and the bull- or ram-horned god, who is unnamed. Cernunnos, wearing his antler headgear, with two gold torques, one around his neck and the other in his right hand, is shown sitting among his beasts on the Gundestrup caldron (p. 73). In this guise he is seen at his most typical, accompanied by a stag and a horned serpent. Clearly a deity of some antiquity, Cernunnos may well reflect a hunting god of the pre-farming period. Pierced antler frontlets have been found at the camps of Mesolithic hunters, and the wearing of antlers by shamans (magicians and seers) is well attested among the later pastoral communities of Russia and the circumpolar zone. The torque, was widely regarded in the Celtic period as having magical properties in warding off evil, while a serpent is a frequent attribute of the Celtic version of the war god. The other, unnamed, horned god must also be associated with warfare, since he is often depicted naked but armed. The serpent may be a reminder of the god's other attribute as a healer. There is nothing inconsistent in this suggestion; the Celtic tribal god was, after all, skilled at all things. There is an interesting example of just such

The tribal gods appear in many artworks as blacksmiths or other craftsmen. *Left:* Dis Pater (father of the gods) from Visp, Switzerland. *Above:* Wood-cutter god from Trier, Germany.

is well attested in Irish mythology and reappears in Wales as Govannon, but it is not certain whether we are dealing here with a separate deity or merely with an aspect of the all-competent tribal god.

Taranis sometimes appears in another form, holding a wheel. In this guise, he is intended to be a sky god, comparable to the Roman Jupiter. In Romano-Celtic iconography he may also appear as a bearded horseman, dressed in Roman style, trampling on a giant (p. 51). Representations of this kind, set on columns, have a restricted distribution from the Middle Rhine to northeastern Gaul, where the cult was evidently very popular.

The tribal goddesses were all, in one way or another, deities of fertility and of bounty. We have already discussed the triads of *matres* (mothers), which gained wide popularity in the Celtic world, where the emphasis was always on plenty (the cornucopia) or fertility (infants). Female deities also presented themselves in other styles. The Irish Flidais was evidently a woodland spirit who commanded the animals. As a huntress she was clearly the counterpart of the Roman Diana, whose other concerns were, of course, fertility (so vividly demonstrated in her appearance as the many-breasted Artemis).

Another female deity who gained great popularity in the Romano-Celtic world was Epona, whose cult seems to have been based in the region of Alesia in eastern France. Epona is usually shown riding a horse sidesaddle and may be accompanied by a bird, a dog, or a foal. In one dedication she is referred to in the plural—*Eponabus*—a hint that she, like the *matres*, may have been conceived of as triple. Although

Rider-goddess Epona, Gallo-Roman statuette from Alesia, France, one of the main centers of the cult. Other female deities popular in eastern France were the "three mothers," a triad of fertility and plenty.

a combination of skills in the Irish literature. In the *Túatha Dé Danann*, one of the gods, renowned as a warrior, heals the wounded hero Cú Chulainn with magical chants and sacred herbs.

Another aspect of the tribal deity, which is sometimes emphasized, is his ability as a smith—his identity proclaimed by association with the tools of the trade. In this guise he is presumably Taranis "the thunderer" mentioned by Lucan—and conflation with the Roman Vulcan would have been inevitable. The divine smith, Goibniu,

Epona was a Gaulish deity, later introduced into Britain, there already existed native equivalents in the British Riannon and the Irish Macha.

Female deities endowed with healing powers are frequently associated with rivers or springs. The great thermal springs at Bath in England were presided over by the native goddess Sulis, who was inevitably conflated with the Roman Minerva, while at the source of the Seine the native shrine of Sequanna has yielded a range of votive offerings (discussed below, pp. 90–91) which dramatically emphasized her powers to cure the sick.

On the other hand, the goddess could be vengeful, as was the great Mórrígan of the Irish sagas, whose sexual advances the hero Cú Chulainn ignores. Enraged and craving revenge, she attempts to distract him while he is locked in deadly single combat with Lóch:

So the Mórrígan came there in the guise of a white red-eared heifer accompanied by fifty heifers.... Cú Chulainn made a cast at the Mórrígan and shattered one of her eyes. Then the Mórrígan appeared in the form of a slippery, black eel swimming downstream and went into the pool and coiled herself around Cú Chulainn's legs.... Then the Mórrígan came in the guise of a shaggy russet-colored she-wolf. While Cú Chulainn was warding her off, Lóch wounded him. Thereupon Cú Chulainn was filled with rage and wounded him ... and pierced his heart in his breast.

A great weariness fell on Cú Chulainn. The Mórrígan appeared to him in the shape of a squint-eyed old woman milking a cow with three teats. He asked her for a drink and she gave him milk from the first teat.

"Good health to the giver!" Cú Chulainn said. "The blessing of God and man on you."

And her head was healed and made whole. She gave him milk from the second teat and her eye was made whole. She gave him milk from the third teat and her legs were made whole.

"You said you would never heal me," the Mórrígan said.

"If I had known it was you I wouldn't have done it," Cú Chulainn said.

To a Celt the shadowy world of the gods was to be avoided if possible, but if contact was inevitable the correct form of propitiation was essential—otherwise unknown catastrophe might ensue.

Overleaf (pp. 78–79): On the bronze funerary cart from a grave mound at Strettweg in Austria, a goddess directs the procession accompanying a soul to the afterlife. The Hallstatt peoples, many of whom practiced cremation, occasionally placed such miniature carts in the grave as a symbol of the death journey. Bronze wagon, 35 cm (14 in.) long; seventh century B.C.

The poet Lucan named three Celtic gods of which one was Esus, shown on this relief from Paris as a war god. The inscription above his head identifies him.

Below: A gallery of deities from all over the Celtic world, some of them as they were represented in the Roman period: *From left to right:*

Boar-god wearing a heavy torque around his neck, from Euffigneix, France. Gallo-Roman period.

Mother goddess holding fruit and foliage, emblems of productive fertility, from Caerwent, Wales. Romano-British.

God of unknown speciality sitting cross-legged. He wears a torque giving him magical protection. From Bouray, France. First century A.D.

Hunting god of the second century A.D., from Touget, France.

Horned god from Burgh-by-Sands, northern England. It was from powerful depictions of this type that the medieval vision of the devil was derived.

A goddess of serpents, possibly a healing goddess. From Ilkley, northern England. Romano-British.

Celtic god of the pre-Roman Iron Age, from France.

The Celts, unlike their contemporaries in eastern Europe, were not particularly interested in mythical animals. The beasts which they chose to represent were those they saw in their everyday lives or encountered in the hunt. Because the gods could take on animal form if they wished, all animals could be gods in disguise. For this reason animal iconography became well developed.

Sometimes the deities were associated with their related animal, like Epona and the horse (p. 78) or the bear and goddess Artio shown here *(top right)* from Muri, Switzerland. The style of this particular piece suggests a date in the second to third century A.D.
Other favorite animals were the bull (Lillebonne, France), the horse (Freisen, Germany), and the dog (Moudon, Switzerland).

The Irish myth of the Mórrígan harassing Cú Chulainn (p. 77) is a reminder that the Celtic gods had the power to transform themselves into animals at will. Thus animals were often regarded with respect, not least because they might be a god who had indulged in shape-shifting. Some animals, moreover, were believed to possess magical powers.

Of the sacred animals the most important was the boar. The symbol of strength and of power, the boar was a suitable animal with which to adorn one's armor. For this reason, crests in the shape of boars are sometimes found on Celtic helmets. A stylized rendering of a boar was also applied to the surface of a bronze shield dredged from the River Witham in England. In contexts such as these we may assume that the

beast was intended to protect the wearer from the blows of his opponent. Perhaps the most famous representation of a boar is carved on the stone sculpture of a god found at Euffigneix in France (p. 76), but the identity of this boar-god remains unknown. It may also be relevant to the animal's magical status that joints of pork and sometimes whole carcasses were buried with the dead. While this could mean merely the provision of a meal in the afterworld, the animal's presence might have been intended to offer strength and support for the journey.

Another animal of considerable cult significance was the dog. Hunting dogs were well known among the Celts, and in this capacity the dog accompanied the Celtic goddess of the forest. Dogs are also found in association with the goddess Epona and with a local god Nodens, the Irish Nuadu, who, traditionally, had an artificial hand made of silver. Nodens was worshiped at a late Roman temple found at Lydney in Gloucestershire where excavations brought to light votive offerings in the form of hands, and, significantly, a small bronze casting of a dog of a breed which closely resembles an Irish wolfhound.

Of the other animals invested with super-frequent. The swan, in particular, is a recurring motif on bronzework of the Urnfield and Hallstatt period. The Irish literature is full of bird symbolism. The raven, a dangerous and menacing creature, was the form the Irish goddess of war might assume, while the crane was thought to be wholly evil. The variety of European folklore about birds reflects the considerable range of beliefs which once surrounded them.

The bird-god Abraxas inspired numerous portrayals of the cock, as in this relief from Nyon, near Geneva.

natural powers, we have already mentioned the stag, so often associated with Cernunnos, and the horse, from which Epona was inseparable. To these should be added the bull and the ram. The bull, usually with three horns, was popular in certain areas of Gaul, while ram-horned serpents and occasionally gods with ram's horns have been found, but they are only of subsidiary significance.

Birds too were a potent force in Celtic mythology and representations of them are

The power of the boar, its loneness and its ferocity when hunted, helped to endow it with magical properties in the Celtic mind. This fine specimen, from Neuvy-en-Sullias, France, dates from the Gallo-Roman period.

THE CULT OF THE HUMAN HEAD

They embalm in cedar-oil
the heads of
the most distinguished enemies
and preserve them carefully in a chest
and display them
with pride to strangers
saying that for this head
one of their ancestors, or his father,
or the man himself,
refused the offer of a large sum of money.
They say that some of them
boast that they refused
the weight of the head in gold.

Diodorus Siculus

The cult of the severed head is dramatically revealed in the two famous temples of southern Gaul, Entremont and Roquepertuse. In the pillars of the portico of the temple of Roquepertuse, niches were carved to hold human skulls. At Entremont *(opposite)* the same concept is transformed into stone and stylized. Both temples were destroyed when the Romans colonized the area in the late second century B.C.

They cut off the heads of enemies slain in battle and attach them to the necks of their horses. The blood-stained spoils they hand over to their attendants and carry off as booty, while striking up a paean and singing a song of victory; and they nail up these first fruits upon their houses.... They embalm in cedar oil the heads of the most distinguished enemies, and preserve them carefully in a chest and display them with pride to strangers saying that for this head one of their ancestors, or his father, or the man himself refused the offer of a large sum of money. They say that some of them boast that they refused the weight of the head in gold.

This explicit account by Diodorus Siculus typifies the head hunting that was so common among the Celts. The practice was not merely bloodthirstiness, however. In common with many primitive peoples, the Celts believed that the soul resided in the head. The head symbolized the very essence of being, and consequently could exist in its own right. By possessing someone's head, one controlled that person and his spirit. These beliefs are manifest in the archaeological evidence, the classical tradition, and the Irish and Welsh literature.

The same theme is echoed by Livy writing of events in the third century B.C.:

The Consuls got no report of the disaster until some Gallic horsemen came in sight, with heads hanging at their horses' breasts, or fixed on their lances, and singing their customary songs of triumph.

Elsewhere the same writer gives an account of the aftermath of an ambush in northern Italy in which the Roman consul-elect Lucius Postumius was killed. The Boii (a Celtic tribe at this time occupying part of the Po valley) "stripped his body, cut off the head, and carried their spoils in triumph to the most hallowed of their temples. There they cleaned out the head, as is their custom, and gilded the skull, which thereafter served them as a holy vessel to pour libations from and as a drinking cup for the priest and the temple attendants."

Several points of considerable interest are contained in these accounts. First there is the carrying away of the spoils in triumph accompanied by battle songs, then their subsequent deposition, as trophies placed over the gate, or as specially revered items accorded some place of honor. The conqueror now owned the power of his vanquished foe. By attaching heads of lesser enemies to the gate, he was doing more

than boasting, he was using the power of the heads for the protection of his own community. A pictorial representation of just such a scene is shown on Trajan's Column. In this instance the heads are those of Roman soldiers captured by the Dacians in Transylvania. Each is shown elevated on a stake, looking out from behind the Dacian fortifications.

The special treatment afforded to the heads of high-ranking or famous enemies sets them aside as part of the portable history of the society. Such collections were maintained either by the community as a whole (in the case of the head pressed into service in the temple of the Boii) or by the individual family, in whose care they became priceless heirlooms, giving protection and providing a constant demonstration of their owners' greatness.

Skulls are often found in excavation on quite ordinary domestic sites, such as farms and hillforts which otherwise have no special ritual association. In one instance, at Stanwick in Yorkshire, a skull, which had presumably been nailed over the gate, was found nearby in the ditch where it had fallen. At Danebury, in southern Britain, skulls were sometimes found on the bottom of storage pits, placed there presumably when the pits had ceased to be used but before they were refilled. It is difficult to know how to interpret this phenomenon unless the head was being dedicated to the gods as thanks for a successful period of storage. Fragments of skull have been found amid the domestic remains of a number of settlements, often worn smooth by handling and occasionally perforated so that they could be worn as amulets. These were perhaps treasured relics handed down from one generation to the next in a manner similar to that described by Diodorus.

But the Celts were not mere head hunters. The head represented an aspect of divinity, and as such was an appropriate offering with which to adorn a temple. The most dramatic evidence for the cult of the severed head comes from the south of France. Within the oppidum of Entremont in Provence (a defended settlement destroyed by the Romans in 124 B.C.), a shrine was uncovered on the highest part of the hill, approached by a pathway lined with statues of heroes. Within the shrine itself stood a tall pillar carved with twelve simplified human heads (opposite). The

The Celtic head cult probably has very ancient origins. The early prehistoric inhabitants of eastern France, in sites such as this cave in the "Dame Jouanne" hills (Seine-et-Marne), practiced a severed head cult long before the Celts.

The head remained a powerful motif throughout the Christian period in Ireland and indeed in the rest of Britain. The gargoyles, corbels, and other decorative heads which decorate many churches, particularly of the eleventh to twelfth centuries A.D., owe much to the Celtic interpretation

of the head. Often it is impossible to distinguish Celtic from Christian carvings. In a Christian context, heads would have encapsulated and made safe the spirits that haunted the folk memory.
Above: Doorway from Dysert O'Dea, Ireland. *Right:* From the church at Clonfert, Ireland. Both Romanesque.

same site has produced a remarkable array of severed-head sculpture, including individual representations of men, women and children as well as groups of heads (picture, p. 86).

Even more vivid evidence of the cult has been uncovered at the nearby sanctuary of Roquepertuse. Here the shrine, arranged on two terraces, was adorned with a portal of three upright columns carrying a horizontal lintel, upon which perched a huge bird, poised to fly away—a symbol perhaps of the flight of spirits to the Other World. Particular interest attaches to the columns which were each carved with a series of niches to take human heads, some of which are actually in position (shown on p. 82). The columns were originally painted with fish and foliage. In addition to these structural monuments, the shrine also produced two carvings of squatting figures, possibly priests or gods, one with a torque and armlet and the other with a belted tunic

painted in bright colors in a check pattern. From the same shrine came a fine sculpture of two heads clasped in what appears to be the beak of a bird of prey (p. 87).

Finally, from the same region comes the famous "Tarasque" at Noves, a fearsome monster covered in scales depicted in the act of devouring a human being and holding, in both paws, severed human heads (illustrated on p. 107).

Together this remarkable group brings us close to the reality of the cult of the severed head, a cult evidently well established in the hinterland of Marseilles. The richness of the surviving evidence is, in part at least, due to the influence of the classical world which taught the native Celts the art of stone building and sculpture; but what we are seeing is nevertheless a purely Celtic religious expression. The apparent uniqueness of these sites should not obscure the fact that all over the Celtic world there were probably similar sanctuaries, similarly adorned, but built of timber, leaving few traces save for a few post-holes in the bedrock.

The cult of the severed head is a recurring theme in the Irish literature. The hero Cú Chulainn, by the end of his exploits, had an enormous collection to his credit. His arrival at Emain Macha is described thus: "A single chariot warrior is here... and terribly he comes. He has in the chariot the bloody heads of his enemies." The exuberance of his approach has its counterpart in war songs of the triumphant warriors described by Livy and Diodorus. On another occasion, however, he leaves the heads of his enemies at the ford where he had slain them. The grim scene is described by a traveler who arrived after the encounter was over: "He saw only the forked pole in the middle of the ford with four heads on it dripping blood down the stem of the pole into the current of the stream, and the hoof marks of the two horses, and the track of a single charioteer and of a single warrior leading eastward out of the ford." This practice of leaving the heads where they were taken is again mentioned when, as the result of another encounter, Cú Chulainn acquired twelve heads which he proceeded to display on twelve stones. This particular behavior pattern may reflect the belief in the need to propitiate the spirits of the location who had allowed the victory to be achieved.

The head was regarded as the dwelling place of the soul and thus it had both a divine and a protective aspect. To possess the head of an enemy was to control his power. It is hardly surprising therefore that the motif of the head pervaded Celtic art.

The face was depicted in a variety of ways, a range of which are shown here. *Below:* In repoussé, female head from a caldron found at Kraghede Denmark. The hair style compares with a mount *(center)* from a wooden flagon of ca. 400 B.C. from Dürrnberg, Austria, though the figure is male.

The cult of the severed head is also reflected in the Welsh literature. In the *Mabinogion* the severed head of the god Bran goes on actively directing events long after it has been removed from its wounded body. The story is a fascinating example of the power with which the head was believed to be endowed. Another expression of the same belief, continuing into later centuries, is amply demonstrated by the popularity of the head in medieval religious architecture in the Celtic fringes of Britain and in Ireland. The remarkable door of the church of Cloufert (picture on p. 85) is a sharp and unexpected reminder of Roquepertuse.

The Celtic iconography of the head, as the selection of illustrations on this page will demonstrate, is extremely varied. The head

Above: The cult of the severed head led to the development of a lively representational art in the region around the mouth of the Rhône, influenced by Greek styles. This group of four heads from the shrine at Entremont includes two females with tight-fitting headdresses, and two males (below them), their hair brushed back in the Celtic manner.

Several stone carvings from Germany, however, illustrate male deities with turban-like headdresses as on the Pfalzfeld pillar *(far right)* and the Heidelberg head *(bottom right).*

The heads on coins derive ultimately from Hellenistic prototypes, but Celtic genius has usually been at work restructuring the elements according to Celtic taste. This coin of the Parisii tribe is worthy of Picasso.

is a recurring theme in most forms of artistic expression, on coins, on decorative fittings and of course in religious sculpture. There were two traditions of religious sculpture among the free Celts; that of the Mediterranean fringe, which we have briefly mentioned in discussing Roquepertuse and Entremont, and a somewhat earlier expression which appears in the Middle Rhine and is thought to owe its origins to inspiration from the Etruscans. The Rhenish carvings are far less representational than those from Provence, the head being conceived of as a series of patterns, resulting in a degree of similarity between the individual pieces: the nose is wedge-shaped, the brow is usually furrowed, and the eyes are often lentoid. Some of the heads are also shown with a turban-like head-dress, which is sometimes, rather unconvincingly, referred to as a "leaf crown." Within the same general tradition, though

showing striking innovations of its own, is the famous stone head from Mšecké-Žehrovice in Bohemia. The swept-back hair and neck torque belie its Celtic origins; while the face itself, less austere than its Rhenish contemporaries, is a masterpiece of Celtic art, with the eyes and mustaches rendered as simple scroll-like motifs. Here the face has been simplified to become an elegant symmetrical pattern—the essence of a face, interpreted by an artist who thinks abstractly.

The face, broken down into its different elements, pervades Celtic art—particularly the art of the bronzeworker. Sometimes it is perfectly clear, on other occasions obscure. The flavor of this kind of enigmatic expression was elegantly summed up by the great art historian Paul Jacobstahl. Referring to the Alice-in-Wonderland quality of Celtic art, he likened the face to the Cheshire cat who appeared and disappeared in the tree: sometimes the whole cat was visible, sometimes just its grin. The bronze disk from Ireland illustrated on this page is a perfect example—is it a face or is it not? We have advanced some way from the vision of warriors clutching their bloody trophies. The cult of the severed head was indeed widespread across the Celtic world, but its more gruesome aspects should not obscure the philosophical and artistic context; the head, because it housed the soul, was endowed with dignity and divinity.

> Amongst the Celts
> the human head was venerated
> above all else,
> since the head was to the Celt the soul,
> center of the emotions
> as well as of life itself,
> a symbol of divinity
> and of the powers
> of the other-world.
>
> Paul Jacobsthal

Variation in the treatment of a single theme is exemplified in the selection of Celtic heads illustrated here.

Left: A highly individual evocation in bronze from Tarbes, France; third century B.C. The hollow neck would have allowed the head to be mounted on a pole for display.

Middle row, left: Two heads held in the beak of a massive bird, from Roquepertuse, France. *Right:* A triple, mustached head, presumably a god, from Reims, France; Gallo-Roman.

Bottom row, left to right: Stylized stone head, with prominent, close-set eyes and scroll-like eyebrows and mustache, ca. 150 B.C., found near Prague.
Female head, rough stone sculpture from pre-Roman Gaul.
Head of a divinity, with typical Celtic treatment of the beard, from the Gundestrup caldron.

Top: An enigma of the kind frequently seen in Celtic art: this bronze disk from Ireland, first—second century A.D., could be either an entirely abstract design, or else the witty, far-fetched suggestion of a face.

And there were
many dark springs
running there,
and grim-faced
figures of gods
uncouthly hewn by the axe
from the untrimmed tree-trunk,
rotted to whiteness....

Lucan

THE SACRED PLACES

They prepare
a ritual sacrifice
and feast
under the tree,
and lead up two white bulls
whose horns are bound
for the first time
on this occasion.
A priest (sacerdos) attired
in a white vestment
ascends the tree
and with a golden
pruning-hook cuts the mistletoe
which is caught
in a white cloth.

Pliny, *Natural History*

Such an intense supernatural life as that of the Celts required a large number of sacred places where the gods and man could communicate. We have already discussed two elaborate sanctuaries, at Entremont and Roquepertuse, but these are likely to be atypical, influenced by the Greek community at nearby Massilia. More commonly, according to the classical writers, the Celtic sacred places were architecturally unadorned. Quite often they were sacred groves situated deep in the solitude of ancient forests, as Lucan's poem so vividly describes.

When the Roman army was campaigning through north Wales in A.D. 59, one of the last strongholds of the druids was attacked and destroyed on the island of Anglesey. Tacitus describes the Roman soldiers hacking down the groves, sacred to savage rites and drenched with the blood of prisoners. Some indication of the prevalence of these sacred groves is given by the distribution of the place-name element *nemeton*, which can be traced across Europe from Spain and Britain in the west, to Asia Minor in the east. Reference to a wood called Nemet in an eleventh-century cartulary in Brittany further emphasizes the strength of the tradition.

Woodland locations were but one setting for Celtic ritual. The countryside would have abounded with others: weird-shaped rocks, ancient gnarled trees, and springs and bogs—the gods could be reached almost anywhere. There is extensive archaeological evidence, particularly of offerings made at rivers and springs, and an increasing body of new material is showing us that, contrary to the impression given by the ancient writers, the Celts also constructed permanent shrines of timber and ritual enclosures where the gods could be propitiated.

SACRED SPRINGS

Fresh, limpid water catching the light as it wells up from the ground exerts an undeniable fascination. To the Celtic mind a particular sanctity was attached to springs, especially those at the source of a great river. Spring water had a special quality, usually curative, which could be enjoyed by man so long as he placated the deity who presided over the location. Since water came from the earth, it was appropriate for the deity of the source to be female, reflecting one of the powers of the earth mother. The continuing strength of this pagan tradition throughout the medieval period and indeed to the present day is shown by the way in which springs and wells were rapidly Christianized and were almost invariably associated with a female patron saint, as at Lourdes.

At Coventina's well on Hadrian's Wall, a spring, presumably of some note in the pre-Roman period, was enclosed by a roughly built wall forming a small pool into which offerings such as coins were thrown. This kind of simple treatment is likely to have been common throughout the Celtic world. But other springs, by virtue of their special sanctity or impressive physical form, might be more elaborately adorned. The thermal spring at Bath, where hot water gushed out of the ground at the rate of a quarter of a million gallons a day, was, under Roman auspices, provided with a most elaborate complex of monumental buildings. Yet beneath the grandiose façade there lurked the native goddess Sulis whose name continued to be associated with the spring throughout the Roman period.

Sacred springs were usually presided over by female deities who were sometimes shown in triple form. The sacred spring at Carrowburgh, on Hadrian's Wall, where Coventina was all-powerful, produced this triad. The goddess is shown here as three water nymphs each of whom holds a beaker in one hand, while in her other she supports an upturned urn from which the sacred water gushes. Although the relief has many classical aspects (and indeed dates to the period of the Roman occupation), the style and the iconography are purely Celtic.

The Seine rises in a secluded valley in the wooded hills to the west of Dijon. Totally undramatic in aspect, the source was an ideal place for the development of a healing shrine, presided over by the goddess Sequanna. There the pilgrims could rest in peace after making their offering to the deity and wait for her curative powers to work.

The shrine at the source has remained a place of fascination for the French. It was romanticized by Napoleon III and is still visited by coach loads of present-day pilgrims.

VOTIVE OFFERINGS

The Celtic religious sense was strongly marked by the principle of reciprocity. To save a life, another would be sacrificed. Similarly, if sacred waters were used by someone wanting a cure, a gift in exchange was expected of the user.

To a warlike people like the Celts, the rituals associated with victory were of great significance—a victory granted had to be paid for with the spoils of war. It was for this reason that great quantities of arms were thrown into lakes and rivers: indeed virtually all the fine metalwork associated with warfare found in Britain has been recovered from under water.

Two sites deserve particular attention. A remarkable collection of metalwork was found in a bog at Llyn Cerrig Bach in Anglesey in 1943. The collection—composed of swords, spears, shields, chariot and harness fittings, ironworkers' tools, trumpets, caldrons, and a slave chain—had been thrown from a projecting rock into a pool some time in the first century A.D. The exact circumstances of the deposition are unknown, but the collection may well have comprised loot collected during the intertribal fighting preceding the Roman advance, and have been consigned to the care of the gods in thanks for victory.

A somewhat similar deposit was found in a bog at Hjortspring on the Danish island of Als. Here, during peat cutting, a long boat was discovered, some 16 meters in length and large enough to carry about 20 men. It had been sunk in the bog together with a range of war gear including 150 wooden shields, 169 spears, and 8 iron swords, together with a number of other objects. Although strictly a Germanic rather than a Celtic find, the equipment—particularly the shields—is clearly Celtic in form. Once more we must suppose that the boat and its contents were dedicated to the gods.

Strabo, writing of the Celtic tribe called the Volcae Tectosages, who occupied the region of Toulouse, offers an interesting insight into ritual deposits. Quoting Posidonius, he tells us that a considerable treasure of unworked gold and silver bullion was stored in the temple enclosures and in sacred lakes—"the lakes in particular provided inviolability for their treasures, into which they let down heavy masses of silver and gold." He goes on to say that the treasure stored in these sacred sites was quite safe because no one would dare to profane them—except, that is, the Romans, who, when they conquered the region, "sold the lakes by public auction, and many of the purchasers found there hammered millstones of silver."

It is an interesting comment on the power of superstition over the people that objects of great value dedicated to the gods were safe from theft. The same point, in a different aspect, is emphasized by Caesar when he mentions that the heaviest sanction that can be imposed on a Gaul is to be banned from taking part in sacrifice to the gods. "Those who are laid under such a ban are

regarded as impious criminals. Everyone shuns them and avoids going near or speaking to them for fear of taking some harm by contact with what is unclean." Here is the essence of Celtic religion: to be whole a man has to be in communion with the gods through the medium of sacrifice and offerings.

We have already mentioned the ritual significance of springs. One, the source of the

Top: The female Celtic deities who presided over the waters were often equated in the Roman mind with the healing goddess Minerva. But this was not always so; many of the native goddesses maintained their own identity. This relief of a native water goddess is from Carrawburgh, England.

Votive offerings from the springs are a poignant reminder of the hopes of the pilgrims. The shrine at the source of the Seine has produced many *ex votos*, some, like this blind girl, reflecting the ills of the visitors. Others are of organs or limbs *(right)* presumably to focus the god's attention on the diseased part; or complete figures such as those shown on the opposite page.

Seine, stands out in particular for the great fascination of the evidence which excavations over the last hundred years have brought to light. Here, in a secluded valley some thirty-five kilometers from Dijon, lay the shrine to Sequanna, a Celtic deity who continued to be revered throughout the Roman period (and whose shrine received a new lease of life when Napoleon III erected a charming if irrelevant grotto on the site to house the statue of a portly water nymph). In addition to the buildings with which the Romans monumentalized the shrine, the excavations have yielded a rich collection of votive offerings which allow us to glimpse something of the hopes and beliefs of the pilgrims.

Of particular interest are the wooden votives, found in 1963, in waterlogged deposits. Most of them were simply carved from the heart wood of oak to represent all or part of the human form. Twenty-seven complete human figurines were recovered, mostly wearing cloaks, but the collection

feet. By offering the goddess a physical representation of a diseased organ or limb, the pilgrims were hoping with the aid of the deity to transfer the ailment to the inanimate object and thus effect their cure. Judging from the range of *ex votos* represented, the goddess seems to have been thought able to cure arthritis, respiratory diseases, hernias, tumors, infertility, and blindness.

Another sacred spring has recently been examined at Chamalières, near Clermont-Ferrand. Once more, it seems to have been presided over by a goddess, unnamed but depicted as a seated matron. The shrine —little more than a pool enclosed by a surrounding wall—seems from coin evidence to have been in active use for only a century or so following Caesar's conquest. Thereafter attention was transferred to the springs at Vichy. The waters at Chamalières, unlike those at Sequanna's spring, were heavily mineralized and thus possessed real curative properties. The people's belief

Votive offerings and portrayals from various sites in the Celtic world. *Left to right:*

Relief from Wilsford, Lincolnshire.

Wooden *ex voto*, from Montboux.

Limestone pilgrim figure, holding a small dog, from the source of the Seine, France.
Wooden *ex voto*, source of the Seine.

Bronze votive of Minerva, from Ehl, near Strasbourg, second century A.D.

Female statue of wood, 1.5 meters in height, from the source of the Seine, first century A.D.

Votive statuette, also from the Seine shrine.

also included heads, limbs (usually legs but occasionally arms and hands), and trunks. Even more interest attaches to a group of twenty-two wooden plaques carved in relief to represent internal organs, one of which is an anatomically accurate depiction of the trachea and lungs. Other remarkable items include a collection of bronze and stone votives illustrating eyes, sex organs, and breasts, as well as heads, hands, and

in these powers is reflected in the magnificent and excellently preserved collection of *ex votos* discovered in the mud of the pool. The collection is similar to that found at the source of the Seine but with an emphasis on the eyes, for the cure of which, no doubt, the waters had a particular renown.

Among the Graeco-Roman cultures of the Mediterranean, it was believed that contact could be made with the underworld by means of ritual shafts dug into the ground. The Greeks called such an excavation a *bothros*, while in Latin it was a *mundus*. The Celts seem to have held to a similar concept. Although there is no clear reference to it in the classical or Irish literature, archaeological evidence for these ritual shafts is becoming increasingly common.

One of the best-known examples of a religious complex containing shafts was found at Holzhausen in Bavaria, where a rectangular earthwork, presumably a ritual enclosure, preceded by timber palisades of the same plan, contained three shafts of which the largest was about forty meters deep. In one of the shallower shafts, eight meters deep, the excavators found a wooden pole, set upright in the bottom of the pit, surrounded by an organic substance

While it is possible that the Celts learned the practice from the Mediterranean world, it is now becoming clear that ritual shafts have an ancient origin in barbarian Europe and, in particular, in Britain. Groups of shafts, apparently nonutilitarian in function, have now been found as far back as the Neolithic period in Hampshire and Norfolk, and other examples have been excavated belonging to the Bronze Age. At Wilsford, close to Stonenenge, a shaft some thirty-four meters in depth had been cut into the solid chalk in the fourteenth century B.C. Although it had functioned as a well, and nothing that could be regarded to be of ritual character was found in it, its size and its situation close to Stonehenge strongly suggest a religious use. Perhaps we are seeing here a combination of the superstition associated with a shaft and the belief in the special properties of spring water.

Shafts were filled with votive offerings, apparently to propitiate the gods residing underground. In the Holzhausen shaft *(above right)*, wooden scaffolding was installed for safety during excavations.

which, according to subsequent analysis, resulted from the decomposition of flesh and blood. The practice of burying a pole or a trunk is also demonstrated by a shaft at Vendée in which was found a four-meter-high Cyprus tree. The ritual nature of these shafts seems indisputable.

A more convincing example of a Bronze Age ritual shaft was found in a brickworks at Swanwick, Hampshire. Here a pit nearly eight meters in depth was excavated. As at Holzhausen, a vertical post was found in the bottom, packed in position with clay, and in the soil around were traces of dried

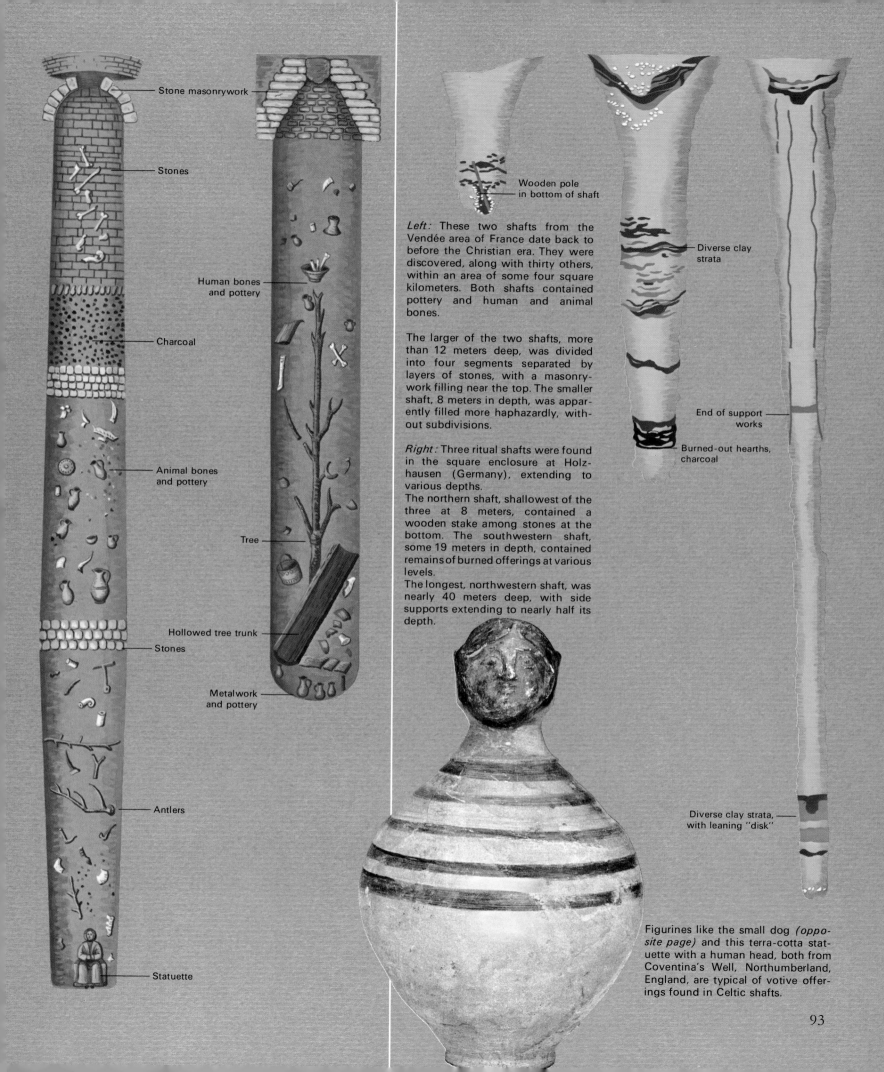

Stone masonrywork

Stones

Human bones
and pottery

Charcoal

Animal bones
and pottery

Tree

Hollowed tree trunk

Stones

Metalwork
and pottery

Antlers

Statuette

Wooden pole
in bottom of shaft

Diverse clay
strata

End of support
works

Burned-out hearths,
charcoal

Diverse clay strata,
with leaning "disk"

Left: These two shafts from the Vendée area of France date back to before the Christian era. They were discovered, along with thirty others, within an area of some four square kilometers. Both shafts contained pottery and human and animal bones.

The larger of the two shafts, more than 12 meters deep, was divided into four segments separated by layers of stones, with a masonry-work filling near the top. The smaller shaft, 8 meters in depth, was apparently filled more haphazardly, without subdivisions.

Right: Three ritual shafts were found in the square enclosure at Holz-hausen (Germany), extending to various depths.
The northern shaft, shallowest of the three at 8 meters, contained a wooden stake among stones at the bottom. The southwestern shaft, some 19 meters in depth, contained remains of burned offerings at various levels.
The longest, northwestern shaft, was nearly 40 meters deep, with side supports extending to nearly half its depth.

Figurines like the small dog *(opposite page)* and this terra-cotta statuette with a human head, both from Coventina's Well, Northumberland, England, are typical of votive offerings found in Celtic shafts.

Typical Roman Celtic temples consisted of a central cella and a surrounding ambulatory *(reconstruction, top)*. The plan was derived from a

flesh and blood. Although precise dating evidence is not available, a date about 1000 B.C. seems probable. Thus the Swanwick shaft presents a convincing predecessor for a tradition that later became widespread in Europe: it is even possible that the belief which required the shafts to be dug originated in Britain and spread from there. The ritual site at Holzhausen was, as we have mentioned, associated with rectangular enclosures. Enclosures of this kind, generally referred to by their German name, *Viereckschanze*, are commonly found north of the Alps concentrated in the triangle between Zurich, Salzburg, and Frankfurt and extending into eastern France. For the most part, they date to the end of the free Celtic period and continued

Libenice in Bohemia provides a particularly interesting example, where, in the third century B.C., an oblong area some eighty by twenty meters was enclosed with a continuous ditch. At one end was an irregular floor created in a hollow dug down into the subsoil containing a stone stela and nearby the holes for two timbers, the charred remains of which were found together with two bronze torques. Apparently the shrines had been adorned with large wooden statues wearing torques. In the floor of the shrine were found several pits, probably dug to take libations, and in addition, there was evidence of human and animal sacrifice together with the burial of an elderly woman who might possibly have been a priestess. Another enclosure, closely com-

There are also other accounts
of their human sacrifices;
for they used to shoot men down with arrows,
and impale them in the temples,
or making a large statue
of straw and wood,
throw into it cattle
and all sorts of wild animals and
human beings,
and thus make a burnt offering.

Strabo

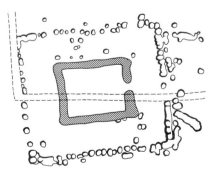

purely Celtic type of which the only example so far known was excavated at Heathrow Airport, London *(diagram above)*, some 10 meters in length. The photograph shows the hilltop shrine, or *cromlech*, of Castlerigg, Cumberland, England: an arrangement of 39 stones in a circle 30 meters in diameter—a religious site of an earlier period.

in use into Roman times. Some are devoid of features, many are associated with burials, and a few with shafts. In all probability they served a ritual function, perhaps simply defining a sacred location where open-air religious practices could be enacted. Once more, a prototype can be found in Britain among the complex of Neolithic ritual monuments excavated at Dorchester-on-Thames in southern Britain, but to suggest a direct relationship is to exceed the reasonable limits of the evidence.

The procedure of defining a ritual area with a fence, bank, or ditch is very ancient and common to many cultures. The *Viereck-schanze* is but one manifestation of this practice in the Celtic world. The site of

parable in size and shape but dating to the Late Bronze Age, was found in the Marne at Aulnay-aux-Planches. Within the enclosure there were several human burials, including what is thought to have been a sacrificed infant, and two large post holes, by one of which was a complete ox skull, which had possibly once been attached to one of the posts. It is, of course, impossible to say exactly what went on at Libenice and Aulnay, but we can reasonably classify both enclosures as ritual structures. The seven-hundred year interval separating them is a reminder of the strength and continuity of religious traditions.

Reading the classical sources, one would get the distinct impression that Celtic

Artist's impression of the Romano-British temple of the Celtic god Nodons, at Lydney Park, on the banks of the Severn River. The temple was built late in the Roman period in an old Iron Age hillfort and may represent the revival of an ancient native shrine. Under Roman rule, Celtic sanctuaries became larger and more complex than before.

observances took place in the open or in clearings in woods, perhaps at places like Aulnay and Libenice. Yet sites like Roquepertuse and Entremont show that sacred locations were sometimes monumentalized. Outside the Mediterranean fringe, however, evidence for temples or shrines is still not extensive, but that they did exist is demonstrated by Strabo (quoting Posidonius) in his description of a community of priestesses who inhabited an island close to the mouth of the Loire. "It is their custom," he says, "once a year to remove the roof from their temple and to roof it again in the same day before sunset."

Other evidence of religious buildings comes from excavations, perhaps the best example being a timber-built temple found at Heathrow Airport, London, where a small rectangular cella surrounded by an ambulatory (or corridor), was discovered dating, apparently, to the third century B.C. Similar cella-like structures have recently been found in the hillforts of Danebury and South Cadbury in southern Britain. The particular interest of the Heathrow temple lies in the fact that its plan is exactly mirrored by many hundreds of masonry-built temples erected in Gaul and Britain during the Roman period. The continuity of building form is impressive; so too is the actual continuity in use, which can be demonstrated at a number of locations, where rather ill-defined Iron Age structures were replaced by distinctive Romano-Celtic temples.

While it is true that the rectangular temple is the normal type throughout most of

Europe, circular shrines are not uncommon in western France and in Britain. It may be that the two styles simply reflect the different traditions of house building prevalent in these regions.

Map of the principal Celtic religious sites, according to archaeological and literary evidence. Our knowledge of Celtic religious centers is incomplete, particularly because so many shrines were simple outdoor sites, rather than monumental buildings in the style of Greece or Rome.

The Celts favored the forest clearing, as in the reconstruction sketch (left), as a place of worship.

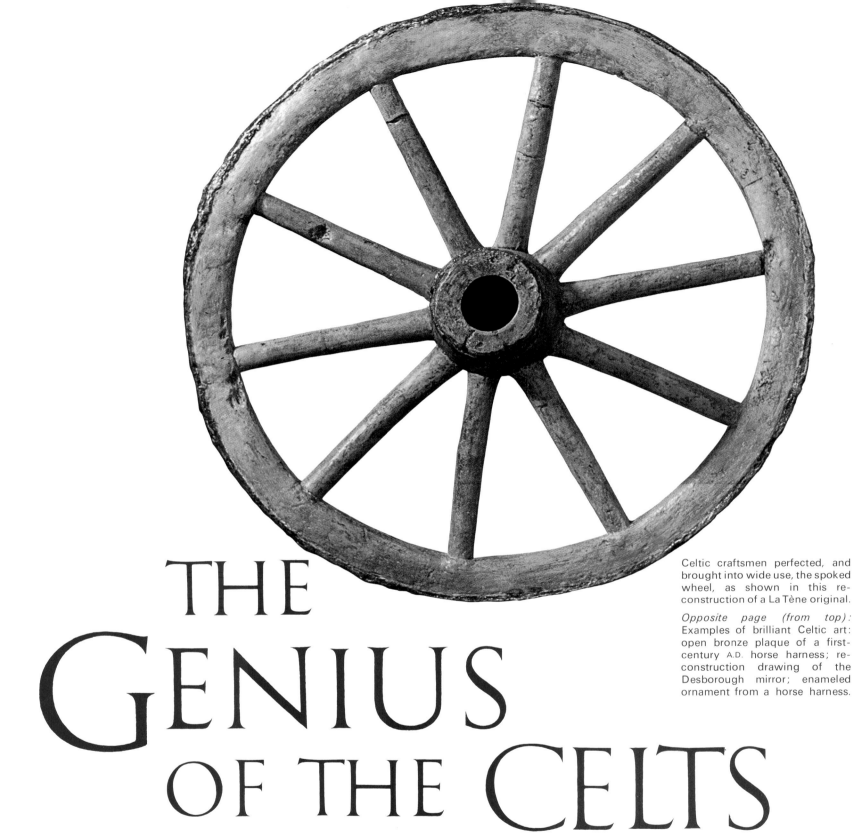

Celtic craftsmen perfected, and brought into wide use, the spoked wheel, as shown in this reconstruction of a La Tène original.

Opposite page (from top): Examples of brilliant Celtic art: open bronze plaque of a first-century A.D. horse harness; reconstruction drawing of the Desborough mirror; enameled ornament from a horse harness.

THE GENIUS OF THE CELTS

Their man-sized shields
are decorated, each in individual fashion.
Some include projecting bronze animals
of brilliant workmanship
which serve for defense as well as decoration.

Diodorus Siculus

The arts of war, in time of crisis, absorbed the efforts and talents of the Celts. Their opponents might thus dismiss them as backward, incapable of seasoned thought, refinement, or the development of sophisticated socio-political institutions. Indeed, their gifts lay in a different area from those of classical Mediterranean civilization. At an early stage the Celts excelled at mining and metalworking, skills that led to all-important mastery of the wheel and the plow. The Celts produced an art that might be called baroque rather than classical: In place of Greek abstraction, a whimsical profusion of detail and daring line. Rather than sober balance and harmonious proportion, a taste for stylization and grotesquery. The Celtic freedom could shock the spectator—force him to rediscover the world, see reality anew. The same creative freshness was to burst upon the European literary scene centuries and centuries later, when the fantastical Irish and Breton legends would fertilize medieval literature.

In recognizing the *Keltoi* as one of the four peoples of the barbarian world, the Greek geographers were tacitly admitting that a vast area of temperate Europe, stretching from Transdanubia to the Atlantic, shared one culture. The linguistic evidence, the documentary evidence bearing upon society and behavior, and the iconographic evidence reflecting the supernatural—all combine to demonstrate a remarkable degree of unity linking all parts of the Celtic territories.

The Celts were one of the last barbarian peoples of temperate Europe, their culture representing the culmination of six thousand years of indigenous development. It had evolved slowly but surely, aberrant developments quickly dying out while beneficial changes were retained and integrated into the communal experience. By the middle of the first millennium B.C. a technological equilibrium had been reached. Comparing Celtic technology with that of preindustrial Europe of the eighteenth century A.D., one finds surprisingly few significant differences apart from knowledge of gunpowder and its associated developments. Iron was not cast and the horse collar had not yet been introduced from China, nor had the Celts shown any aptitude for hydraulic engineering. (This is not surprising: engineering would not have appealed to the Celtic temperament.) The Celt was immediate and spontaneous in his responses, able to carry out communal projects like the building of defenses when they became necessary to protect his social institutions, but with no particular facility for abstract calculations.

From whichever direction we approach the Celts, through literature, art, or archaeology, the overriding impression one gets is of immense energy. Celtic society was coiled like a spring, tensed ready for action. This shows in the boisterous nature of social gatherings and in conduct in battle; it also pervades Celtic art—one has only to look at the mirror back (p. 99) to sense the restlessness of it all.

The quick, agile mind of the Celt, his love of riddles and of the half-stated are characteristics noted by classical observers: this sense of enigma lies behind the best of his abstract art. Free Celtic society at its most developed cannot be regarded as a mature expression of a people; it was a society in its adolescence.

To the Greeks anyone who did not speak Greek but made unintelligible sounds was called a barbarian. The word was not overtly derogatory; it implied that one was non-civilized, but it did not have its modern connotation of lacking in culture and sensitivity. No one who has looked at items of decorated Celtic metalwork or has read the Irish sagas could accuse the Celts of that. In the visual arts, Celtic craftsmen working under the patronage of the aristocracy produced a style that was both original and exciting. It was an abstract art which, from a close observation of the natural world, distilled the essence of line and form. There was no desire to depict reality, but instead to capture the spirit, the intangible, and the fleeting. Just as Celtic literature is ridden with illusions, surprise, and shape-shifting, so too is Celtic art.

THE SO-CALLED BARBARIANS

Although, in its first flowering, Celtic art was reserved to the aristocracy, it soon became the art of the people. An Iron Age potter was as concerned to produce a satisfying decoration on his cooking pot as was the bronzesmith. His medium of expression may have been less exotic and his skill less developed, but the essential love of form was shared by both. The humble domestic pottery and decorated wooden vessels from the Somerset marshes are a vivid reminder that decoration, and presumably bright color, formed a normal part of everyday experience.

Most of the Celtic world was eventually submerged beneath the tide of Roman imperial aggression, and the hand of classicism lay heavy upon Celtic creative abilities. There could be no turning back; nor was there submission. Although representation became the accepted mode of display, it was often representation on Celtic terms, with pictorial accuracy subservient to line and movement.

At every level of their lives the Celts liked to be surrounded by ornaments and decoration. Even quite humble items like safety-pin-type brooches were frequently elaborated. This little brooch from Reinheim, Germany, was worked into the form of a cock, inset with pieces of imported coral. It dates from the late fifth or early fourth century B.C.

He saw a woman
at the edge of the spring,
with a bright silver comb
ornamented with gold,
washing her hair in a
silver bowl with four
golden birds on it, and little
flashing jewels of purple
carbuncle on the rims
of the bowl. She had a
shaggy purple cloak made
of fine fleece, and silver
brooches of filigree work
decorated with handsome
gold, in the cloak;
a long-hooded tunic on her,
stiff and smooth, of green
silk with embroidery
of red gold. Wonderful
ornaments of gold and
silver with twining animal
designs, in the tunic on her
breast and her shoulders
and her shoulder-blades
on both sides.

Irish poem, ninth century

Schools of craftsmen developed local styles in many parts of Europe. In Britain, for example, in the first century B.C. and early first century A.D., decorated mirrors became popular and were made by many different hands; at least one was exported to Holland. This brilliant example is from Old Warden in Bedfordshire, England.

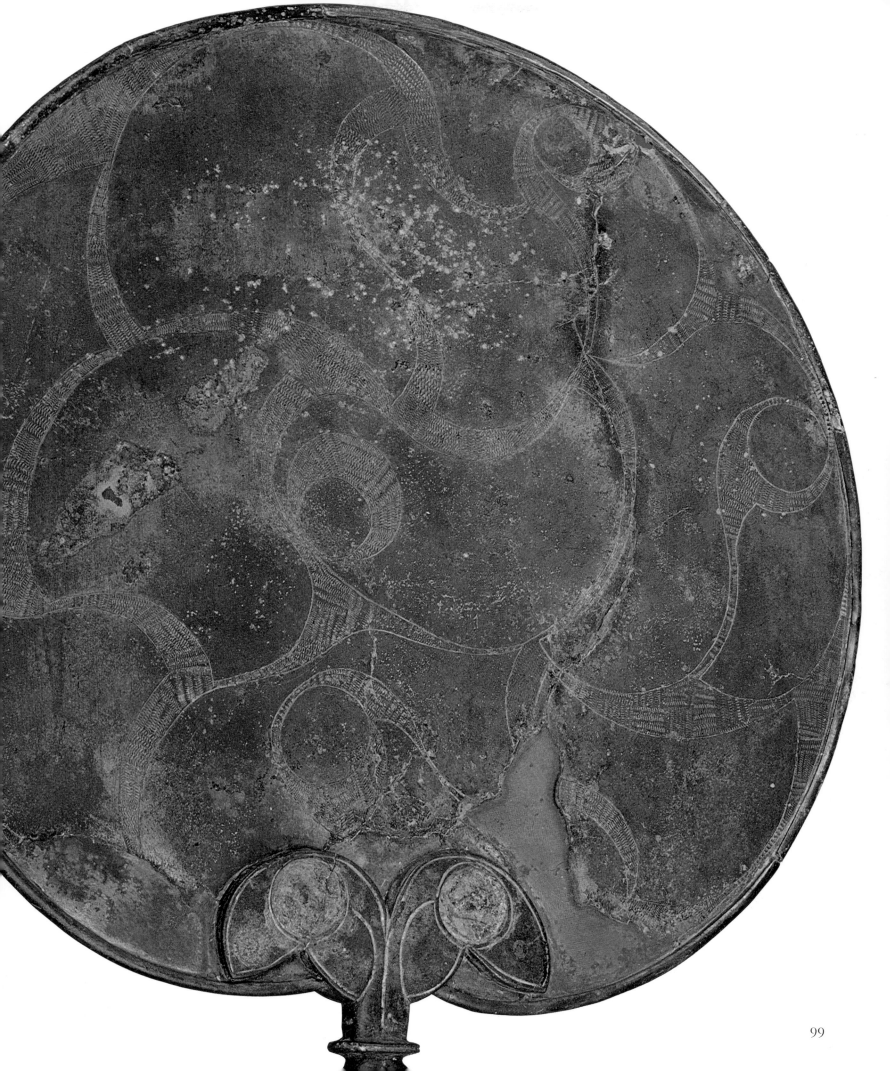

The genesis of Celtic art lay in the molding together of several disparate styles into something quite unique and distinctive. Beneath everything lay indigenous Hallstatt modes of decoration—a sense of contrasting colors and textures, but a style essentially four-square and geometric. Superimposed upon this was the art of the classical world interpreted particularly through its Graeco-Etruscan manifestations. Bronze vessels decorated with palmettes and tendrils flooded into the Celtic world and into the households of the chieftains. A third, more shadowy, element came from the east, though by what mechanism is unknown. Eastern Europe had for some while been settled by peoples closely related to the Scythians practicing their own exquisite style of animal art. Upon this was superimposed a Persian flavor. Perhaps the craftsmen serving this strange hybrid of Greek, Scythian, and Persian migrated to the west—perhaps it was little more than traded goods, saddle cloths, leatherwork, and fabric wall hangings that brought the eastern flavor to the courts of the Celtic aristocracy. At any event, in the latter part of the fifth century we can see the different elements coming together in the earliest manifestation of a truly Celtic art known as the Early Strict Style—Celtic, yet of recognizable parentage.

In the ensuing centuries Celtic art became an expression of the Celtic spirit. There developed what is called the Free Style: free graphic for its two dimensional form, free plastic when in three dimensions. It is a style which eschews bilateral symmetry and adapts design to form—elements grow and die away again and everything is in a state of tense balance. Finally, growing contact with the world of Rome, introducing new standards of formality and leading to the emergence of more stable, urban forms of government, gives rise to a more staid art style which reflects the change of the times.

100

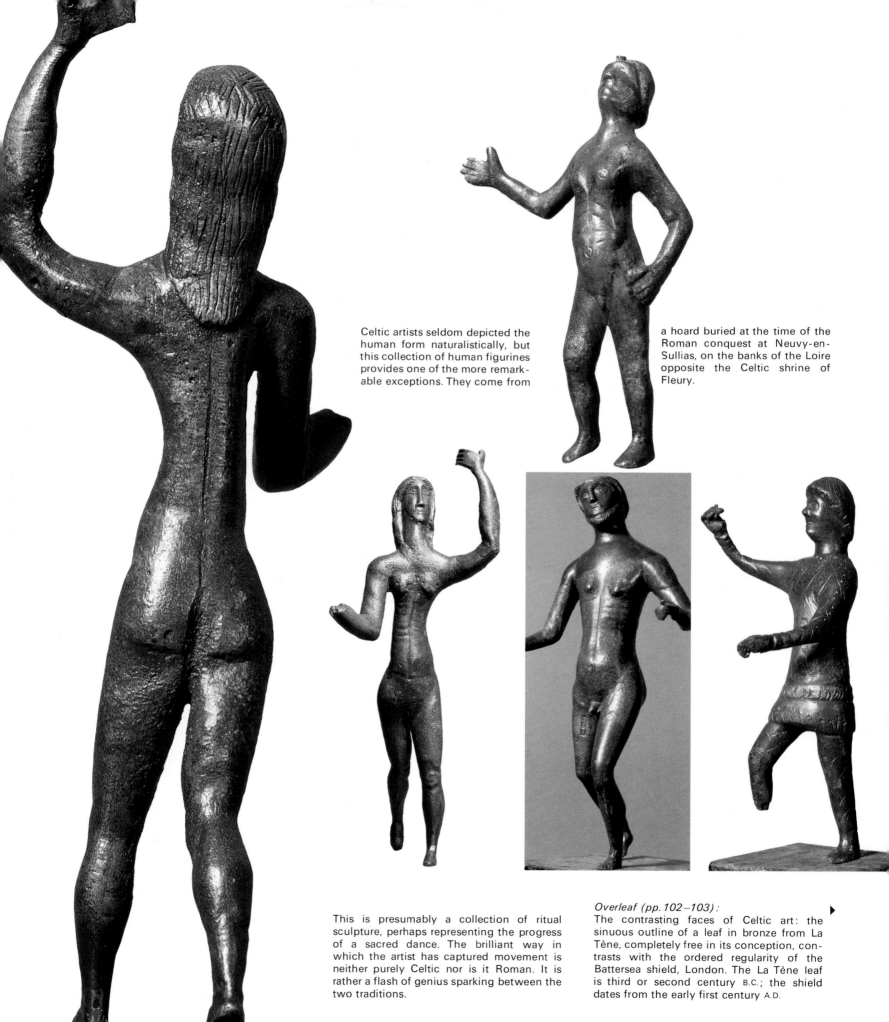

Celtic artists seldom depicted the human form naturalistically, but this collection of human figurines provides one of the more remarkable exceptions. They come from a hoard buried at the time of the Roman conquest at Neuvy-en-Sullias, on the banks of the Loire opposite the Celtic shrine of Fleury.

This is presumably a collection of ritual sculpture, perhaps representing the progress of a sacred dance. The brilliant way in which the artist has captured movement is neither purely Celtic nor is it Roman. It is rather a flash of genius sparking between the two traditions.

Overleaf (pp. 102–103):
The contrasting faces of Celtic art: the sinuous outline of a leaf in bronze from La Tène, completely free in its conception, contrasts with the ordered regularity of the Battersea shield, London. The La Tène leaf is third or second century B.C.; the shield dates from the early first century A.D.

One can recognize in the earlier manifestation of Celtic art the disparate influences which led to its genesis. The palmette and lyre motifs of the Graeco-Etruscan world can readily be distinguished in two gold openwork designs illustrated here: the cup from the chieftain's grave at Schwarzenbach, Germany *(right)*, and the gold mounting from Eigenbilzen, Belgium *(bottom)*.

The flagon from Basse-Yutz in the Lorraine *(far right)* is a fine example of the fusing of the different traditions. In form, and in the decoration beneath its spout, the flagon is clearly dependent on Etruscan inspiration, but the magnificent beast which forms its handle is ultimately Scythian in style.

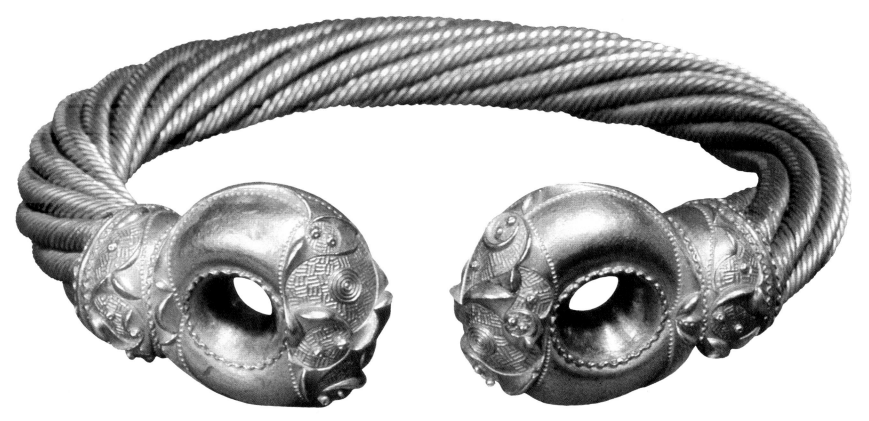

Although Celtic art in its later stages became a folk art, there were still some schools of craftsmen working in precious metals for aristocratic patrons. One of these schools, probably located somewhere in the east of England, made gold torques of enormous value, of which the example illustrated above from Snettisham in Norfolk is justly the most famous.

Opposite : Celtic artists were so adept at capturing the essence of a figure or face with an economy of detail that it is often very difficult to be sure of the dating of some pieces, like the god from Bouvray, France. His features strongly suggest the work of a Celt in the first century B.C.

THE DRUIDS: PRIESTS, SEERS, JUDGES

Within the upper echelons of Celtic society was a learned class, respected for their wisdom and for their special powers as intermediaries between the tribe and the gods. These men were known as druids—a word which probably derives from a term for "knowledge of the oak" or alternatively "profound knowledge." They were wise men: in their hands lay all the intellectual activities necessary for the satisfactory running of society. Caesar is quite specific about the duties of the druids: they "officiate at the worship of the gods, regulate public and private sacrifices, and give rulings on all religious questions. Large numbers of young men flock to them for instruction, and they are held in great honor by the people. They act as judges in practically all disputes whether between tribes or between individuals." Here then is a succinct summary of their powers; priests and magicians, teachers and judges, they command respect well beyond that of their own tribe of origin.

The order was under the control of an arch-druid appointed by his fellows by virtue of his outstanding merit. Caesar mentions that election ensues if several people of equal ability present themselves, and adds that orderly voting sometimes degenerates into an outright fight between the contestants— a not unexpected eventuality in the Celtic world.

The druids formed a privileged class exempt from taxes and from military service, attractions which apparently encouraged large numbers of young men to seek admission to the order. Training, however, was rigorous. The initiates were required to memorize a great volume of oral learning; so much, says Caesar, that some of them spent twenty years at their studies. "The druids believe that their religion forbids them to commit their teachings to writing... but," he adds, "I imagine that this rule was originally established for other reasons—because they did not want their doctrine to become public property and in order to prevent their pupils from relying on the written word and neglecting to train their memories." His explanation was superfluous since the real reason was that Celtic was not a written language. What the druids committed to memory was the entire knowledge store of the community: magic formulas, ritual procedures, medical knowledge, law, folk history, and genealogies. To aid the memory a simple verse form with repeated epithets would have been adopted. It was by this means that the Irish folktales were passed from one generation to the next until they were eventually written down by Christian scribes in the eighth century.

Caesar recognized the druids as the only class of intellectuals in Gaul, but this seems to be an oversimplification. Other writers —Strabo, Diodorus, Athenaeus—supported by the Irish literature, distinguish three distinct categories: the bards, in whose poetry the history and traditions of the tribe were immortalized; the augurers, who oversaw the sacrifices and foretold the future; and the druids proper, versed in law and philosophy—the conservers of the ancient wisdoms. An occasional overlap in function may have obscured the differences and led Caesar into his somewhat inaccurate generalization.

The function of the bards was clearly defined by Athenaeus (quoting Posidonius). He refers to them as entertainers. "These are the poets who deliver eulogies in song"—it was they who were responsible for extolling the virtues of their aristocratic patrons. In Ireland the *fili* shared some of the functions of the *bard*: he learned by heart the traditions and genealogies of his people and composed his own verses, often in praise of his patron or of other aristocrats. Bardic schools, where these skills were taught, flourished in Ireland even as late as the seventeenth century.

The judicial functions of the druids were very important to the stability of society: their powers were wide ranging. Disputes

The wise men of Celtic society, who were sometimes classed together and called "druids," were healers, teachers, musicians, poets, augurers, priests, and judges. Some of the contemporary writers recognize their specialities and distinguish between them. One function of the druids was to officiate at sacrifices, often the sacrifice of human beings. The more forbidding side of Celtic supernatural belief is intimated in this sculpture from Noves in southern France, dating to the third or second century B.C. The fearsome scaly beast squats on the ground: he is in the act of devouring someone and holds severed heads in each paw.

Control of healing plants figured among the responsibilities of the druids. Healing was also a function of some of the gods. The Dagda, in Irish mythology, was usually accompanied by a caldron, the contents of which, among its other properties, had healing powers. According to one interpretation, this scene on the Gundestrup caldron shows the Great God allowing a mortal to partake of the caldron. Another suggestion, no less plausible, is that the small figure is a sacrifice being thrown into a sacred shaft!

between individuals, crimes including manslaughter, disagreements over boundaries or inheritances, all came within their jurisdiction. According to Caesar, an annual gathering was held each year near Chartres in Gaul on an appointed day. "Those who are involved in disputes assemble here from all parts and accept the druids' judgments and awards." Their decisions were final. "They ... adjudicate the matter and appoint the compensation to be paid and received by the parties concerned. Any individual or tribe failing to accept the award is banned from taking part in sacrifice." The power of the druids, then, transcended tribal boundaries: they were even able to come between opposing forces and halt battles.

The druids were also the philosophers of society. They studied the movements of the heavenly bodies, and according to Caesar they gave instruction to young men in astronomy, the size of the universe and of the earth, and the power and abilities of the gods. Another aspect of their teaching concerned life after death. They believed that the soul did not perish, but after death passed from one body to another—a philosophical concept which the military mind of Caesar interprets somewhat mundanely: "They think that this is the best incentive to bravery, because it teaches men to disregard the terrors of death." These tantalizing references to a philosophical tradition among the Celts imply a degree of sophisticated thought which some modern writers believe to have been influenced by the stoic philosophy of Greece.

Caesar is explicit about the sacrificial duties of druids: they officiate at the worship of the gods and regulate public and private sacrifice. Other writers, however, imply that the actual augury was undertaken by special officials, though it is of course possible that a druid had to be present at these ceremonies to make sure that the correct procedures were followed.

Strabo explains:

They used to strike a man whom they had devoted to death in the back with a knife, and then divine from his death-throes, but they did not sacrifice without a druid.... We are told of still other kinds of sacrifices; for example they would shoot victims to death with their arrows, or impale them in temples....

The point to emphasize here is the essential presence, though not necessarily the participation, of the druid.

The rite of human sacrifice is emphasized, with explicit disgust, by several Roman writers (though it comes incongruously from a society that relished as entertainment mass slaughter in the amphitheater). The poet Lucan writes of a Celtic shrine near Massilia where "there were many dark springs running, and grim-faced figures of gods roughly hewn by the axe from the untrimmed tree-trunk rotted to whiteness"—these places were steeped in human blood from victims sacrificed to the gods. Exactly the same point is made by Tacitus in describing the Roman attack on the druid stronghold on Anglesey in A.D. 59, as the result of which the army hacked down the groves "sacred to the savage rites... for their religion enjoined them to drench their altars with the blood of prisoners, and to find out the will of the gods by consulting the entrails of human beings."

The self-satisfied Pliny concludes, "We can hardly realize how much is owed to the Romans, who swept away the monstrous conditions in which to kill a man was the highest religious function, and to eat him was even more highly salubrious." No doubt human sacrifice was unpalatable to some Romans. More to the point, it provided Roman propagandists with an excellent self-righteous excuse to annihilate Celtic religion, when really what they feared was the ability of the druids to unite the Celts in resistance to Rome. To the Celt human sacrifice was simply a means by which their augurers could communicate with the gods.

We know little in detail of the ritual procedures guided by the druids, but in one unique and charming passage, recorded by Pliny, we can come close to the reality of a Celtic ceremony. He tells us that mistletoe is a well-known healing plant and that if it is found growing on an oak tree it is thought to be particularly potent, if cut according to a strict ritual. First of all two white bulls have to be brought to the spot. Then the white-robed priest clutching a golden sickle climbs the tree and cuts the mistletoe, which is caught in a white robe by those standing below. The bulls are then sacrificed, while prayers to the gods ask that they allow the gift to be propitious. Mistletoe, harvested in this way and taken

The bronze calendar of Coligny is one of the most remarkable Celtic objects to be discovered. Dating to the late first century B.C., it is wholly Celtic in concept and is the oldest document written in the Celtic language.

It was divided into 16 columns, each of four months, representing a five-year cycle (62 lunar months plus two intercalary months). It may be that the surviving section was part of a larger 19-year calendar. Each month, of 29 or 30 days, is divided into a dark and a light half, and the days in each one are separately numbered. The months are divided between good ("MAT") and not good ("ANM"), and some of the festivals, those corresponding to Beltine and Lugnasad, are indicated. The months are also named.

The calendar uses Roman lettering, but this should not obscure its purely Celtic nature.

in a drink, could make barren animals fertile and was an antidote for all poisons. "Such are the religious feelings that are entertained towards trifling things by many peoples" adds Pliny. The record is fascinating not only for the immediacy which it imparts to Celtic ritual, but as a reminder that the druids were also responsible for preserving the medical knowledge of the community. It is an aspect upon which other contemporary writers are silent.

The reference to the fertility of herds is a reflection of the importance of the druids in ensuring the well-being of the community, particularly with respect to seasonal activities and the appropriate rituals which accompanied them. Everything was determined by the calendar, which it was the druids' responsibility to maintain and observe. In Celtic Ireland the year was divided into two halves, which were each once subdivided. The old year ended and the new year began at the festival of *Samain* (the first of November), which marked the beginning of the dark half of the year. The second (light) half began at *Beltine*, celebrated on May the first. Between these two major ceremonies were two other of lesser importance, *Imbolc*, held on the first of February, and *Lugnasad* on the first of August. The calendar was regulated by the druids and calculated by lunar observations, the passage of time being measured by the passing of nights.

The famous calendar found at Coligny *(opposite)* shows just how well-ordered Celtic astronomy was. The year, divided into twelve lunar months, was adapted to the solar year by adding an extra month of thirty days in every three-year cycle. Each month, of thirty or twenty-nine days, was divided into two halves, a light and a dark half, echoing the division of the year. The thirty-day month was auspicious and the twenty-nine-day month inauspicious, and within each some days were lucky while others were not. Clearly, for the good of the community, it was essential that certain acts, the beginning of the planting season, the bringing in of the herds, or the initiation of a conflict, should be undertaken on the most auspicious day possible, and only the druids could advise on this. By controlling the calendar, the druids controlled society. It is easy to understand their preeminent position in the Celtic world.

Then by slow degrees
the iron sword
came to the fore,
the bronze sickle
fell into disrepute,
the plowman began to cleave
the earth with iron,
and on the darkling
field of battle
the odds were made even.

Lucretius

NEW TOOLS AND SKILLS

The importance of the craft of the ironworker in the Celtic world is demonstrated by the fact that the tribal god is sometimes shown in the guise of a smith, conflated, in the Roman period, with the god Vulcan. Representations of this kind (this example is Romano-British) provide evidence of the smithying tools of the period.

By about 1000 B.C. bronzeworking technology had reached its peak of achievement. The metal could be cast into a variety of complex forms: it could be beaten into thin sheets and riveted to form vessels, and alloys could be produced of varying composition with qualities suitable for a range of different uses. These skills marked the culmination of some three thousand years of practice and experiment. In the eighth century B.C., barbarian Europe was introduced to a new metal—iron. Knowledge of iron extraction can be traced back to the second millennium in the east. By 1500 B.C. the metal was being produced in significant quantities by the Hittites of the New Empire in Anatolia, but the skills involved were a closely guarded secret. In the thirteenth century B.C., King Hattusilis III wrote to the king of Assyria:

As for the iron which you wrote to me about, good iron is not available.... That it is a bad time for producing iron I have written. They will produce good iron, but as yet they will not have finished. When they have finished I shall send it to you. Today I am dispatching an iron dagger blade to you.

This fascinating insight implies that the Hittites held a monopoly over iron production, while the reference to the wrong season hints that iron extraction may well have been in the hands of peasants working in the winter when agricultural demands were slack. The rarity of iron is further emphasized at this time by a letter from the pharaoh of Egypt to the king of the Hittites asking for a supply of the metal. A little earlier, in the mid-fourteenth century, we find iron armlets and an iron dagger among the treasures buried with Tutankhamen.

In the twelfth century, partly as the result of barbarian attacks, the Hittite empire collapsed and in the chaos of folk movement which engulfed the Aegean world at this time, knowledge of iron smelting spread to Europe. The links are tenuous in the extreme. Cyprus and Palestine soon shared the new technology, and from the former, in the early eleventh century B.C., knowledge of ironworking spread to the isolated communities along the Aegean coasts of Greece. With the emergence of Greek civilization an iron industry became firmly established in Europe.

By the eighth century the Greeks had established a colony at Pithekoussai on the island of Ischia near Naples. Here, in eighth-century contexts, there is indisputable evidence that iron, imported from the island of Elba some 250 miles to the north, was being smelted in quantity. However, there is evidence of even earlier ironworking in Italy, suggesting that the Greek colonists merely intensified a production which had probably already been initiated by direct contacts between Cyprus and the east and Italy. Once established on the Italian mainland, a knowledge of ironworking could naturally have spread northward into Europe.

112

The new technology may, however, have reached the Celts by another route. Recent work in Hungary, in the northern part of the Great Hungarian Plain, has unearthed iron trinkets located in tombs dating to the eighth century. These graves and their contexts have similarities to the culture which extends from the north Pontic region into the valley of the lower Danube. We have seen (p. 19) that these peoples may well represent horse-riding communities who moved into Europe as the result of Scythian pressures on their Pontic homeland in the ninth and eighth centuries; if so, they could well have brought a knowledge of ironworking with them into Hungary. Trade and exchange with the communities to the west would have led inevitably to the spread of the new technology. Thus from the east and the south the Late Bronze Age communities of the Alpine fringes were introduced to the benefits of iron.

Although ironworking spread rapidly across central and western Europe, reaching the western parts of Britain by the seventh century B.C., the metal was at first by no means common. Presumably broken weapons and worn-out tools were reforged to make new implements rather than being discarded in the rubbish heaps of the farmsteads. In burials and votive deposits, on the other hand, iron weapons occur quite frequently. By the first century B.C., rejected implements are commonly found, and the extensive use of nails in the ramparts of *murus Gallicus* type (300 tons at Manching) shows that the community could afford to be lavish with its iron. Clearly, production methods had so improved, as the result of industrial intensification, that the metal was in plentiful supply.

Iron had many advantages over bronze, not the least of which was its durability. Moreover, its natural distribution was wider than that of copper and tin and it was comparatively easy to work. The ore occurred in many forms, quite close to the surface and could therefore be gathered without elaborate mining. After initial roasting, the ore was mixed with charcoal and heated in a small bowl furnace, to about 900°C. At this temperature the ore was reduced to iron and the impurities melted to form a slag which accumulated in the bottom of the furnace, leaving the

iron as a spongy mass known as a bloom, which had to be reheated and beaten to remove the remaining slag inclusions.

At an early stage, production was no doubt organized on a cottage industry basis, most communities being able to produce sufficient for their own needs. With increasing specialization, however, a few centers began to concentrate on iron extraction, forging the crude metal into ingots of various shapes for transport and exchange. Thus, by the first century B.C., the majority of iron used, whether by the small farmers

or by the specialist smiths in the towns, reached them in ingot form from well-organized production centers. Those tribes who could control the main iron deposits grew rich on the proceeds. It is hardly a coincidence that several of the newly developing urban centers of Celtic Europe grew up in close proximity to rich supplies of iron ore.

A durable testimony to the metal-working technology of the Celts is the sword sheath, a fourth-century B.C. product found at Hallstatt, Austria. In this detail view, two warriors are holding a wheel believed to be a symbol sacred to the war god. A sketch of the whole sheath is found on pages 24–25.

113

MINING TECHNOLOGY

While iron ore could, for the most part, be gathered from shallow surface workings, certain mineral deposits—in particular, rock salt and copper—were only obtainable in some regions by deep mining. Mining technology in Europe had a considerable ancestry going back to the Neolithic period when extensive shafts and radiating galleries were dug through the chalk of southern Britain and the Low Countries to reach the bands of flint required to make tools. At about the same time, in parts of southeastern Europe, pits were being sunk to reach rich lodes of copper. Thus by the Late Bronze Age some two thousand years of experience had been gained in the intricacies of mining engineering.

The extraction of rock salt is best exemplified in the mines of the eastern Alps, in the region of Salzburg, Hallstatt, and Dürrnberg. At Hallstatt, using socketed bronze picks and winged axes, the miners hacked their way deep into the mountain side, their shuttered galleries extending as far as 350 meters from the surface. In the salt-laden conditions within the galleries a wide range of organic material survived, including the wooden shovels of the miners and the framed leather sacks which they used to transport the rock salt from the mine face.

While the rock salt was comparatively easy to extract, the copper lodes embedded in hard crystalline rocks in the vicinity of Salzburg presented more formidable problems to the miners of the Late Bronze Age. The best known of their workings occurs on the Mitterberg in the Mühlbach-Beschofshofen region where a vein of copper pyrites some two meters thick outcropped in the mountainside over a distance in excess of 1,600 meters. The two principal problems faced by the miners were how to break up the excessively hard rock and how to remove water from the shafts which followed the vein into the mountain sloping down at between 20 and 30 degrees below the horizontal. Although simple mining tools were available, the method used to break the rock was firesetting. A fire was lit against the working face and after the rock had been given time to heat, cold water was thrown on it inducing extensive cracking. This allowed the face to be more easily worked with picks and axes. The technique was, of course, very wasteful of wood: it was estimated that for each cubic meter of ore extracted nine cubic meters of wood were required. When it is remembered that the galleries needed extensive propping and shuttering, it is no surprise that lumbermen were estimated to constitute one-third of the total labor force.

The mining operation began by attacking the vein where it outcropped on the surface, but gradually as the tunnel deepened, an intermediate platform was introduced upon which debris could be piled to form a suitable basis for fires set against the roof of the shaft. An added advantage of this system was that the two levels provided ample means for air to circulate, and indeed the heat from the fires set up a vigorous convection current. The lower shaft also allowed surface water to be collected behind a dam, from where it could be bucketed out of the workings. In this way, and with the insertion of additional staging where necessary, the shaft bored deep into the mountain, the largest reaching a length of 160 meters and a height of 30 meters. The ore would have been dragged out of the shaft on sledges and then sorted, roasted, and smelted. To facilitate this, ancillary works like water channels for the ore washing and roasting ovens for the secondary preparation had to be built and maintained. The entire enterprise was evidently thoroughly co-ordinated and heavily manned—one estimate suggests that to service each fully developed shaft about 180 men would have been needed. How they were recruited we will never know, but in all probability they would have worked together for several months at a time, returning home to their families in spring in time to take part in the activities of the farming year. Their life in the high mountain valleys cannot have been easy. Camping out among the waste heaps of the workings, the atmosphere heavy with smoke belching from the mine shafts and sulfurous fumes from the roasting furnaces, their daily routine was rigorous. Felling and dragging timber for the shuttering and the fires, hacking rock from the work face and carting it to the furnaces—the simple life of the farmer must have seemed idyllic in comparison. Something of the immense effort involved can be gauged when it is said that the Mitterberg mines are estimated to have produced twenty thousand metric tons of crude copper during their life.

A La Tène swordsmith's trademark, stamped on the blade of a sword. In a warrior society the role of the swordsmith was important and the manufacture of weapons became a highly skilled craft in the La Tène period. We may suppose from the evidence of such surviving trade marks that the work of specific armorers whose identities are otherwise lost to us was particularly valued for its excellence.

Extensive Celtic salt mining operations are known in the Eastern Alps, with tunnels running up to 350 meters into the mountain side. The actual extraction of the salt was in some cases effected by the use of waterpower, as shown in the sketch, left. A nearby stream was diverted to flood into the mineshaft. The rock salt was thus washed out of the mine, and led through a conduit system into large vats, where the water was evaporated off, using heat from the sun, or wood fires under the vats.

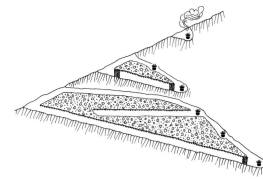

The diagram above shows the development of the deep shafts necessary to extract copper ore at Mühlbach-Bischofshafen. At the top is the first stage in the technique, known as firesetting; the building of a fire at the start of the shaft. Alternate heating and cooling with water cracked the stone and enabled the shaft to be deepened. In the second stage, as the tunnel lengthened and widened, a platform was erected, built up with debris from the excavation. On this further fires were built, to attack the roof of the shaft, and also to assist the circulation of air in the workings. This system could be extended, as in the third stage, up to 160 meters into the mountain. Damming the bottom shaft also enabled the water level in the mine to be controlled.

MASTERY OF THE WHEEL

The Celts learned how to shrink an iron tire on a wooden wheel. This seventeenth-century French engraving by Benard shows a contemporary wheelwright at work using techniques and tools which would have been wholly familiar to a Celt. The

Wheeled vehicles were extensively used in the Celtic world to carry warriors into battle, dead chieftains to their graves, and for a whole range of more mundane purposes about the village or farm. To judge from the surviving remains, the art of the wheelwright was both widespread and highly developed: indeed the craft has shown little significant improvement since the second century B.C. It was during the first millennium B.C. that the spoked wheel as we know it today was perfected.

The early prehistory of the wheel is not our concern: suffice it to say that plank-wheeled vehicles had reached all parts of Europe long before the emergence of the Celts and

cast in bronze in a single piece. On average these bronze wheel centers were about fifty centimeters in diameter, and clearly they were meant to be fitted with a wooden tire set into a channel in the bronze wheel rim and secured by rivets. How wide these tires were cannot now be determined, but they are unlikely to have exceeded ten centimeters. Thus the completed wheel would be quite small, never more than seventy centimeters in diameter. Since the spokes were of cast bronze, they were strong and needed only to be few: normally there were four, five, or six. Finally to create a durable running surface nails with expanded heads were sometimes set in the

wheel is first constructed of its wooden parts. Then an iron tire is made fractionally too small for the wheel. The idea is that when the tire is heated, it will expand and can be forced over the wheel *(left)*, burning itself into position. On cooling, the iron will contract and the tire will shrink on to the felly, binding all parts of the wheel tightly together.

that spoked-wheeled chariots were evidently in use among the Mycenaeans of Greece in the thirteenth century B.C. The wheels of the Mycenaean chariot, however, insofar as one can judge from contemporary representations, were of a specific type which appears to be identical to Late Bronze Age wheels from the rest of Europe. Essentially the hub, spokes, and rim were

wooden tire. This then was the prototype from which the more advanced wheel type was to develop.

The next stage is represented by a wheel found in a late seventh-century grave at Salamis in Cyprus. It was composed largely of wood with eight spokes set into a wooden felly made up of two strips of wood both bent into a circle, their overlapping ends being secured with nails. Strictly speaking, the inner felly, the spokes, and the hub together formed that part of the wheel which, in the earlier examples we have described, had been made of bronze; while the outer felly of wood was the equivalent to the wooden tire. How it was attached to the inner member is uncertain, but in all probability some kind of tongue-and-groove joint was perfected, much as the wooden tire had been set into the channel of the bronze wheel center.

Wheels of this type are depicted on Assyrian reliefs and frescoes, and it may have been from this region that the technique

with a broad felly was found in Transcaucasia. Which route of introduction had precedence over the other it is impossible to say. It may be that the Celtic wheelwrights, already adept at wheel making, simply absorbed new ideas brought to their attention by travelers and traders from surrounding areas, and created a concept of their own.

The resulting spoked wheel found in graves of the seventh century in Germany and Bohemia, was a sophisticated device. It was composed entirely of wood with iron fittings. In general construction it resembled the wheels from Cyprus, but there were significant differences. The fellies were of double thickness, the inner one being composed of a single piece of wood bent into a circle, while the outer one was made up of several separate sections each bent

Below: Cast bronze wheels, as on this ritual model from Schlesien, Germany, were well known in central Europe in the Late Bronze Age. But the spoked wheel of wood did not

make an appearance in the archaeological record until the seventh century, and then it is found only in chieftains' graves. These early wheels were cumbersome, but from the fifth century onward the technology of wheelmaking had been mastered and elegant vehicles, like the cart from Dejbjerg, Denmark *(left)*, became more widely distributed. The wheel was a recurring motif in Celtic iconography, ultimately deriving perhaps from a solar symbol. *Far left:* A Romano-Celtic deity holding a wheel, from Carlisle, England.

into an arc to suit the curvature of the inner felly. They were joined with iron clamps which also bound the two fellies together. The wooden parts of these wheels have rotted, but the structure can be reconstructed because the separate wooden sections have left grain impressions preserved in the rust on the iron clamps.

To give the wheel added rigidity, the ends of the spokes penetrated both inner and outer fellies and the whole was bound by an iron tire which was attached to the wood with large-headed iron nails, the nail heads forming the actual running surface.

These early Hallstatt wheels provide a fascinating glimpse of technology in a state of change: they owe much to the earlier bronze type but have adopted the double-thickness felly of the Assyrian type of wheel to which has been added the sig-

The shrinking-on of iron tires was a technique used by the barrel-maker. Celtic barrels are unknown, but Roman wine was imported in bound barrels of this type. *Above:* Detail of wine barrels on a river boat; Gallo-Roman relief from Cabrières-d'Aygues.

spread to the eastern Mediterranean and thus to the European mainland, perhaps via the Etruscans in northern Italy. But rather like the problem of the spread of iron technology (pp. 112–113), the idea of the multiple felly wheel may have penetrated Europe by another route: that is, from the east, overland along the Danube valley since the oldest known spoked wheel

nificant innovation of the iron tire. Wheels of this kind were resilient, strong, and hard wearing, but they were still rather heavy; and although the weight did not matter much in general-purpose vehicles, the emergence of chariot warfare in the fifth century B.C. demanded a lighter structure but one of great strength. It was quite possibly this need that encouraged the final improvements to be made in the technology of the Celtic wheel.

The perfected wheel is best demonstrated by the four-wheeled ritual vehicle of the first century B.C. found in a bog near Dejbjerg in Denmark. The felly was now a single piece of wood, as little as five centimeters thick, bent and clamped at the joint,

harness pole to the chassis was a somewhat cumbersome arrangement which must have affected maneuverability. The Dejbjerg cart was, however, designed for stately ritual processions in which rapid changes of direction were likely to have been unnecessary. In war chariots we might expect this problem to have been overcome. With the Celts, as in so many cultures, it was the need to perfect war gear that forced technological improvements.

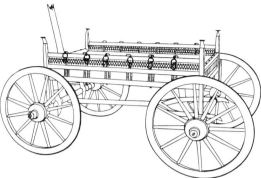

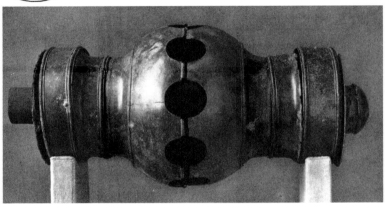

Wheelwrights of great skill were employed by the Celtic chieftains, and fine examples of their work have been found in aristocratic graves of the Hallstatt and early La Tène periods. *Above:* Reconstruction of the funerary cart from the grave at Ohnenheim, Germany. *Above right:* Bronze hub binding from one of the four wheels of the cart buried with the "princess" of Vix, Burgundy.

kept rigid with a nail-less iron tire which had been shrunk on. Wheels of this type, which became common in the La Tène period, are elegant in their simplicity—the unnecessary wood of the double felly has been pared down to a minimum, while the heavy iron nails, which originally attached the tire, have been omitted altogether. What remains is a highly efficient device which it was impossible to improve upon until the development of twentieth-century technology.

Although we have concentrated here upon the evolution of the wheel, it should be remembered that there would also have been improvements in the frame of the vehicle itself. The well-preserved Dejbjerg cart, already referred to, showed one particularly interesting innovation. In the hub-box, between the hub and the axle, several hardwood pegs of circular cross-section had been placed to ease the rotation of the wheel—much the same idea as the modern ball-bearing! Yet the attachment of the

The ritual concept behind the wheeled vehicle is difficult to untangle, but many different cultures in far-flung parts of Europe produced what are evidently ritual vehicles: Trundholm, in Denmark; Strettweg, in Austria (p. 78/79); Mérida, in Spain (p. 53); and the example from Glasinac, in Yugoslavia, illustrated here, dating to the middle of the first millennium B.C. The tradition is clearly deep-rooted. In Yugoslavia a

similar vehicle made in clay, this time carrying a god and drawn by water birds, was found at Dupljaja (Serbia) and dates to the middle of the second millennium. The rich cart burials of the Hallstatt period are therefore only one manifestation of a very ancient cart ritual.

The plow, so vital to prehistoric society, was an invention of great antiquity. To sow crops efficiently it was necessary first to pulverize the soil, and the simplest way to do this was with a digging stick or hoe. It would not have taken a great feat of inventive genius to realize that a hoe dragged through the soil created an acceptable furrow, and it was only a matter of time before man was replaced by yoked oxen as a means of traction.

Evidence for the use of the plow in prehistoric Europe is of four kinds: plow marks preserved in ancient ground surfaces below later earthworks; field banks (lynchets) caused by the movement of soil consequent upon plowing; contemporary illustrations, usually rock carvings, showing plow teams in action; and the remains of the plows themselves. Taken together, the evidence points to an intensification of cultivation taking place some time in the middle of the second millennium.

There are two principal classes of plow—light plows, or ards, and heavy plows—the difference being that while the ard scratched a furrow in the soil, the heavy plow could turn a furrow. It was the ard that was in common use throughout the pre-Roman Celtic period.

Discoveries of ards preserved in the peat bogs of northwestern Europe show that there were two basic types of construction: The simplest, called a "crook ard," has the plow beam (for harnessing to the oxen), and the sole (i.e., the cutting edge) made from a single piece of wood. In the more complex, and presumably later, type known as the spade ard, the stilt (guiding handle) and share were inserted through a hole in the base of a separate plow beam. It is this type which appears to be illustrated on the rock engraving from Val Camonica (far left).

For the most part the simple ards were made entirely of wood, the inherent weakness in the implement being the actual point which was in contact with the soil. Under normal conditions a wooden point would have quickly worn out, but in the case of the spade ard a new wooden shear could easily have been slipped into place. In some areas, stone shears were used, but among the Celtic communities iron shears are found sufficiently frequently to suggest that they were in common use. In fact, two types of iron strengthening were employed: long

bars of iron could be wedged in position on top of the wooden shear base but projecting in front of it so that the iron tip ripped through the soil. This type had the advantage that when the tip had worn out, the bar could be hammered forward to become once more the effective cutting point. The other type entailed enclosing the tip of the wooden share with an iron shoe. The arrangement was perfectly effective but was liable to wear out.

By means of simple ards of this type, drawn by two yoked oxen and guided from behind by a plowman, vast areas of temperate Europe were opened up to agriculture. Well before the emergence of the Celts the forest clearings were beginning to coalesce into an ordered arable landscape. It was, however, the spread of iron that so accelerated

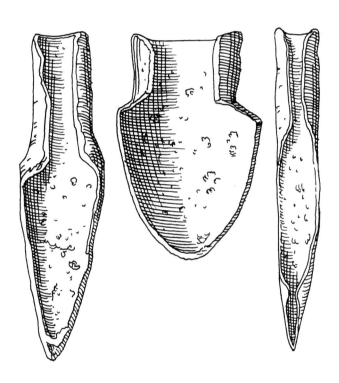

the process, for the iron axe and iron-shod plow were highly efficient implements for hacking down the forest and breaking the land. Thus equipped, the Celtic farmers could penetrate regions previously impossible to tame.

The Celtic ard, unlike the medieval plow, simply scratched a furrow in the soil; it did not turn the sod, but by careful tilting, the displaced soil could be ridged upon one side of the furrow. To break down the soil to produce an adequate seed bed, it appears to have been necessary to plow each field

Rock engravings depicting agricultural scenes occur in Scandinavia, in the Ligurian Alps, and in particular at Val Camonica, north of Milan, where this example was found. Several plowing scenes have been recorded, usually with a single ox team and a man guiding the plow. Occasionally a second man is shown leading the team. In the scene from which this example is extracted, the plow team is followed by five men (or women) with hoes, suggesting that it may have been necessary to break up the soil by hand after the plow had loosened it.

beam, which made a vertical cut through the soil at the same time as the shear sliced horizontally. Behind the coulter was a mold board so angled that the loosened soil was turned over upon itself. The problem, archaeologically, is to know how to recognize the improved implement: a number of iron blades have been found which *could* be coulters, but simple blades of this sort could have many functions. However, towards the end of the free-Celtic period heavy land was being broken for the first time—a fair indication that the improved heavy plow was coming into general use in many areas.

The regular plowing of defined areas gave rise to regular fields, the boundaries of which, fenced or otherwise, soon became distinctive landscape features as soil accu-

Not all plows were pulled by animals. On the island of Skye, off the west coast of Scotland, this crofter used a foot plow into the early decades of this century. On steep slopes and rocky ground this method of cultivation was far less cumbersome than trying to maneuver a team of horses or oxen.

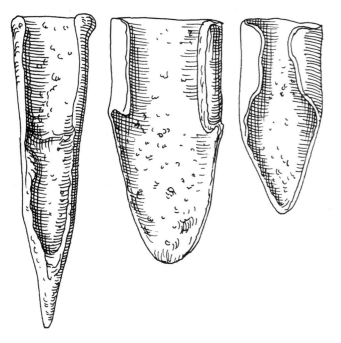

Above left: Plowshares of various types, as shown in these sketches, have been found on many Celtic sites. Strictly they are only the iron shoes which clad and strengthened the wooden shear. Although of course far cruder than the modern shears *(above)*, which cut and turn the soil in one operation, the plowing principle in both cases is the same and the shape of the blades has changed little in the intervening millennia.

twice, the second plowing being at right angles to the first. Grooves formed by this kind of cross-plowing have been recognized in ground surfaces now preserved beneath later earthworks in Holland and Denmark, and it is reasonable to assume that the technique was widely adopted elsewhere in Europe.

Whether or not the Celts had developed the heavy plow before the Roman period, is a difficult question. The essential difference was that the heavy plow was provided with a *coulter* (or knife) attached to the plow

mulated on downhill slopes and rocks were thrown off the field and piled along the boundaries where hedges grew. In this way checkerboards of little fields blanketed the landscape. They can still be seen in marginal areas of Britain, beyond the present limit of agriculture, a tribute to the skill and persistence of the Celtic farmers.

ART COMBINED WITH PRACTICALITY

Celtic art has a humor of its own: faces peer out of designs when they are least expected. The delightfully doleful horse *(right)* from Stanwick in Yorkshire is brilliantly captured by placing two simple trumpet scrolls together and adding eyes. The cleverness of the design would have amused a Celt.

Horses and chariots were enlivened with elaborate decoration wherever opportunity presented itself. Even functional objects were ornamented.

Below, left to right:
This linchpin from Kings Langley in Herefordshire served to keep the wheel from slipping off the axle, but its head provided a convenient medium for decoration.

Bridle bit from Attymon, Galway, Ireland. Here again, the craftsman could not resist the temptation to enliven a functional object with decoration.

Celtic art of the fifth and early fourth centuries B.C. was essentially the art of the aristocratic class, an art style developed by specialists to adorn the luxury objects of their masters. But during the migration period in the fourth and third centuries, Celtic art styles became widely dispersed both geographically and socially, and decorative skills are found lavished on quite mundane items. In other words, Celtic art became the folk art of the people.

A warlike people like the Celts inevitably lavished considerable skill in decorating their arms and armor. Flamboyance and display were the keynotes of the fourth and third centuries. Simple functional items were frequently chosen for decoration. Bronze scabbards for swords, for example, were enhanced with chased, tendril patterns. Indeed, so popular did decorated scabbards become that schools of craftsmen grew up specializing in these matters in Hungary and in Switzerland, each area producing its own distinctive repertoire of designs. The horse and the war chariot were

Chariot mount from a fourth-century burial at Waldalgesheim, Germany.

Harness ornament (phalera) from Horovicky, Czechoslovakia, late fifth to early fourth century.

Detail from a bronze shield, Wandsworth, third to second century.

Phalera from Manerbio sul Mella, Italy, third to second century.

Right: Reconstruction drawing showing an elaborate harness of the Hallstatt period.

also favorite items of display. After all, the warrior driving up and down in front of the enemies' lines, while hurling abuse at his adversaries, wanted to look both frightening and spectacular. The harness of his horses and the metal fittings of his chariot allowed him plenty of scope for decoration, as we can see from the items illustrated on this page. Every fitting, however simple, was a vehicle for flashy display: the bright red enamel contrasting with the glint of

polished bronze must surely have been an impressive spectacle.

Horse fittings of this kind were comparatively simple to manufacture. They required skillful handling of materials but no bulky equipment. A single craftsman with a few bars of iron, a bag of scrap bronze, some crude glass, beeswax, and a few basic tools could have made everything required to deck out a chariot and its team. Sheets of bronze could easily have been produced from scrap. Attached to some suitable yielding base—perhaps a slab of leather or soft wood covered with layers of cloth— the sheet could quite quickly have been indented, using wooden hammers and punches, to create repoussé designs. If more complex items were required, they could be cast. Inscribed or chased decoration could later be worked onto the surface, or heat-softened glass or enamels could be applied to reserved areas.

The exact social position of the craftsman who produced such work is not immediately apparent. The Irish literature recog-

So far we have been concerned with items of display made by specialists, but love of decoration went far deeper, to pervade all aspects of everyday life. A good example is seen in Celtic pottery, particularly the folk pottery made in the home or village. During manufacture the leather-hard vessel would have provided an irresistible medium for design—simple stamped pottery of elegant simplicity in Hungary, energetic curvilinear designs drawn with a shallow pointed tool in Brittany, or the combination of curvilinear and geometric patterning found in the south of Britain. Although there is great regional variation, the essential Celtic spirit shines through them all. Nor should we forget the importance of wood as a medium for decoration. Wooden vessels, handles, as well as the furniture and fittings for the house, would, for the most

Reconstructed harness based on items found at La Tène, third to second century B.C.

nizes the skilled craftsman as a man of status in society, implying that he was free of the necessity to produce his own food. In all probability each warrior of any status had one or more metalworkers among his clients. Such a man might be allowed to work for others from time to time, or more likely, the surplus to his master's needs might have been distributed as gifts, since a single craftsman working fulltime could have provided for many families.

part, have been decorated in some way— by carving, painting, or a combination of both. Brightness and visual liveliness must have characterized the Celtic environment.

The first century A.D. in Britain saw the development of the art of enameling. Both of these pieces functioned as harness mounts; they were inlaid with red enamel.

Above: From Santon, Norfolk. *Below:* from the Polden Hills, Somerset.

123

A WIDE RANGE OF IMPLEMENTS

Right: Reconstruction of various tools from the La Tène period hanging on the inside wall of a reconstructed La Tène house. From left to right: sickles, a scythe, and an adze.

The introduction of iron gave a new flexibility to the toolmaker. Bronze, because of its comparative softness, needed careful attention paid to hafting arrangements, which affected the form of the individual tool. Iron, on the other hand, was much tougher and was therefore far more flexible. Thus socketed hafting, common during the Late Bronze Age, was replaced by the shaft-hole technique, while cutting tools could be attached to their handles by means of quite simple tangs. The introduction of iron technology, therefore, paved the way for the development of the modern tool kit. Indeed, with the exception of scissors and screws, the hand tools we use today were all anticipated by types in use by the first century B.C.

Apart from the plow the most important tools were those of the wood worker: axes, adzes, saws, drills, files, and chisels. It was, after all, the axe which allowed land to be cleared for farming and provided the raw material necessary for practically every kind of construction, from houses to war chariots. The skill required in making the moving parts of a chariot or the yokes for harnessing the horses leaves little doubt that carpentry had reached a high degree of proficiency. The tools of the smith were of equal importance. They would have included a range of heavy hammers for forging the iron, the tongs to hold it, and iron anvils. The smith would also have needed heavy points and chisels with which to cut and perforate the metal. A distinction seems to have been made between the heavy tool kit of the resident smith, and a lighter range of implements which could be taken into the fields to make running repairs on agricultural implements in active use. One characteristic type is the small field anvil which could be hammered into a convenient tree stump to enable tools like sickles to be repaired.

The farming community would have needed several specialized types of tool. We have already considered the plow (pp. 120–121). In addition, there was a range of reaping tools in common use: sickles for cutting the corn; long-handled reaping knives for collecting reeds or for hacking branches from trees to provide fodder for cattle; and smaller hooks for stripping off the leaves. These little hooks were also well suited for trimming and splitting branches to make wattle work. Then, of course, there would have been knives of all sizes and a great variety of minor fittings, such as nails, bolts, rings, pivots, clamps, and bindings.

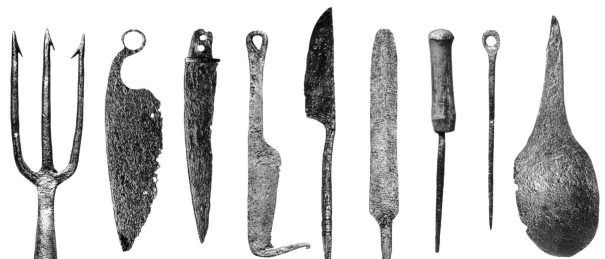

Iron was, after all, a highly flexible material that could be turned to almost any use. One activity that needed little iron was the manufacture of woolen fabrics. Many of the sheep could quite easily have been plucked of their wool, but some breeds may have needed shearing with sharp knives and less commonly with sprung two-bladed shears. Once the wool was collected, spinning could take place on a hand spindle weighted with a whorl of baked clay; then followed the weaving of the cloth on an upright timber-framed loom. Apart from the loom weights, of clay or stone, no special fittings were needed that could not be made in wood—the shuttle and the sword (for beat-

Decorated Celtic pottery was discovered at Sopron (Hungary) in 1900. The drawing, left, shows a woman spinning. The second woman plays a musical instrument. The patterns on the stylized figures are similar to cloth weaves used by the Celts.

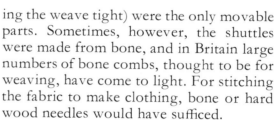

ing the weave tight) were the only movable parts. Sometimes, however, the shuttles were made from bone, and in Britain large numbers of bone combs, thought to be for weaving, have come to light. For stitching the fabric to make clothing, bone or hard wood needles would have sufficed.

Of the wooden tools in use we know very little, but water-logged deposits have ensured the survival of a sufficient quantity of material to show just how important wood was, for making tool handles, containers, shovels, mallets, spoons, and a wide range of other items. Nor should we forget the basketry, matting, and nets which would have been made for home use as well as for fishing. Each community would have been essentially self-sufficient, capable of making everything it needed to live a comfortable and well-provided existence.

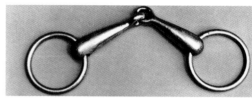

The Celts were renowned as exceptionally able horsemen. They were able to make perfectly functional snaffle bits over two thousand years ago. Below is shown a modern snaffle bit for comparison.

Highly developed tool manufacture from the La Tène period. From left to right: tweezers, shears, fishing trident, four various types of knife, file, awl, needle, cutter, pick, saw, edgetool, pointed hook, pruning-knifes and sickle, two mattocks.

From the Pyrenees to the Alps,
the Cevennes, the Rhine,
and the Rhone—
Caesar reduced all Gaul to a province.

Suetonius

Clasp from St. Margarethen, Austria, showing a rider and two men fighting; Hallstatt period.

Opposite page: Head of a Gaul, on a first-century B.C. coin commemorating Caesar's conquests. The relief statue is a Praetorian guard, second century A.D.

THE
DESTINY
OF THE CELTS

A thanksgiving of twenty days
was celebrated
in Rome.
The whole of Gaul
was now conquered.

Caesar

A time of upheaval came in the fifth century B.C. in the Celtic world. Social unrest, population expansion, possibly also climactic deterioration, combined to force large sections of the community to migrate from their central European homelands southward into Italy and eastward to Greece and beyond. Their exploits are vividly recounted by the Mediterranean peoples with whom they clashed. Rome fell to them, and sacred Delphi was overrun. These Celtic warriors, however, were no match for the citizen armies of Greece and the might of Rome. Pushed back once again beyond the Alps, the Celts were destined to suffer a still more momentous defeat in the last century B.C. It would be their fate, ironically, to be crushed between new barbarian forces—the Germans to the north, the Dacians to the east—and the efficient, modern Roman legions under Julius Caesar. Celtic Europe came under Roman rule, forced to surrender its identity in the Imperial melting pot. Gallo-Roman art, a new hybrid, was the cultural fruit of this domination. Gauls would henceforth gain military glory only as auxiliaries serving under Rome. The conquerors of old—once the terror of Europe—had now been conquered.

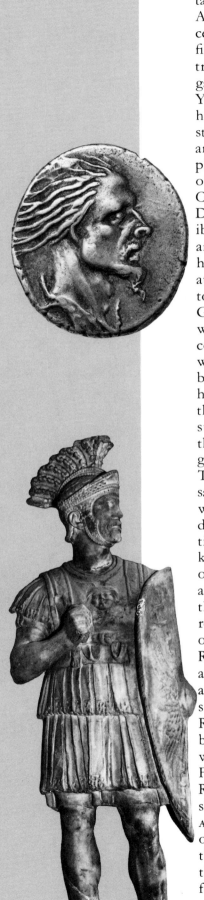

The rise and fall of the Celts was spectacular. From their homeland north of the Alps, migrating bands in the fifth to third century spread in all directions. They infiltrated south through the Alpine passes, traveled east along the Danube into Hungary, and sailed across the North Sea to Yorkshire. From the Po valley warrior hordes spilled across the Apennines to strike terror into the hearts of the Etruscans and the Romans. Even Rome itself was pillaged. In the east, the combined effort of the Greek city-states failed to prevent Celtic hordes reaching Apollo's shrine at Delphi. These initial thrusts were irresistible, but they lacked long-term planning and purpose. Once the first flood of energy had subsided, the warrior bands remained at large in the countryside, always willing to sell their swords to the highest bidder. Gradually, as the Roman and Hellenistic world gained strength, the barbarians were controlled and evicted. For a while they were allowed to remain in the Po valley, but the Second Punic War showed Rome how dangerous the Celtic settlement on their northern boundary could be, and subjugation ensued. In Anatolia, however, the Celts (Galatians) were settled on marginal lands and there remained.

The beginning of the second century B.C. saw the Celts in retreat: Cisalpine Gaul was annexed by Rome after a series of decisive victories, and at about the same time the Galatians were defeated by the kings of Pergamum. It was the beginning of the end. Germanic tribes from the north and the emerging Dacian state in the east thrust against the Celts, causing further reverberations which were to be quieted only when Caesar intervened to extend Roman domination over the whole of Gaul as far north as the Rhine. Under Augustus and Tiberius the rest of Celtic Europe was subjugated, and new campaigns across the Rhine aimed at annexing yet more barbarian territory in the belief that the empire was ever expanding.

For a while Britain remained free, but the Romans could not be stopped—Caesar had shown the way and Claudius followed. By A.D. 84 the armies had reached the north of Scotland, leaving only the Highlands, the Western Isles, and Ireland to continue their old way of life undisturbed. It was from here, after the Roman Empire had collapsed, that Celtic culture reemerged.

127

SOCIETY IN CRISIS

In the fifth century B.C., early Celtic aristocratic society burst apart, unleashing waves of population across Europe, which smashed against the monoliths of Mediterranean civilization. So great was the disruption that repercussions were still felt as late as the first century B.C., long after the full force had been spent. It was these minor convulsions that provided Caesar with his excuse for moving against the Gauls in 58 B.C.

Population expansion, overpopulation, and the excessive consumption of the aristocratic class were among the factors which brought Celtic society to the point of crisis (pp. 40–41). In the areas of the aristocratic heartland—in Germany and northern France—the effects can be seen in the disappearance of the wealthy chieftains' graves and the abandonment of their fortified

When the three envoys asked
by what sort of justice they demanded land,
under threat of violence,
from its rightful owners,
and what business Gauls had to be in Etruria,
they received the haughty reply
that all things belonged to the brave
who carried justice
on the point of their swords.
Passions were aroused and a fight began—
and then it was that the envoys
took their fatal step.

Livy

The aggression and conflict which pervaded the Hallstatt and La Tène period are brilliantly captured on this belt clasp of the Hallstatt period from Vace in Yugoslavia. Two mounted warriors, each supported by foot soldiers, confront each other. Their dress and weapons reflect their different ethnic origins.

courts; but the actual processes of the dispersal elude us. Livy, however, offers a plausible hypothesis in his story of Ambitgatus, king of the Bituriges who, finding it difficult to rule his rich and populous land, "decided to relieve his kingdom of the burdensome excess of population." To do this he sent his nephews Bellovesus and Segovesus, "both adventurous young men, out into the world to find such new homes as the gods by signs from heaven might point the way to; he was willing to give

them as many followers as they thought would ensure their ability to overcome any opposition they might encounter." Here then is a historian of the first century B.C. looking back on the distant past and interpreting it according to traditional beliefs. He goes on to tell us that the gods directed Segovesus to the uplands of southern Germany, while Bellovesus was sent to Italy. Bellovesus collected the surplus population (Livy's phrase) from a number of tribes and set out with his "vast host, some mounted, some on foot, and reached the territory of the Tricastini at the foot of the Alps." Eventually they found a way through the mountains and emerged in the valley of the River Po to found the city of Mediolanum (Milan). In this way began the Celtic colonization of what soon became Cisalpine Gaul.

Livy's account should not, of course, be accepted as accurate history. It was little more than a rationalization of dimly remembered folk tradition, but it provides some indication of the processes which led to the great migration. Livy believed that the movement began during the reign of the Elder Tarquin (traditionally 614–576 B.C.). Polybius, on the other hand, writing in the middle of the second century B.C., tells us that the Celts did not arrive in northern Italy until about 400 B.C. and came not from the west but from the Danube Basin via the eastern Alps. The conflict is more apparent than real, since both accounts are likely to reflect isolated historical events in what was, in all probability, a long and complex process.

An amusing, but not irrelevant, aside to the problem of the migration is provided by the Greek playwright Aristides of Miletus. Etruscans were often portrayed as figures of fun. Such a man was Aruns of Chiusi, whose wife had been seduced by another Etruscan. To take his revenge on society, Aruns filled wagons with wine, oil, and figs and set off for the Alpine passes to display the riches of the south to the Celts. Thus he enticed them to migrate into Italy, bringing destruction (and retribution) with them. This literary invention is an interesting reminder that, to the Celts of the transalpine regions, the south was the source of great luxury. The gods, says Livy, directed Bellovesus along "the much pleasanter road into Italy."

The classical writers give the impression that the Celtic migrations were sudden and very rapid, but in reality this was not so. The initial movements were probably slow and deliberate—a kind of bow wave in advance of a greater displacement. We have already seen that during the period of the aristocratic chiefdoms, there appears to have been a gradual movement north and west of the main centers of power and wealth. This could be seen as a preliminary manifestation of the much greater disruptions which were soon to follow.

The initial stages of expansion to the south can be recognized in the archaeological evidence recovered from the cemeteries clustering in the valleys along the southern flanks of the Alps, in particular in the region of the Lombard lakes. Here, in the warrior burials of Sesto Calende and the wagon burial of Ca' Morta, it is possible to recognize distinct cultural links with the Celtic world of the north, dating to as far back as the seventh century B.C. The Ca' Morta cemetery continued in use and in the late fifth century served as the resting place for warriors clad in La Tène equipment. It was during the fifth century that the dead buried in other cemeteries in the region of Bellinzona began to be provided with objects of early La Tène type and were also graced with Etruscan wine flagons of the kind exported from the Etruscan workshops to the Celtic world. Although alternative explanations are possible, we could reasonably conclude that the Alpine population had become increasingly Celticized during the fifth century, quite possibly as the result of the infiltration of people southward into the valleys along the trade routes between north and south. Because objects of La Tène A type have been found south of the Po in the region of Marzabotto, the Celts may have penetrated this area in the

fifth century, decades before the main Celtic movements southward gained momentum. The second line of Celtic advance indicated by Livy, eastward into the mountainous region between the upper Rhine and the Carpathian Basin, does not appear to have been opened up by earlier Celtic settlers. At present, the earliest archaeological evidence suggests that the Celtic (La Tène) settlement of northeastern Hungary did not begin until about 400 B.C., by which time the migrations were in full swing.

The fifth-century B.C. social crisis coincided with a phase of growing Etruscan influence north of the Alps. At Hirschlanden, near Tübingen, the grave mound of a warrior of the early fifth century was found, capped with a remarkable stone figure *(above)*—a full-scale representation of a warrior—carved in a style reminiscent of Etruscan work.

It is difficult to judge how many men were involved in the migrations and to assess the composition of the migrating forces. Did these armies consist only of warriors, or were whole families on the move? The classical sources give some indication, but they were prone to exaggerate and to oversimplify. That the numbers were large is, however, certain.

Livy's account of Bellovesus's force is particularly interesting: he actually enumerates the tribes from which the "surplus population" was enlisted—some seven in all. While we cannot accept the list as necessarily accurate, it clearly implies that the migratory movements were not confined to

ing the Illyrians (in modern Yugoslavia) and by the beginning of the third century were ravaging Macedonia and Thrace, penetrating deep into Greece in 279. Other groups crossed to Asia Minor where they caused widespread disruptions, until they were finally brought to heel by the kings of Pergamum in the early second century. Thus in southeastern Europe and Asia Minor the main period of Celtic aggression lasted just over two centuries after about 400 B.C. By about 180 their energies were spent, and they had either settled in peace with their neighbors or had been driven back into central Europe to Hungary and Czechoslovakia.

The dislocations caused by this onslaught must have been considerable. One effect was on the Celtic hordes themselves. It seems that in many instances, the fragmentation of the group ensued, and not infrequently we read of Celtic mercenaries in the service of foreign rulers. As early as 369, Celtic mercenaries were employed in Greece by Dionysius I in his battle against the Boetians. Later, in 277, the Hellenistic ruler Antigonus Gonatas used Celtic mercenaries against Pyrrhus, king of Epirus, but Pyrrhus too employed Celts—apparently he kept them under control by allowing them to plunder the graves of the Macedonian kings. Celtic mercenaries also played a significant part in the conflicts among the different rulers of Asia Minor, but, frequently got out of hand. We also hear of them in the service of the Ptolemies in Egypt in the third century, and as late as 187–186 Celtic mercenaries were involved in suppressing a revolt in upper Egypt. There can therefore be little doubt that a considerable part of the force that poured into the Balkans in the fourth century, and their successors, found gainful employment in the conflicts consequent upon the interminable power struggles of the Hellenistic rulers. What percentage of the original horde found its way back into Europe we will never know.

The migration of the Celts southward and eastward into Italy, Greece, Macedonia, and Asia Minor is tolerably well recorded in the works of the Greek and Roman historians. Such is the quality of record that the individual events can be considered in some detail (pp. 132–139). But if the Celts were known to have migrated in these directions, is it not possible that they also

The migration of the central European Celts, by the second century B.C., spanned Europe. South into Italy and east into Greece and Asia Minor, their progress is recorded in some detail by the classical authors. The

movement northeastward into Transylvania and beyond is well attested by the discovery of cemeteries of the La Tène culture; but western movements into Spain and Britain are more problematical, since the evidence could be interpreted as little more than intensified trading contacts. However, one group appears to have crossed the North Sea and settled in Yorkshire.

a single tribe but were confederacies of splinter groups enlisted from a number of regions.

The main force of the migration burst upon the classical world about 400 B.C. By 390 the Celts were at the gates of Rome, and they remained in Italy, a constant irritation to the Roman government, until the early decades of the second century B.C. In southeastern Europe they were no less a menace. In the mid-fourth century they were fight-

expanded to the northeast and northwest? To answer this question, it is necessary for us to examine the archaeological evidence, for upon these matters the classical writers are silent.

The eastward migration of Celts from the area of southern Germany, and possibly Switzerland, is well attested in the spread of cemeteries containing early La Tène objects (principally La Tène B). One possible line of advance led eastward along the Danube into the northwestern part of what is now Hungary. Once through the constrictions imposed by the Alps and the Little Carpathians (in the area of Vienna and Bratislava), the migrants spread out into Transdanubia, where the number of their cemeteries suggests that settlement was dense.

This may well have been the route taken by the hordes who attacked the Balkans. At the same time there was a separate movement eastward into Transylvania (the heart of modern Romania), where once more Celtic cemeteries attest settlement. These groups would have come into contact with local inhabitants, culturally related to the Scythians, contributing to an ethnic mix-

ture from which the Dacian state emerged. In the west, much of France was already settled by communities that had adopted a La Tène style of culture. Even remote areas of western Brittany were producing pottery decorated with elaborate La Tène motifs. While there is no direct evidence of folk movement, minor shifts and readjustments must have taken place. One of the principal areas of innovation at this time was the Marne region, where a vigorous La Tène culture developed, sufficiently distinctive to be called the Marnian culture in archaeological terminology. From here it seems that direct contact was established with parts of the Low Countries, and it may well be that small bands of settlers spread northward. It is, however, difficult to distinguish on archaeological grounds between distribution patterns created by folk movement and those resulting from exchange systems. Much the same problem is posed by the evidence from Britain. It used to be thought that bands of Marnian invaders poured across the Channel to colonize the south and spread northward into Yorkshire. More recent work, however, has emphasized that, while it is true that the southeast of the country was in direct contact with the Continent, that contact is simply a continuation of a long-established relationship which had already existed for half a millennium. Commodities were traded back and forth, but there was no recognizable change in settlement pattern or in burial ritual which would signal a folk movement— with one exception: Yorkshire. Here, in the late fifth or early fourth century, a novel burial rite was introduced: bodies were inhumed, sometimes with their two-wheeled carts or chariots, in graves which were often set in rectangular enclosures delimited by ditches. This style of burial, hitherto completely alien in Britain, is well known among the early La Tène cultures of France and Germany. Perhaps then we are seeing, dimly reflected in the archaeological evidence from the Yorkshire Moors, the trace of one of the most far-flung of the Celtic migrations, equivalent in its daring to the movement of the Celts into Anatolia but unsung in contemporary literature.

The following account has come down to us of the Gallic migration. During the reign of Tarquinius Priscus in Rome, the Celts, one of the three Gallic peoples, were dominated by the Bituriges, and their king was consequently a member of that tribe. At the time we are concerned with the king was one Amitgatus, who by his personal qualities, aided by the good luck which blessed both himself and his subjects, had attained to very considerable power; indeed under his rule Gaul became so rich and populous that the effective control of such large numbers was a matter of serious difficulty.

Livy

The great strength of the migrating Celtic force lay in its infantry. Most men, even the poorest, could arm themselves with a sword and shield. This Celt-Iberian warrior on a first-century B.C. relief from Osuna, Spain, wears a helmet typical of the region and holds the usual oval Celtic shield.

The opposing forces in northern Italy were well matched. Etruscan warriors, like the one depicted in the second-century B.C. bronze *(far right)*, were armed in much the same way as the Celts; but their small round shields, for fending off the blow rather than protecting the whole body, were better designed for more open fighting than the massed onslaught of Celtic type.

Right: Celts occasionally wore body armor, as the warrior shown here from Grézan, Gard, France, but this was unusual and was more likely learned from contacts with their Mediterranean opponents.

Terrified townships
rushed to arms
as the avengers
went roaring by;
men fled from the field
for their lives;
and from all the immense host,
covering miles of ground
with its straggling masses
of horse and foot,
the cry went up
"To Rome!"

Livy

Throughout the fifth century, Celts (or Gauls, as they are frequently called by the classical writers) began to settle in the Po valley. According to the classical writers, the first to come were the Insubres, who captured and destroyed the Etruscan city of Milan. The Cenomani settled around Brescia and Verona, the Lepontii around Lake Maggiore, and the Libici and Salluvii on the banks of the Ticina. A little later the Boii and Lingones crossed the Alps to take up their position south of the Po, while the Senones, coming still later, passed farther south into Umbria to settle on the Adriatic coast. By about 400 B.C. the land was densely settled and incapable of absorbing more. Polybius, writing a little later, describes the small scattered farmsteads and the neat fertile fields growing wheat, barley, millet, vines, and figs.

The next stage of the advance came soon after 400 B.C. when tribes from the Po valley, possibly under pressure from further immigrants, decided to move southward, through the Apennines, to explore and plunder Italy.

In about 391 B.C. (the traditions of Livy and Polybius give slightly differing dates)

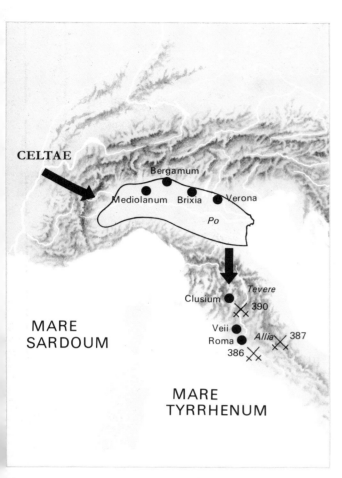

CELTAE

Bergamum

Mediolanum Brixia Verona

Po

MARE
SARDOUM

Clusium Tevere
✕✕ 390

Veii
Roma Allia ✕✕ 387
386 ✕✕

MARE
TYRRHENUM

thirty thousand Celts, led by Brennus, marched on the Etruscan town of Clusium, which had recently established a treaty relationship with Rome. "The plight in Clusium was a most alarming one: Strange men in thousands were at the gates, men the like of whom the townsfolk had never seen, outlandish warriors armed with strange weapons who were rumored already to have scattered the Etruscan legions on both sides of the Po; it was a terrible situation" (Livy). Rome sent envoys to negotiate peace, but the demands of the Celts—land upon which to settle—were unacceptable, and battle ensued in which, contrary to international convention, the envoys took part, one of them actually killing a Celtic chieftain. This is the reason given by Livy for the Celts' turning on Rome, but it is unlikely that they really needed political provocation; visions of plunder would have been quite sufficient. In four days the Celtic hordes, composed of Senones and Lingones, covered the eighty miles to Rome. The mood of the city was captured by Livy in a speech which he puts into the mouth of the consul M. Popillius Laenas: "You are not facing a Latin or Sabine foe

who will become your ally when you have beaten him: we have drawn our swords against wild beasts whose blood we must shed or spill our own."

On the eighteenth of July at Allia on the left bank of the Tiber, the Roman army was routed, leaving the city entirely undefended. The Celts entered and in a frenzy of destruction reduced everything to a heap of smoldering ruins: only the Capitol held out, its defenders remaining under siege for seven months. Eventually, after plague had ravaged the Celtic armies, terms were agreed and the Celts moved off, their booty almost intact.

For more than fifty years following the destruction of Rome in 390 B.C. the Celtic armies in Italy remained a serious threat to Rome, and their presence encouraged the allied cities of central Italy to revolt. Many battles were recorded. One, of particular interest, took place at Anio in 367. Polybius describes how a Roman, T. Manlius, confronted a Celt in single combat in front of both armies and killed him, taking his neck torque. Such was the magnitude of his achievement that he assumed the name of Torquatus. The 350s saw an intensification of the conflict, but in 349 the Celts suffered a resounding defeat and a general stampede from the Romans began. Raids ceased altogether by about 335, and in 332–331 a treaty was concluded between Rome and the Senones.

The Celts were now in full retreat; in 295 they suffered a major defeat at Sentinum, and in 225 at the famous battle of Telamon, so vividly described by Polybius, a Celtic army was cut to pieces.

The Celts of the Po valley continued to be an irritation to Rome, particularly during the Second Punic War when Hannibal used them as somewhat uncontrolled allies. By taking the Punic side, the Celts had sealed their own fate. In 197 in the battle of Lake Como they were defeated and Latin settlement began. The Boii rebelled, but in a series of encounters culminating in the battle of Bologna in 191 their resistance was destroyed; massive spoils passed to Rome; vast territories were annexed; and the tribe, having suffered great losses, moved away to find a new home north of the Alps. The wheel had come full circle.

The actual area from which the initial movement into the Po valley came is uncertain, and thus the arrow in the Alpine area of the map is hypothetical. Livy mentions that it was the Bituriges who migrated first. Several hundred years later this tribe was living in central France, but at the time of the migrations it may well have occupied land north of the Alps. Expansion through the Apennines began about 400 B.C. after the Po valley had been extensively settled.

The assault on Rome (around 390 B.C.) caught the city totally unprepared. Although an earthwork defense protected the eastern approach, the Celts had no difficulty in sweeping through the city, destroying and looting as they went. The debris of this destruction has been found below the Forum and on the Palatine.

After the Celtic threat had abated, a massive new defensive system was built to protect the city. The so-called Servian Wall, constructed of large blocks of tufa, was ten kilometers long and served Rome well for centuries.

Overleaf (pp. 134–135):
The conflict between barbarian Celt, fighting naked, and the Etruscan warrior is vividly portrayed on a relief found at Bologna dating to the fifth to fourth century B.C.

VIOLATION OF DELPHI

The Celts who penetrated south-eastern Europe came into conflict first with the world of Alexander the Great and, after Alexander's death in 334 B.C., with the rival faction of the Hellenistic dynasty who succeeded him. In the confusion of the period, Celtic mercenaries were sometimes used by the rival Hellenistic leaders, but more often the Celts moved around in raiding bands, several of which combined in 279 for the concerted attack through Greece to Delphi.

Above: Coins of the Macedonian kings. Head of Alexander, on coin minted in 297–281 B.C. by Lysimachus, to demonstrate his legitimacy; and (at right) coin of Antigonus Gonatas, 277–239 B.C. It was the death of Lysimachus in 281 that opened up new opportunities for the Celts in Macedonia. Antigonus Gonatas employed Celtic mercenaries in his army, but in 277 was defeated by Pyrrhus, king of Epirus.

While the Senones and their confederates were plundering their way through Italy, other Celtic tribes traditionally led by the Sigoves were moving through the foothills of the eastern Alps and raiding both Pannonia (Hungary) and Illyria (Yugoslavia). In all probability, the Danube formed the boundary of their easterly advance, for beyond lay the powerful tribes of Scythian extraction. Apart from the movement into Transylvania (pp. 130–131), these eastern territories were avoided, and the main thrust of the advance was concentrated on the Balkans.

Celts were active in Illyrian territory in the mid-fourth century. In 358 clashes with the Illyrians were recorded, and in 335 we hear that Alexander the Great had to undertake campaigns in Bulgaria as the result of unrest caused by the displacement of tribes resulting from the Celtic advance down the Adriatic coast. Indeed he actually received Celtic envoys at this time.

The advance continued. In 310 Celtic raids created panic among the Illyrian tribes, and a few years later, in 298, one group of Celts had reached Bulgaria while another had penetrated Thrace. Fighting in Bulgaria intensified during the 280s.

The culmination of this gradual buildup of forces came in 279 when a vast Celtic horde marched into Macedonia to plunder and to settle. The attractions of Greece were many, not least the vast treasures at the great sanctuaries, of which Delphi was the most famous. At Delphi resided the oracle of Apollo, who through the accuracy of her prophecy had gained worldwide recognition. The shrine was sacrosanct and thus was the appropriate place for the city-states of the Greek world to deposit their treasures for safekeeping. Rumors of untold wealth would soon have reached the invading armies, and it is hardly surprising therefore that Brennus advanced with his thirty thousand men towards the shrine.

The route southward led through the famous pass of Thermopylae, which they found to be strongly held by the Greeks. A direct frontal attack showed that the Celts were no match for the spears of the Greek hoplites. Faced with repulse, one group of Celts decided to move off and plunder the territory of the Aetolians; they sacked the town of Callium and butchered its in-

habitants. Their action drew the Aetolian contingent away from Thermopylae. The Greeks were bent on revenge, and using the tactics of guerrilla warfare, cut the Celtic raiders to pieces—but their absence from the pass gave Brennus and his warriors the opportunity to outflank the remaining defenders using unguarded mountain passes.

Delphi was reached in midwinter; but though without substantial defenses, its position high on the side of Mount Parnassus gave it a degree of protection. The events of that fateful winter are not recorded in detail, and obscurities remain; but it would seem that the Celts achieved some measure of success. Strabo tells us that one of the participating tribes, the Tectosages, carried off a huge quantity of

Triumphant, Brennus ravages
the whole of Macedonia
without hindrance.
Then, as if the spoils of men
have no further attraction
for him, he turns his eyes
to the temples
of the immortal gods,
joking that they, who are rich,
must make presents to men.
So he marches on Delphi....
The Gauls, still
under the influence of
the previous night's
drunkenness, hurl themselves
into battle, without
considering the danger.
The Delphians fight back,
trusting more in the God
than their own forces....
His presence is soon apparent:
rocks, split from the mountain
by an earth tremor,
crush the Gallic army,
and scatter the strongest units,
which at the same time
break under the blows
of the defenders.
Finally, a storm breaks
and hail and cold put
an end to the wounded.

T. Pompeius

spoils to the region of Toulouse, where they eventually settled. But other parts of the Celtic force fared less well.

The story is told that the Greeks asked the oracle of Apollo for advice and received a reply couched in the usual enigmatic terms: that the god would send white maidens to the aid of the Greeks. The white maidens turned out to be a blizzard accompanied by a monstrous thunderstorm causing rockfalls. Under this cover, the Greeks attacked the Celtic camp, raining arrows down on the invaders. The Celts, thoroughly demoralized and in complete disarray, retreated, having first killed off their wounded. The Celtic temperament could not sustain reverses of this magnitude. During the long, hard retreat northward, constantly harried and attacked, the wounded

leader Brennus committed suicide. The remainder of the force continued their retreat to join the melee of dispossessed warriors in Macedonia.

Some groups moved back westward along the Danube, settling in the region of Beograd: they were known as the Scordisci. Others moved farther north to join the Celtic groups already settled in Transdanubia. But a number of tribes decided to move off eastward. The Tolistoagii and the Trocini, who had separated from Brennus in Macedonia, reached the Dardanelles in 278 and crossed with difficulty into Asia Minor. Another group, the Tectosages, who had been with Brennus, followed them. In Asia the Celts were to find a congenial land in which to pursue their warlike activities.

Delphi claimed to be the center of the world. By the seventh century B.C. it had risen from obscurity to a position of dominance, largely as the result of the fame of its oracle at the shrine of Apollo. Excavations, which began in 1892, showed the sanctuary itself to have been quite small, ca. 200 by 150 meters, but a city of some proportions spread out in front of it. Nearby was the sanctuary of Athena Pronaia within which is the circular shrine (or *tholos*), shown above. It was built about 400 B.C. Some of the earlier buildings had been destroyed by landslides in ca. 480 and 373, similar to the landslide which so demoralized the Celts in 279.

A CELTIC KINGDOM IN ASIA

The growth of the kingdom of Pergamum was spectacular. A place of obscurity in the fourth century, it rose to dominance under Philetaeros, who inherited a vast fortune follow-

ing the death of Lysimachus in 281 B.C. The dynasty he founded began with his nephew Eumenes I, the first of the Attalid kings. Eumenes's son Attalus I beat the Gauls in a great battle in 230. Eumenes II *(above right)* ruled from 197 to 159, during which time he enslaved forty thousand Celts (Galatians).

The Celtic force that crossed into Asia Minor—in all some twenty thousand men, women, and children—were immediately enlisted into the service of two local rulers, Nicomedes of Bythinia and Mithridates of Pontus, who controlled the northwestern part of Anatolia. Those Celts without weapons were armed by their employers to prepare them for their new role. Quite simply, their function was to raid and plunder the lands to the south ruled by the Seleucid king, Antiochus—a task, one would imagine, not uncongenial to the Celtic mentality. The raids were well-organized affairs: the Tolistoagii took the wealthy lands of Aeolis and Ionia; the Trocini were given the Dardanelles; while the Tectosages were allowed the interior. The Celtic onslaught was quite unprecedented and threw the cities of Aegean Turkey into turmoil. Whereas in Greece the city-states had combined to repel the invader, here in Anatolia there was no cohesive resistance; each city fended for itself, suspicious of its neighbors. One by one they came under attack. Some paid protection money; others, like Miletus and Ephesus, fought. Priene would do neither, but one of its citizens, Sotas, organized a private army and managed to save many of the inhabitants from the countryside around. Only Pergamum managed successfully to drive off the attackers—a success which brought the city renown.

The raids persisted over several years, but in 275 Antiochus, his armies strengthened with elephants, took the field and resoundingly defeated them. The Celts now withdrew to northern Phrygia, where they were settled in a land which became known as Galatia, their presence on the northern fringe of Seleucid territory serving as a buffer between the two power blocks.

For some years, they continued to extract money from the Seleucid monarchy in payment for leaving the cities of the south unmolested, but the comparative calm was short-lived, and raids became increasingly persistent. Eventually, in the 230s, the kingdom of Pergamum felt strong enough to resist. Payments were stopped, with the inevitable result that the Celts marched on the city. In the great battle which ensued, the armies of Pergamum, led by their king Attalus, scored a spectacular victory, after which the Celts retreated to Galatia and Attalus assumed the title King and Savior. The political situation in Asia Minor now became even more complicated. By brilliant political maneuvering, Pergamum managed to involve Rome on her side against the Seleucids, and in 189 at the battle of Magnesia the army of Antiochus was defeated: at the same time forty thousand Galatians (as the Celts were now called) who served with him were enslaved—an act which effectively marked the end of the Celtic raids. The historian Polybius put events into perspective: "All those who dwelt on this side of the Taurus did not rejoice so much at the defeat of Antiochus as at their release from the terror of the barbarians."

To celebrate their great victory, and to demonstrate their leadership of western Anatolia, the Pergamenes erected an altar to Zeus high on their hilltop capital. The outer wall of its podium was decorated with a magnificent relief portraying the battle between the gods and earth-borne giants, a composition of great brilliance and originality symbolizing the success of the Pergamum kings (the gods) against the barbarian Celts. At about the same time (during the reign of Eumenes II, 197–159) the balustrade of the nearby temple of Athene Nikephoros was decorated with a relief illustrating piles of captured Celtic armor, presumably of the type in use at the end of the third and beginning of the second centuries. All the familiar items are there: the carnyx, mail armor, shields, spears, swords, helmets, and a yoke, either from a chariot or a baggage cart. The temple frieze is the last monument to Celtic aggression in Asia.

Although much is known of the Asian Celts (the Galatians) in their relationship to their neighbors, our knowledge of their social and economic organization in their own territory remains vague. Their land, although comparatively infertile, provided them with a convenient and well-protected referred to as kings, were elected for the purpose of leading a raid. Annual meetings of a council composed of three hundred elders were held at a location, called Drynemetos—the *nemeton* element of the name suggesting that it was a sacred clearing in a wood. These isolated scraps of evidence,

The great altar of Zeus dominated the hilltop city of Pergamum. Constructed between 180 and 160 B.C., it was decorated with a series of energetic sculptures showing the conflict of the gods and the earth-

base from which to raid. It appears that the indigenous Phrygian peasants continued to till the land, presumably serving as the clients of their Celtic masters and thus giving them the freedom of mobility they required. Each of the three tribes was ruled by four tetrarchs; but war leaders, gleaned from the classical writers, give the impression that the Celtic way of life had changed little in the migration. Indeed the Galatians still maintained a distinct identity into the first century A.D., when St. Paul could address them as "O foolish Galatians."

born titans, symbolizing the battles of the Pergamum kings against the Celts. Only the foundation of the altar now remains. All the sculptures and architectural fragments, removed by the German excavators in the nineteenth century, are now displayed in a full-size reconstruction in Berlin.

The Gauls in the Po valley (the Cisalpine Gauls) were a constant menace to Rome, and during the Second Punic War gave some assist-

ance to Hannibal *(coin, above)* after he had crossed the Alps in 218 and had beaten the Roman army, led by Scipio *(top)* at the River Ticinus. The Romans were haunted by the memory of their vulnerability from the north, and when, at the end of the second century, the Cimbri and Teutones began to threaten the region, Marius *(bottom)* attacked them with his reorganized Roman army.

Where the boundary between the Celts and the Germans lay is a matter of dispute. Caesar believed it to be the River Rhine, but this may be little more than the military commander's desire to use the river (a convenient military boundary) as the symbolic dividing line between his potential Gallic allies to the south and the Germanic enemy to the north. Indeed he himself admitted that there were groups of Germans settled on the left bank and reports the belief that both the Belgae and Treveri were ultimately of German origin. In other words, the boundary line had been so blurred and obscured by folk movements in the past that it could not be precisely defined.

Caesar's account of the tribes living north of the Rhine was designed to highlight their differences from the Celts. The economy was more pastorally based, the people less civilized, and because they were untouched by the luxuries of the south, they tended to be far more warlike. Although allowance must be made for some exaggeration, these generalizations are borne out by writers who observed the situation from closer quarters in the first century A.D., when the Roman armies were more intimately involved in the German problem. In 113 B.C. a hitherto unknown tribe, called the Cimbri, suddenly burst into Noricum, in the eastern Alps, and there defeated the Roman consul who had moved into the area to defend the Celtic inhabitants. The event took the Romans completely by surprise—that a barbarian horde could appear so close to Italy, and savage a Roman force, was a cause for considerable concern.

The identity of the Cimbri raises interesting questions. Having first appeared in southeastern Europe about 120 B.C., they attempted to settle in the land of the Boii, but their advances were repelled and they had to turn west through the land of the Scordisci into the territory settled by the Taurisci and Norici. Posidonius, who made a special study of the problem, admitted that he did not known who they were, but Caesar proclaimed them to be Germans, and it is now generally accepted that the migration started in Jutland and gathered strength as it moved south. That the personal names of their leaders are all purely Celtic would suggest, however, that the Cimbri acquired a strong Celtic contingent during their movements.

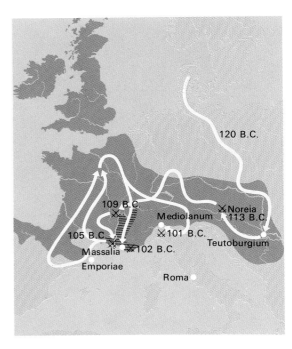

The origins of the Cimbri and Teutones is obscure. The homeland of the Cimbri may have been in Jutland, but as they moved south they gathered other groups to their cause. The Teutones, possibly a Celtic tribe, joined them at a later stage.

A few years later, in 109 B.C., they appeared in southern Gaul, their strength further augmented by another tribe, the Teutones. Although Caesar claimed that the Teutones were also of Germanic origin, their name contains the Celtic word meaning "the people" (the same as *túath* in Irish) and in all probability they were a northern Celtic tribe. Posidonius regarded them as a branch of the Helvetii who were of undisputed Celtic origin.

In southern Gaul the Cimbri and Teutones came into conflict with Rome, and after a number of undecisive battles they succeeded in annihilating a Roman army at Arausio, near Orange, in 105. Thereafter the two forces split up, the Cimbri moving south into Spain, while the Teutones caused havoc in northern Gaul. After a while the Cimbri returned, and the combined horde continued to ravage the Gaulish countryside. Finally they parted once more, the Teutones moving back to southern Gaul, where in 102 at Aquae Sextiae (Aix-en-Provence) they were met and destroyed by the Roman army of Marius. The Cimbri had meanwhile crossed the Alps into the Po valley but were intercepted by Marius, and at Vercellae (Vercelli) the barbarians were annihilated. It had been a frightening time for Rome, with the fearsome barbarian hordes on their very doorstep, and memories of the devastating Celtic invasion nearly three centuries earlier would have been very much in mind. Whatever the true ethnic origins of the invaders, to the Roman world they came from the north, from beyond the semi-civilized Celts with whom the Romans were becoming increasingly familiar. A few years later it was both convenient and politically expedient for Caesar to categorize them as Germans. The effects of the invasion on the Celts who were settled in Gaul were no less disruptive. The Helvetii, who at this time lived between the Rhine and the Danube, moved south into present-day Switzerland,

the tribes in Gaul only the Belgae of the north were strong enough to stand up to the invaders.

The overall situation in Gaul in the last decade of the second century B.C. was confused. The movement of the Cimbri and Teutones had caused widespread disruption among the Celtic tribes. Indeed it may have been at this time that groups of settlers crossed the Channel into southeastern Britain. But to present the situation as a German-inspired invasion (as the later Roman writers were inclined to do) is a gross oversimplification. Whatever the origins of the Cimbri, the majority of the tribes on the move were probably Celtic from the northern fringes of the Celtic world. Pressure from the north would make

Now the infantry of the Cimbri began to move slowly forward from behind their fortifications. They marched in a square, each side of which was thirty furlongs in extent. Their cavalry, 15,000 in number, were a splendid sight as they came riding out. They wore helmets like the heads and gaping jaws of terrible wild beasts and other strange creatures.

Plutarch, Life of Marius

The Germanic tribes shared many elements of culture and religion with the Celts. Their war god, Woden, was often depicted as a mounted warrior like his Celtic equivalent. *Left*: Germanic tombstone, eighth century A.D., representing Woden. It is quite possible that the *Germani* were originally a Celtic tribe living in the region beyond the Rhine. Indeed the author Dionysius of Halicarnassus, writing at the end of the first century B.C. but using older source material, says of Celtica that that part of it beyond the Rhine was called Germania. From Caesar's time onward, any tribe from across the Rhine was called German regardless of ethnic origins.

while the Tigurini, who were of Helvetian stock, joined the raiding hordes. Later another Celtic tribe, the Volcae Tectosages, joined the melee: it was they who, together with the Tigurini, in 107 B.C. near Bordeaux, defeated the Roman army led by Cassius Longinus and forced the humiliated troops to march under the yoke. Of all

the neighboring tribes of the south so vulnerable that a single, and possibly quite small-scale, event like the migration of a few Cimbri could cause sudden and widespread dislocations. It was a situation of instability that was to remain for more than six centuries.

THE RISE OF THE DACIANS

The Dacian state rose to power in the first century B.C. in central Romania—an area already crossed and fringed by migrating Celtic tribes. The

By the fifth century B.C., a people in Romania known as the Getae had developed an advanced and impressive civilization. Described by Herodotus as "the noblest as well as the most just of all the Thracian tribes," the Getae were also formidable as a fighting force. They opposed the advances of the Persian leader Darius and later were active against Alexander the Great as he marched northward to subdue an uprising among their southern neighbors, the Triballi. For decades they were a thorn in the flesh of the Macedonian rulers.

the plain of Wallacia, north of the lower Danube. In the early second century, however, Dacians are recorded within the arc of the Carpathians—the area now called Transylvania—and during the reign of King Rubobostes (before 168 B.C.) we learn of a further buildup of Dacian strength in this area. By the turn of the century, ascendancy had passed to Transylvania, and the Dacian state had begun to emerge.

Transylvania was a well-endowed region. It yielded a wide range of mineral deposits, including iron, copper, silver, and gold; the land was fertile, and it was well protected by the Carpathian range, defended moreover with strong Dacian fortifications. Their capital was centered in the Orăştie mountains, in the southeast of the region, within reach of the fertile valley of the Mureş.

In the eighties of the first century B.C., one of the Dacian tribes, led by Burebista, rose to a position of dominance and within twenty years or so had succeeded in establishing its preeminence over the rest of the Dacian communities of present-day Romania. Burebista, now extremely powerful (Strabo estimated that he had 200,000 troops at his command), began a policy of aggressive expansion. In 60 or 59 B.C. he marched westward against the Celts. First he overcame the Scordisci (in southern Hungary and northern Yugoslavia) and then turned northward through Hungary to attack the Boii and Taurisci. So successful were his campaigns that, according to Strabo, the devastation he wrought gave rise to the nickname "the Desert of the Boii" for the northern part of the Great Plain.

Burebista justified his attacks by claiming that he was simply winning back Dacian territory from the Celts. He was perhaps referring to the fact that the Celtic tribes in this area were relative newcomers, having arrived no more than three centuries before. The archaeological evidence shows that the sphere of Dacian influence now engulfed the region of the River Tisza (in the Great Hungarian Plain), spread across Slovakia, and extended west of the Danube, in the region of the Danube Bend (north of present-day Budapest). Even though Burebista died soon afterward and his kingdom began to fragment, the Celtic tribes had lost their driving energy and were unable to regain their former territories. In-

white outline on the map shows Burebista's empire at its largest extent. The arrows indicate Celtic raids.

Below: Bronze boar, which once adorned a Celtic helmet from Bata, Hungary, first century B.C. or A.D.

The material culture of the Getic tribes was a complex amalgam—a long-established folk culture overlaid by Scythian and Greek influences—giving rise to a tradition of magnificent gold and silver work made to adorn the graves of the aristocrats. Indeed the characteristics of Getic society and art in the sixth to third centuries B.C. seem to have marked similarities to those of the Celts: the same love of display, the same powerful aristocracy, and the same warlike tendencies. This Geto-Dacian culture (as the Romanian archaeologists prefer to call it) formed the basis from which Dacian civilization was soon to emerge.

In the second century B.C. a shift of power can be detected. Until then, Geto-Dacian culture was centered upon the Dobruja and

The Celtic tribes that occupied Transylvania were soon subsumed by emerging Dacian culture, but those that had settled along the lower Danube retained their own distinctive culture and issued coins of striking originality *(below).*

The capital of the Dacian state was the strongly fortified hilltop town of Sarmizegetusa, set at the end of a strongly protected valley in the Onesti mountains of Transylvania. The town was defended by a massive wall and was provided with a spacious religious precinct containing circular and rectangular temples *(left).* All were destroyed by the Roman armies led by Trajan early in the second century A.D.

stead they fell back westward. After having unsuccessfully besieged Noreia, the Boii joined forces with the Helvetii, who at this very moment had decided to move out of Switzerland to seek new lands in Gaul. In all there were 32,000 Boian refugees among the 368,000 migrants.

The Dacian advance was yet another example of the pressures which came to bear on the Celtic population. With the Atlantic in the west, the new vigorous Dacian state in the east, the Germanic buildup in the north, and the increasingly aggressive Roman presence in the south, it was only a matter of time before the Celts of the European mainland were squeezed out of existence.

143

A PYRRHIC VICTORY

On hearing of his arrival
the Helvetii sent an embassy,
composed of their
most illustrious citizens
and headed by Nammeius,
to say that they intended
to march through the Province
because there was no other
route open to them.
They promised to do no harm
and asked for his consent.
As Caesar remembered
that the consul Lucius Cassius
had been killed by the Helvetii,
and his army routed
and sent under the yoke,
he was not disposed
to grant their request.
If people so hostile to Rome
were permitted to go
through the Province,
he did not think they were
likely to refrain
from damage to persons
and property.

Caesar

The defeat of the Roman army of Cassius Longinus in 107 B.C. at the hands of the Volcae Tectosages was made more humiliating when the captured troops were forced to show their subservience by marching under the yoke. The event captured the imagination of nineteenth-century Swiss artist Charles Gleyre *(right)*.

The victory of the Volcae Tectosages over the Roman army in 107 B.C. is noteworthy in one important sense. It was the only significant battle fought against Romans on Gallic soil which was won by Celts. Although spectacular, the event was an isolated incident of no lasting significance. Roman authority was already well established in Provence, and within sixty years the whole of Gaul was to be in Roman hands.

The Roman foothold in Gaul was established between 125 and 121 B.C. It came about not as the result of outright aggression, but simply because the Celts had attacked the territory of Massilia, a Greek foundation which for centuries had been on friendly terms with Rome.

The political situation in barbarian Gaul in the middle of the second century was changing fast: a degree of unity was emerging under the leadership of the Arverni, a powerful tribe which occupied the Massif Central. Together with their allies, the Allobroges of the Rhone valley and the Saluvii who lay to the southeast, they constituted a political and military force of potential danger to the civilized Mediterranean coastal region. In 125 the Saluvii attacked the territory of Massilia. Rome responded immediately by sending an army, which the next year decisively defeated the Saluvii and destroyed their stronghold at Entremont.

The presence of Rome introduced a new factor into Celtic politics: allegiance with Rome could be used as a vital bargaining counter in the intertribal power struggle. The Aedui whose territory lay to the north of the Arverni (in the region of Autun) rapidly concluded a treaty with Rome and the next year asked for Rome's protection against the Arverni. Once more the Roman armies moved in. The Celts were soundly beaten, with casualties amounting to twenty thousand. The final confrontation came in 121, when a combined force of Allobroges and Arverni, led by the Arvernian king Bituitus, met the consular army, only to be virtually annihilated.

The result of these first entanglements in Gaul was that Rome had gained a new territory—an arc of land stretching from the Pyrenees to Geneva—while the Celts of transalpine Gaul had been given a foretaste of what was to come.

Rome's new transalpine province was rapidly absorbed into the classical world; a new colony was founded at Narbonne, roads were laid out, the Celtic aristocracy were encouraged to assume the Roman way of life, and administrative abuses, so typical of the period, became rife. The situation in the seventies of the first century B.C. is eloquently summed up by Cicero in a speech made on behalf of M. Fonteius, expropraetor of Gaul who was impeached for extortion:

All Gaul is filled with traders, is full of Roman citizens. No Gaul does any business without the aid of a Roman citizen; not a single sesterce in Gaul ever changes hands without being entered in the account books of Roman citizens.

THE TURNING POINT

The appearance of Julius Caesar in the political arena in the middle of the first century B.C. had a dramatic effect on the history of the Celts. His rivalry with Pompey made it essential for him to gain substantial victories in the west to outshine Pompey's achievements in the east. Moreover, all the time he was actively campaigning against the enemies of Rome, he could legitimately maintain a large army at state expense. A brilliant soldier and charismatic leader, his troops idolized him. His grasp of geography and his speed of movement brought him success in Gaul. The coin above was minted in Rome in 44 B.C., the year of his assassination.

An overstatement, no doubt, but a reminder of the energetic commercial activity which followed in the wake of the Roman army.

Apart from the chaos caused by the invasions of the Cimbri and Teutones in the last decade of the second century, and the momentarily successful revolt of the Volcae Tectosages in the region of Toulouse, the new province enjoyed a degree of peace and prosperity. There had been some territorial expansion. The Volcae Tectosages made a further bid for freedom but were finally subdued by Sulla, and Toulouse was incorporated into the province. But elsewhere the original frontiers remained, protected by treaty relationships with the neighboring tribes.

Among the newly conquered tribes, a spate of revolts was only to be expected. In 90 and 83 the Salluvii were up in arms, while in 66 and again in 62–61 it was the turn of the Allobroges to rebel; but to no avail. Each uprising was ferociously quashed. By 60 B.C. the province was firmly under Roman control and already largely integrated with the Roman world. No further problems were expected from within, nor were there any.

It was at this moment that three things happened: the Helvetii and their allies decided to move into Gaul in search of new lands; Ariovistus, king of the Germanic Suevi, began to interfere in Gaulish intertribal rivalries; and Gaius Julius Caesar took up what was to be a ten-year command in Gaul. The coincidence of these three events in the year 59 B.C. was to have a shattering effect on the Celtic world. It was indeed a turning point.

The three events were interlinked. Ariovistus and his tribe were evidently under pressure from tribes living to the north and were intent upon gaining new lands for themselves to the south. An occasion presented itself when the Sequani invited them to intervene in a dispute they were having with their old rivals the Aedui. Ariovistus readily agreed on condition that the Sequani provide him and his followers with a large part of their territory in present-day Alsace. When the Germanic settlers arrived, the Sequani panicked and began to resist. It was at this point that the neighboring Aedui called upon their ally, Rome, for help.

"I myself," said Ariovistus, "am the only man of the whole Aeduan nation who could not be prevailed upon to swear this oath or to give my children as hostages. That was why I fled from my country and went to Rome to claim assistance from the Senate— because I alone was not restrained either by an oath or by the surrender of hostages."

Caesar

Meanwhile the Helvetii, in western Switzerland, had decided that their constricted territory was too small for them. Moreover, they feared German pressures from across the Rhine, and they must have watched the fortunes of Ariovistus with alarm. The only solution was to move off to new lands in the west. Thus, after a year

Caesar in his official guise: marble statue from Rome. Conquests, particularly in Gaul, brought him political power in Rome. This is his only surviving full portrait from Roman times.

of preparation, they and their allies (including Boian refugees fleeing from Burebista), numbering 368,000 men, women, and children in all, set out with the intention of passing through Roman-held territory near Geneva, en route to the land of the Santones in western France, where they hoped to settle.

Although these two events seemed menacing, they were after all only part of a pattern of migration that had been practiced by the Celts for centuries. If events had been left to take their own course, it is unlikely that any repercussions would have been felt in the Roman world. Yet for Caesar, proconsul of Cisalpine and Transalpine Gaul, it was as if history were playing into his hands. He could present the facts as a German threat to Rome (reminding his audience of the Cimbri and Teutones), an appeal for help from an ally, and the potential invasion of a Roman province. Armed with the righteousness of self-justification, he could plunge into Gaul with every expectation of successful campaigns, culminating in the victorious war he so desperately needed both politically and financially. The stage was set for the last act in the tragedy of the European Celts.

The immediate causes of Caesar's intervention in Gaul were comparatively easily dealt with. At the beginning of the campaigning season in 58, he made for Geneva to prevent the Helvetii from crossing the Rhone. Quite undeterred, the migrating hordes moved off to the north to outflank Roman territory by marching around the Jura through the territory of the Sequani with whom they first negotiated permission. It was at this stage that the Aedui, Caesar's principal allies in free Gaul, complained of Helvetic raiding parties pillaging their lands. The Allobroges too were suffering from the invaders. Caesar now summoned all his available troops, some six legions, and after dogging the steps of the Helvetii for a while, moved in for the kill. The campaign was short and totally effective. In the aftermath the stragglers were rounded up; and the Helvetii, Tulingi, Latovici, and Rauraci, supplied with grain, were sent back home to reoccupy and rebuild their farms and villages on the charred remains of those they had burned some months before. Only the Boii were allowed to stay, being settled on the fringe of

147

The migration of the Helvetii and their associates—368,000 men, women, and children who set out across France to escape German neighbors—is the theme of this modern sketch.

After a year of preparation, they were ready to leave their homes in western Switzerland, their last act being the burning of their homes and villages —to remove any incentive to return. Detailed lists in Greek of all the emigrants capable of bearing arms, as well as the numbers of old men, women, and children, were prepared. This attempted migration set off the Gallic wars in 58 B.C.

Aeduian territory, possibly to serve as a buffer against aggressive neighbors. Of the 368,000 migrants who had set out, less than a third survived to return home.

Caesar had tasted power in Gaul. At this moment he could have withdrawn, but the opportunity was too good to miss.

It was now the turn of Ariovistus. "The man was an ill-tempered, headstrong savage," according to the Gauls, "and it was impossible to endure his tyranny any longer." After desultory negotiation, Caesar marched to Vesontio (Besançon), the largest town in the territory of the Sequani, and there prepared to do battle. It was already autumn and with the campaigning season nearly over, a rapid conclusion to the affair was necessary. Six days of uninterrupted marching led Caesar to within a few miles of the German forces. Further negotiations were undertaken, but to no avail: in the ensuing battle, Ariovistus was routed, and the remnants of his army fled back northward into Germany in disarray.

In a single summer Caesar had dealt decisively with the immediate cause for concern in Gaul. Leaving his army, under the command of Labienus, quartered in Sequanian territory, he returned to Italy. Caesar could not, even had he wished, have proceeded farther, but it was now even more essential for him to gain further victories, and in Gaul, with its incessant intertribal rivalries, he could easily find an excuse to intervene. His reason for mounting a second campaign in 57 was that the powerful Belgic tribes of the north were organizing armed resistance to Rome. This was a sufficient excuse to return to Besançon the next spring with reinforcements. The nature of the opposition was carefully explained to him by ambassadors from the Remi, one of the Belgic tribes which intended to stay on good terms with Rome. In all, about a quarter of a million troops were being mustered under the direction of the most powerful tribe, the Bellovaci. The Bellovaci were providing 100,000 troops; while the Suessiones offered 50,000 but, by virtue of their prestige, were allowed to nominate their king, Galba, as the commander-in-chief of the operation. Twelve other tribes agreed to send levies. It was a formidable opposition but no match for the incisive speed with which Caesar acted.

Knowing that he had the support of the

Aedui at his rear and the Remi in the heart of the dissident territory, Caesar advanced quickly towards the massed Belgic forces on the Aisne, somewhere in the region of Bervy-au-Bac. In a massive engagement, the Belgic army was scattered, and without pause Caesar thrust forward into the land of the Suessiones storming their *oppidum* of Noviodunum near Soissons. Next in his line of advance were the Bellovaci and Ambiani, but before he could attack the Bellovacian capital, the tribe sued for peace. Leadership of the Belgic resistance now rested with the Nervii, an austere tribe who occupied the land between the Sambre and the Scheldt: "They were a fierce warlike people who bitterly reproached the other Belgae for throwing away their inheritance of bravery by submitting to the Romans."

In one of the most hard-fought encounters of the war, enacted in the valley of the Sambre, Caesar met the combined force of Nervii, Atrebates, and Viromandui. It was a vicious, long drawn out, engagement, as the result of which "the tribe of the Nervii was almost annihilated and their name almost blotted out from the face of the earth." The pathetic remnants were allowed to retain their territory and *oppida*, protected from the depredations of their neighbors by Caesar's authority.

It remained, now, only to deal with the

Atuatuci, a remnant of the Cimbri and Teutones, who had settled in the middle Meuse region. They had retired to a strongly defended hillfort which Caesar proceeded to storm. Resistance was short-lived, and the army smashed down the gates, capturing the entire population. Caesar laconically sums up the encounter by saying that he "sold all the inhabitants of the place by auction in one lot. The purchasers reported that the number of persons included in the sale was 53,000."

While these events were being played out in the north, Publius Crassus, with a single legion, was sent to demand the formal submission of the tribes of Lower Normandy and Brittany: this was obtained without difficulty. It was now autumn, so, putting his legions into winter quarters among the newly conquered tribes, leaving one on the Loire to keep an eye on the Armorican tribes, he left for Italy. "All Gaul was at peace": his primary task had been accomplished.

During the winter of 57–56 a serious revolt broke out among the tribes of Armorica led by the Veneti who controlled the maritime trade in the region. Hearing of these events, Caesar sent word to Crassus that a fleet should be constructed on the Loire in readiness for the spring campaign. Meanwhile the Celts "fortified their strongholds, stocked them with corn from the fields, and assembled as many ships as possible." As these preparations proceeded, the tribes of Normandy joined the rebels. For Caesar the situation was dangerous, but once more the brilliance of his strategy and speed of his response saved the day. His main concern was to contain the revolt. Accordingly Labienus, with a force of cavalry, was sent among the Belgae, equipped for rapid movement should rebellion spark; Crassus moved to the land of the Aquitani on the Atlantic coast to prevent reinforcements coming through from the south, while Sabinus made a show of strength with three legions in Normandy and northern Brittany. Meanwhile the Loire fleet was nearing completion. The rebels, now isolated, were Ceasar's personal concern. The campaign began on land with Caesar taking a number of Celtic hillforts, but little progress could be made all the time that the rebels had command of the sea. Accordingly Caesar waited for his fleet to be completed and then in a decisive sea battle,

fought off Cape Quiberon, destroyed the Venetic navy. The victory ended the uprising, but to make an example of the rebels, all the senior Celts were executed and the rest of the population were sold as slaves. At the time of this confrontation, Sabinus was smashing the resistance of the tribes of Normandy. The year ended with the submission of the inhabitants of Aquitania and

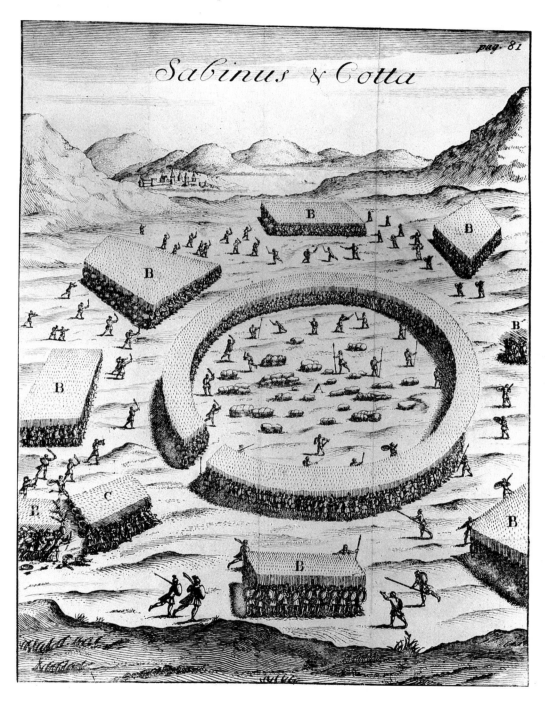

pag. 81

Sabinus & Cotta

a late and indecisive campaign against the Morini and Menapii in Artois and Belgium. After burning farms and villages, Caesar withdrew his troops to their winter quarters in Normandy.

THE LAST HOPE

Two Gaulish resistance leaders stood up against Caesar in the latter stages of his war in Gaul. Ambiorix, chief of the Eburones (seen below through romantic nineteenth-century eyes, in a statue at Tongres), led the Belgic tribes in revolt in 54–53 B.C. but

failed and escaped into obscurity. In the next year Vercingetorix *(right)* staged a far more serious uprising in central Gaul but was forced to surrender and was eventually strangled in Rome at Caesar's triumph. The revolt led by Vercingetorix was the last chance for any united defense on the part of the fragmented, feuding Gauls.

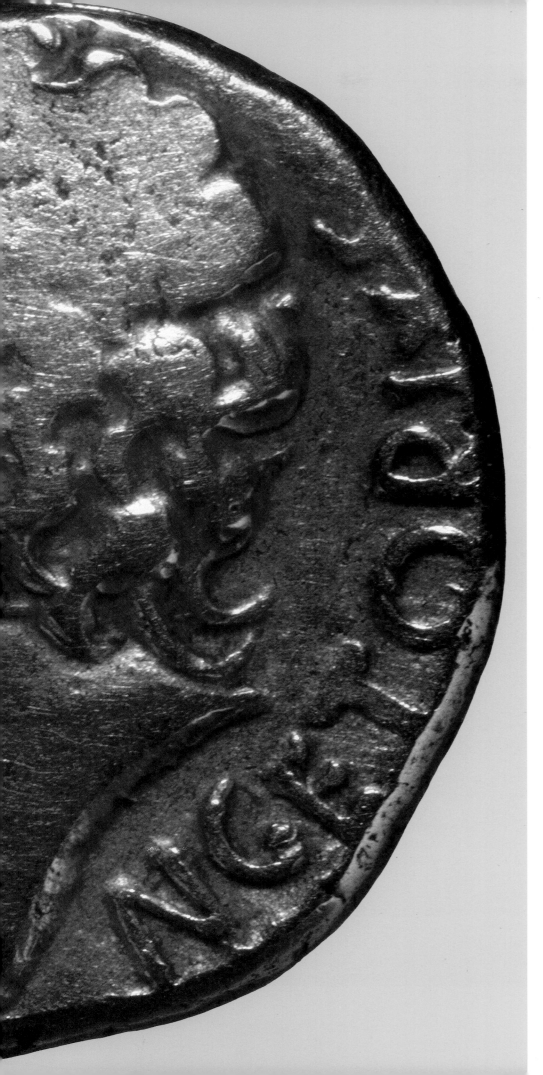

The campaigns of 56 left Gaul firmly under Roman control. So sure was Caesar of his position that in 55 and 54 B.C. he pushed beyond Gaul to explore Britain and Germany. To the Roman audience in Italy these feats of military daring must have been almost unbelievable; in reality they were of little significance.

Gaul had still not been fully stabilized. Caesar returned from his second British expedition late in 54 B.C. to a situation of unrest in northern Gaul. The dissidents were headed by Ambiorix, king of the Eburones, who occupied land along the Meuse in the region of Namur. The spread of this revolt involved Caesar in protracted campaigns throughout Belgica from the land of the Senones and Carnutes, south of the Seine, to beyond the Rhine. Eventually, in the summer of 53 he set out through the Ardennes to attack Ambiorix. The king escaped into obscurity, but his land and people suffered the fury of the Romans. Every village and building was destroyed, animals were slaughtered, and crops consumed. Even if some tribesmen had escaped, "it seemed certain," wrote Caesar, "that they must die of starvation." The revolt had been long drawn out and viciously suppressed, but it was but a prelude for what was to follow.

The dissident Gauls desperately needed a war leader to match Caesar. In Vercingetorix they were to find one. Vercingetorix was the son of an Arvernian aristocrat named Celtillus, whose ambitions of kingship had led to his assassination. Vercingetorix was a headstrong young man whose outspoken anti-Roman feelings led to his expulsion from Gergovia. Undeterred, he gathered a band of followers and returned to the capital to oust the resistance and install himself as king. Caesar describes him thus: "A man of boundless energy, he terrorized waverers with the rigors of an iron discipline." Through sheer force of personality he had secured the allegiance of many tribes in the center and west of Gaul who had previously taken little part in resistance. For Caesar the situation was particularly dangerous: not only was he facing a far more widespread rebellion then ever before, but the rebels lay between him and his legions stationed in the still unstable north. At last, after six years of uncertainty, it looked as if the Gauls stood a chance of success.

THE FINAL DISASTER

The siege works of Alesia, shown in outline.

Outer siege works, 22 kilometers long.

Inner siege works, 14 kilometers long.

Fortifications of Vercingetorix.

Roman camps placed on high points to oppose Gaulish reinforcement forces from outside.

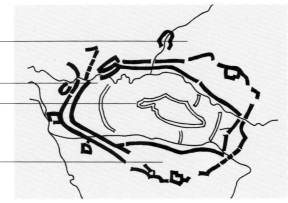

The last rebellion began dramatically with the massacre of the Roman traders who had congregated in the town of Cenabum. Caesar was not to be deflected, and with his customary drive outflanked the rebels in order to join his legions in the north. Speed was now even more vital: one after another, native strongholds fell to his attack: Vellaunodunum of the Senones, Cenabum of the Carnutes, and Noviodunum of the Bituriges. Then, after a prolonged and bitter siege, Avaricum was taken. The Roman soldiers had no mercy: old men, women, and children were slaughtered, and of the forty thousand inhabitants only eight hundred escaped to join Vercingetorix who was camped nearby.

After a brief rest at Avaricum, enjoying the ample supplies found there, the Roman army moved off to capture the Arvernian town of Gergovia, situated on a steep hilltop difficult of access and guarded by Vercingetorix. In front of Gergovia, after a lengthy encounter, the Romans were forced to retreat, severely mauled. The extent of their defeat can be gauged from Caesar's reference to the loss of forty-six centurions —the backbone of the Roman army. The effect of the reverse was dramatic: At last, it seemed as though the Gauls had hope, and even the Aedui, long-standing allies of Rome, transferred their allegiance to Vercingetorix, seizing Caesar's principal supply base at Noviodunum.

For Caesar the situation was highly dangerous; he had two alternatives, either to retire to Provence or to strike at the enemy before they could build up reinforcements.

The first was unthinkable: accordingly, after a series of extraordinarily long marches, he joined Labienus, who had just succeeded in stamping out trouble among the Parisii on the Seine. His army reunited, he then prepared to meet Vercingetorix in open battle. Somewhere in the territory of the Sequani, a cavalry engagement took place at which the Gauls were routed. It was a staggering blow for Vercingetorix, for the Gauls regarded their cavalry with particular pride. Shaken, Vercingetorix

"I did not
undertake the war
for private ends,
but in the cause of
national liberty.
And since I must now
accept my fate,
I place myself
at your disposal.
Make amends to the Romans
by killing me
or surrender me alive
as you think best."

Caesar, quoting Vercingetorix

made for the defended hilltop of Alesia, where he set up camp to await Caesar's arrival. No doubt, in choosing Alesia he was mindful of his successes some weeks earlier when, from a similar position of strength at Gergovia, he had put Caesar to flight. He must have been well aware that the Gauls were no match for the Romans in the open field.

As soon as he arrived, Caesar decided to surround the hilltop with a complex of

siege works, realizing that direct attack was doomed to failure; and in spite of constant harassment by the Gallic cavalry, the first stage of the works were soon completed. A second series of defenses was then undertaken, facing outward to protect the besieging force from attack from the countryside around. This outer circuit, complete with forts and lookout posts, was 22.5 kilometers in length.

Vercingetorix was relying on the arrival of a relieving force which he had sent his messengers to summon. Eventually a vast army of Gauls approached, recruited from all parts of the country—some quarter of a million men in all. Three times they flung themselves at the Roman defenses, but on the last occasion, after a close-run encounter, they were soundly defeated. The years of almost constant fighting, the Gauls were too exhausted to continue: their submission to the Roman will was now final.

The site of Alesia (Mont Auxois) is an extensive diamond-shaped plateau protected by river valleys on both sides. To the north and south rise steep hills, but to the west is open countryside where the Gallic reinforcements mustered.

Map opposite: Caesar's problem was twofold: He had to prevent the rebels from escaping and, at the same time, protect his rear from attack by the Celtic relief forces whom Vercingetorix had summoned. To do this he constructed two massive complexes of siege works (shown here in a reconstruction), an inner series facing Vercingetorix, and an outer line rising up onto the crests of the nearby hills where forts and watch towers were built.

Top and bottom: The siege works (shown in full-size reconstruction) were very complex. The main rampart, four meters high, was reinforced with an embattled breastwork. In front of it was a V-sectioned ditch. In front of this were trenches filled with sharpened saplings interleaved to form an entanglement, and farther out rows of circular pits were dug with sharpened stakes projecting upward from their bottoms. Finally the defenses were completed by a zone of iron spikes set in wooden blocks.

situation was lost: Vercingetorix surrendered, and his starving supporters filed out of their stronghold under Caesar's supervision.

The capitulation of Alesia was not quite the end. Caesar remained in Gaul throughout the winter and the next year (51) put down a revolt among the Bellovaci and besieged a group of dissidents in Uxellodunum. Their heroic stand was the final death agony of the free Celts. After eight

Caesar could not resist the opportunity of crossing to Britain—it was a place of mystery, a land of legendary mineral wealth, and a haven for dissidents. The purpose of his campaigns in 55 and 54 B.C. is unclear. Curiosity, combined with the quite unprecedented prestige which the expeditions brought him, would have been sufficient motive. The outcome was that the Romans had established, by treaties, a political toehold on the island.

For the next ninety years, the effects of Caesar's expedition continued to be felt. Traditional trading links between southern Britain and Armorica seem suddenly to have ceased, and instead the Trinovantes, who occupied part of southeastern Britain north of the Thames—the tribe with whom Caesar had concluded a treaty of friendship —began to grow rich by controlling what appears to have been a profitable trading

The initial stages of the conquest were soon over, and by A.D. 47 a frontier zone based on the Fosse Way had been established across Britain.

Between 47 and 51 the army extended its control over Cornwall and began to spread into Wales. In 51 the resistance leader Caratacus was captured in north Wales. Campaigning in Wales continued until A.D. 60, the year in which Boudicca rebelled.

From 71 to 74 large areas of the north of Britain were overcome and the hold on Wales tightened.

Agricola completed the conquest of north Wales in A.D. 78 and then turned his attention to Scotland, where his campaigns (A.D. 78–84) culminated in the battle of Mons Graupius.

The conquest of Britain was initiated by the emperor Claudius *(top)* in A.D. 43. By the beginning of the second century, it was clear that in the interests of efficiency and security much of Scotland would have to be abandoned, and accordingly, on the instructions of Hadrian *(bottom)* a wall was built across the country to divide barbarian from Roman *(center)*.

monopoly. Mediterranean wine, Roman silverware, and fine pottery from the Gaulish markets now found their way into the sumptuous burial chambers of the wealthy. In parallel with this now active trade, the whole socio-economic structure of the southeast changed: urban centers developed, and a money economy became widespread.

In A.D. 43 Rome looked once more to Britain as a place where its emperor, this time Claudius, could gain military prestige. Thus, under the command of Aulus Plautius, an invasion force once more set out for Kent intent to conquer. After the capitulation of the principal urban center at Camulodunum, the southeast was easily over-

run, only the Durotriges of Dorset putting up any concerted resistance. By the end of the first campaigning season, it was possible to begin work on the establishment of the frontier: a diagonal line marked by a road called the Fosse Way, which ran from Lincoln in the north to the vicinity of Exeter in the southwest. Behind that line the process of Romanization continued apace. The Fosse Way divided Britain into two very different halves: to the southeast was a settled semi-urbanized landscape dependent upon intensive grain production, while to the north and west social organization was more fragmented and the country mountainous, but there lay the mineral wealth.

Who the first inhabitants
of Britain were,
whether natives or
immigrants
is open to question:
one must remember
we are dealing
with barbarians.

Tacitus

Within a few years, the frontier was being so harassed by dissident tribesmen from the Welsh mountains, led by Caratacus, that further advance was essential. The Romans moved first into south Wales, then into the north, and finally, in A.D. 59, destroyed the druid center on Anglesey. It was at this moment that a highly dangerous rebellion broke out among the Iceni of Norfolk led by Queen Boudicca, and spread rapidly in the southeast, until even the Trinovantes took up arms against the Roman troops and administrators. The rebellion was contained, but it took ten years for the province to recover.

The early seventies saw a further advance in Wales, Yorkshire, and the north, cul-minating in a series of northern campaigns under the generalship of Agricola (A.D. 78–84). In the final great battle fought in the far north of Scotland, at Mons Graupius, in 84, the last Celtic army, still ferocious and unpredictable, still using chariots, was virtually annihilated. The conquest of the island was at an end—all but the Highland mountains and the Western Isles had been brought under Roman control. The only part of the Celtic world which had not experienced the force of Rome was Ireland. In 83 Agricola stood on the Scottish coast and looked across to Ireland thinking of conquest. This, however, was not to be.

During the Antonine period the northern frontier was calmed. To mark the satisfactory completion of the campaign a sesterce was issued A.D. 143–144 inscribed "Britannia."

THE ROMAN IMPRINT

Early in his governorship of Britain, Agricola devoted the winter, between campaigning seasons, to promoting schemes for the social betterment of the community. His object, so Tacitus tells us, was to accustom the natives to a life of peace and quiet by providing them with amenities such as elaborate public buildings. Gradually they came to appreciate the benefits of Roman life. They "spoke of such novelties as 'civilization,' when in fact they were only a feature of their enslavement." Tacitus could not resist the twist in the tail, but his statement of the process of Romanization, irrespective of region, cannot be bettered. Once the shock of the invasion was over, most tribes settled down to embrace the new way of life. For most of them it brought peace for the first time from the uncertainties and dangers of inter-tribal conflict.

The Roman administrators were careful to retain as much of the Celtic social and economic structures as possible. Tribal boundaries were formalized to become administrative boundaries, and many of the traditional *oppida* developed into thriving cities on the same spot or at a more convenient road nexus nearby. The old tribal aristocracy became the *equites* from among whom the town council, with its two chief magistrates *(duumvirs)*, were elected annually. Roman citizenship was readily bestowed on the worthy, and by the time of the emperor Claudius, Gauls were even admitted to the Roman Senate. The Roman desire to adapt native structures, rather than to replace, them is well demonstrated by the institution of the *Concilium Galliarum*. This was an annual gathering of representatives from all parts of Gaul held once a year at Lugudunum (Lyons). It was, in essence, a festival held in honor of the divine Augustus and was presided over by the high priest, or *sacerdos*, who was chosen from among the representatives. But it had other functions: provincial business could be discussed and representations made direct to the emperor. Although outwardly Roman in its appearance, the *concilium* was clearly little more than the old pre-Roman institution which used to meet annually at Chartres under the auspices of the archdruid. By focusing the religious fervor of the gathering on the person of the emperor, the Romans were able to harness Gallic energies to the good of the state.

Much the same procedure was attempted

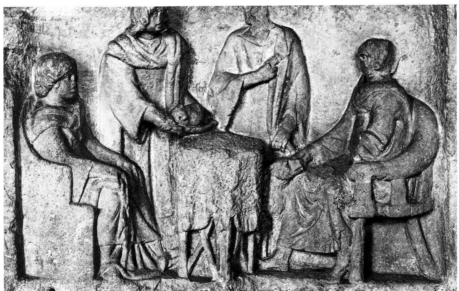

The adoption of the Roman way of life by the Gauls can most readily be appreciated by reference to the large collection of reliefs, which still survive, depicting everyday scenes.

Above left: An armorer at work, one of the many crafts depicted on Romano-Gaulish reliefs.
Above, center and right: On these two reliefs from Neumagen, near Trier, we can compare family life with that of a tavern. The domestic scene shows comfortable middle-class existence: the figure on the left sits in a basket-work chair, while the individual on the right occupies a well-carved wooden seat. Between them is what may be a folding table, on which fruit is being served. The postures, clothing, and furniture in this scene are purely Roman—a far cry from Strabo's description of the Celts sitting on dried grass at their feasts, only a few hundred years

at Camulodunum (Colchester), where a massive temple to the emperor Claudius was built; but the idea badly misfired. The native Britons resented the intrusion, and their resentment turned to outright aggression when the occasion for rebellion presented itself in A.D. 60.

Education, referred to by Tacitus above, was an important tool for Romanization. One of the earliest schools, for the sons of Gaulish aristocrats, was founded in Autun (the town which replaced the Aeduian capital of Bibracte). During a rebellion in A.D. 21 the scholars, all of wealthy parents, provided valuable hostages for the rebels who seized the city. In the late third century it was still a flourishing concern, as is shown by the demands for its restoration after it had been destroyed in a siege in 272. Other famous schools grew up at Massilia, Toulouse, Lyons, Vienna, Reims, Bordeaux, Arles, and Trier. Of these, Massilia was perhaps the most famous, ranking with Athens, Rhodes, and Alexandria. It was renowned for its medical teaching, and it was here that Agricola, a native of Narbonnese Gaul was educated.

The quick-witted Celts were well known for their ability to learn, and it was for this reason that the Latin language spread so rapidly across Europe. Latin was a language that could be written; moreover, it was the language of education and of administration. Until the advent of Rome, Celtic writing was virtually unknown: If records had to be kept, then Greek was used; but after Caesar, Latin provided the means by which the ambitious young man could advance in the newly imposed social system.

Yet the Celtic language did not die out. It must have been widely spoken in rural areas, and indeed a few inscriptions in Celtic, but written in Latin or Greek letters,

Everything else
is shared equally between us.
You often command
our legions in person,
and in person govern
these and other provinces.
There is no question
of segregation or exclusion.
Again, those emperors
who are well spoken
of benefit you
as much as they do us,
though you live far away,
whereas tyrants wreak
their will upon
such as are nearest to them.

Tacitus, *Histories*

earlier. The tavern scene is more rustic: the bearded figure wears a Celtic-style hooded cloak.

The imposition of Roman culture meant the adoption of a complicated way of life. Bartering and simple money exchanges gave place to involved transactions and record keeping. In this scene, *(above)* from Trier, the figure at far left holds open a wooden-based wax writing tablet, while the other two figures appear to be counting out money. A man at far right enters bearing some merchandise (possibly grain) on his shoulder.

Above right: In another craft portrayal, a fuller is shown at work treading cloth in his vat. Other fabric is seen hanging up behind him, carved with realistic attention to the folds of the cloth.

157

are known. Some Celtic words were even taken into the Latin language—words for which no Roman equivalent existed, like *bracae* for trousers, and various specialist terms for types of wheeled vehicles. The Celtic *leuga* was still preferred to the Roman mile, and *vergebret* was sometimes used instead of *duumvir*. The survival of Celtic in the third century is shown by the emperor Severus's agreement that it could be used for wills. We must suppose, therefore, that most Roman Gauls, at least the educated ones, were bilingual, able to speak and write official Latin in their professional lives, but ready to relapse into patois whenever it was necessary.

The new regime provided ample scope for the native population to develop its various skills. The Celtic aristocracy became the urban rich. Strabo records that at Vienna, the new capital of the Allobroges, the chief men of the tribe soon moved into residence, no doubt administering their estates from the comfort of the city while serving the community in official positions. The more outstanding were able to play their part in world affairs. Domitius Afer, from Nîmes, for example, became praetor in A.D. 25 and rose to the position of consul in 39; Valerius Asiaticus from Vienna was consul twice in the mid-first century.

For the lower classes there was of course the army. All provincials were eligible for service as auxiliary troops, and the Gallic cavalry was world famous. Having served his appointed term, a veteran would retire a Roman citizen, able to return with dignity to the land of his birth, if he wished to do so, to take up farming or become a trader. Manufacturing industries and trade developed rapidly, employing an increasingly large percentage of the population. Alongside a vast output of mass-produced goods, pottery, bricks, bronzework, and glass, the Celtic areas continued to produce their own specialities. Woolen goods were particularly popular in Rome; the hooded cloak from Britain, the *birrus britannicus*, was highly prized; so was the Gallic *sagum* of similar type. The poet Martial mentions that these Gallic garments were dyed in bright colors, a reminder of the Celtic love of display. Some cloth merchants, like the Secundinii from Trier, grew rich enough to build elaborate mausoleums for themselves.

Wherever one looks in those Roman provinces which were imposed on Celtic lands something of the Celtic spirit shines through, but nowhere is it better represented than in the religious art of the period. The gods were, after all, Celtic gods, and their shrines existed long before even Caesar was heard of. A sculptor who spent most of his life cutting ovolos and acanthus leaves on cornices, or churning out tombstones for the army, must have sighed with relief when he was asked to produce a triad of "mothers" or an Epona. The ambivalence attached to art, which persisted, in many areas, throughout the Roman period, has been demonstrated many times over by the pieces chosen to illustrate these pages. But nowhere is it better displayed than in the famous Gorgon's head relief from Bath (right). The Gorgon, so evidently a Celtic male with a mane of hair and drooping mustaches, stares out from the pediment of a purely classical temple, a dramatic reminder that one is here on the very fringe of the Roman empire, a few meters from the sacred spring over which the Celtic goddess Sulis presides. She may have been conflated with Roman Minerva, but her Celtic pedigree remains blazoned for all to see.

In spite of the Romanized life depicted on the reliefs shown on the previous pages, there were plenty of visual reminders of their Celtic heritage to be seen about the towns of Roman Gaul and Britain.

Below: On the arch of Narbonne, reliefs of Celtic armor—including helmets, shields, and a pig mounted on a standard—represent captured Celtic war gear, illustrating the troubled early history of the community.

Opposite: At Aquae Sulis (Bath), visitors and residents alike would have been reminded of Celtic antecedents of the shrine by the Gorgon's head which glowered down on them from the pediment of the temple—a fascinating conflation with a purely Celtic male face and the serpent-ridden hair of the classical gorgon.

THE ISLAND CELTS

Aerial view of the monastery of Skellig Michael, on an island off the Irish coast.

Opposite page: Moone Celtic cross, Kildare, Ireland.

Said Patrick to Kieran: "Precede me into Ireland...
and build thou a monastery;
there shall thine honor abide for ever
and thy resurrection be."

Seventeenth-century Irish poem

The long, dramatic saga of the Celts took a new turn soon after the fall of Rome and the disintegration of her Empire. Celtic invaders once more penetrated the heart of Europe, as if repeating history. But these were a new breed of warriors—soldiers of Christ, missionaries from Ireland who bore the Gospel and monasticism to the Continent, beginning in the sixth century A.D., to restore Christianity where Germanic marauders had wiped it out. Behind this wave of renewal there lay centuries of undisturbed Celtic survival in the western fringes of Romanized Europe. In Scotland, Wales, Cornwall, Brittany, and above all in Ireland, the Celts held on to their language and art, their spirit and their traditions. But remote as they were, they were not to remain untouched by Christianity. The Christianized Celts of the fringe lands created a remarkable culture, essentially Celtic in its expression and energy but motivated by the new religious force. Its influence went far and wide in medieval Europe, to spark the monastic movement and to inject Celtic myth—Camelot, the Grail, Tristan, and Parsifal—into the literature of many tongues.

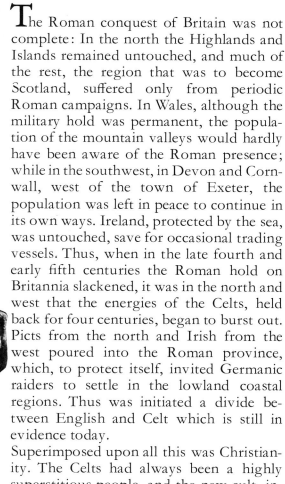

The Roman conquest of Britain was not complete: In the north the Highlands and Islands remained untouched, and much of the rest, the region that was to become Scotland, suffered only from periodic Roman campaigns. In Wales, although the military hold was permanent, the population of the mountain valleys would hardly have been aware of the Roman presence; while in the southwest, in Devon and Cornwall, west of the town of Exeter, the population was left in peace to continue in its own ways. Ireland, protected by the sea, was untouched, save for occasional trading vessels. Thus, when in the late fourth and early fifth centuries the Roman hold on Britannia slackened, it was in the north and west that the energies of the Celts, held back for four centuries, began to burst out. Picts from the north and Irish from the west poured into the Roman province, which, to protect itself, invited Germanic raiders to settle in the lowland coastal regions. Thus was initiated a divide between English and Celt which is still in evidence today.

Superimposed upon all this was Christianity. The Celts had always been a highly superstitious people, and the new cult, introduced to Ireland in the fifth century, rapidly took root. Zealous enthusiasm fueled by their love of wandering ensured that missionaries spread into Wales, northern England, and Brittany, in the wake of settlers and thence, as the movement grew, to Gaul, Switzerland, and Italy. The Celtic Church—austere, highly individualistic, and organized like a Celtic tribe—came into inevitable conflict with the Roman Church, but by its sheer energy was able to maintain its distinctive character. Celtic love of oral learning and poetry, together with the Celtic feeling for design, found a willing patron in the monasteries. There these ancient skills flourished and were perfected. The verse composition, stone carving, fine metalwork, and manuscript illumination of the seventh, eighth, and ninth centuries were in the highest tradition of Celtic craftsmanship; while the "lives" of the saints provided a medium for storytelling, enlivened by miraculous events, in direct descent from the pagan sagas. In the Celtic Christian movement, then, the Celtic ethos was kept alive throughout the Dark Ages, to make its contribution to the culture of medieval Europe.

161

EVENTS ON EUROPE'S WESTERN FRINGE

From the middle of the third century A.D., the Roman frontier in Europe came under increasing pressure from the barbarian peoples of the north European plain. The buildup of population and the folk movements consequent upon it, with which Caesar dealt, were for a while counterbalanced by the energetic advances of the Roman Empire. But by the reign of Hadrian (A.D. 117–138) the Empire had reached its limits: frontiers were formalized and retrenchment set in. Freed from the necessity to respond to Roman aggression, the north European population could begin to organize aggressive campaigns of their own. For a while the Roman government

was able to maintain control, but gradually the barbarians gained the advantage. In the decade 250–260 a large tract of Roman territory north of the Rhine opposite Mainz was abandoned. Soon after, the province of Dacia was let slip.

The first major setback came in about 260 when, taking advantage of dissension in the Roman ranks, one of the Germanic tribes, the Alemanni, burst through the Rhine defenses and swept in a destructive wave through Gaul, reaching the Mediterranean. The incursion was quickly dealt with, but sixteen years later history was to repeat itself. This time the barbarian incursion was far more extensive. Franks crossed the lower Rhine and ravaged northern Gaul; the Alemanni swept triumphantly across the upper Rhine into Burgundy and central France; other tribes attacked Switzerland and Bavaria. The speed of the Roman response once more saved the situation, and the frontier defenses were patched up in readiness for the next onslaught.

The legends surrounding St. Brendan became popular in the medieval period. They are a conflation of many stories, the oldest of which date back to the mid-sixth century. St. Brendan was a typical wandering monk seeking a life of austerity. He and his followers sailed across the western ocean in a curragh, visiting many islands, guided by a miraculous youth and nourished with supernatural fish and fruits. These fanciful stories were taken by some nineteenth- and twentieth-century romantics to mean that St. Brendan reached America.

Britain, though comparatively isolated, was not unaffected by these events. Franks and Saxons had taken to the sea and were raiding the coasts of the North Sea and the English Channel. To protect the island, coastal defenses on both sides of the Channel were put into good defensive order, and campaigns designed to rid the seas of pirates seem to have met with a degree of success.

An uneasy peace prevailed for some decades, but by the middle of the fourth century the Alemanni were again rampag-

Ireland had, in the third and second millennia, enjoyed a rich Neolithic and Bronze Age culture which left megalithic monuments, like this dolmen from Ballina, scattered across the countryside.

Right: Manuscript illustration of British coastal forts, erected by the Romans to withstand raids from Germanic pirates in the late third century A.D. These defenseworks remained in use into the fifth century. This title page from a Carolingian copy of the fifth-century *Notitia Dignitatum* shows the coastal forts under the command of the "Count of the Saxon Shore."

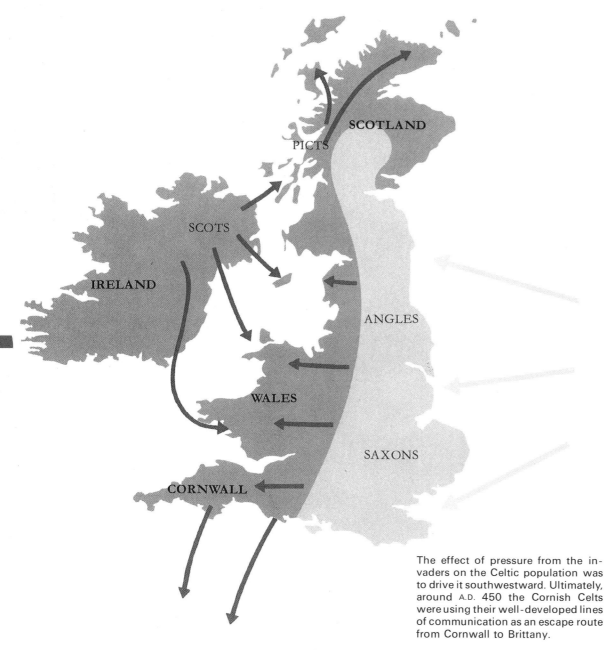

SCOTLAND

PICTS

SCOTS

IRELAND

ANGLES

WALES

SAXONS

CORNWALL

The effect of pressure from the invaders on the Celtic population was to drive it southwestward. Ultimately, around A.D. 450 the Cornish Celts were using their well-developed lines of communication as an escape route from Cornwall to Brittany.

The enemies of Roman Britain came from all sides by land and by sea. The first great attack, called by classical writers the "barbarian conspiracy," took place in 367 and caused chaos south as far as the Thames. The period of folk movement during which Roman Britain was transformed to England was short: it began soon after 350 and was largely over by 450.

SCOTS

The Scotti was the name given to the peoples of northern Ireland, many of whom migrated to the western coasts of what became Scotland and also to north Wales. Other groups of Irish from the midland plain and the south settled in south Wales and in Cornwall.

PICTS

The Celtic and pre-Celtic peoples of Scotland became known to the Romans as Picti—"the painted ones." They were a constant menace to the northern frontiers in the fourth and early fifth centuries.

SAXONS, ANGLES, AND JUTES

The venerable Bede, in writing of the Germanic settlement of Britain, mentions these three tribes. It is not easy to distinguish them archaeologically. The situation in the migration period was more complex. In all probability settlers from the seaboard from Denmark to northern France all contributed to the Germanic settlement of Britain.

Above: The Germanic raiders were warlike peoples not unlike the Celts of the pre-Roman period. This detail is taken from the helmet from Sutton Hoo (early seventh century A.D.).

Overleaf (pp. 164–165): The extreme western fringes of the Celtic world, the cliffs of Moher against which the Atlantic Ocean breaks. ▶

ing through northeastern Gaul. Gradually the situation deteriorated as new peoples moved against the Empire: Visigoths, Ostrogoths, and Vandals. Unable to keep them out, successive emperors allowed groups across the frontier to serve as confederate troops—but the tide of invasion was impossible to stem. In December 406 vast numbers of Vandals, Alans, and Lugi crossed the frozen Rhine near Mainz and wandered through Gaul and Spain, while Burgundians moved into Alsace and Visigoths were allowed to settle in Narbonensis. In the first fifty years of the fifth century, Roman Gaul disintegrated.

Britain fared no better. A concerted attack of Saxons, Franks, Picts (from Scotland), and Attacotti (from the Western Isles)

poured into the province in 367 and caused chaos south to the Thames. Provincial government recovered, but it was seriously shaken. Then in the early fifth century Germanic invasion changed momentum. Previously there had been raids and some limited settlement in Britain under strict Roman supervision; now uncontrolled settlement began—Saxons, Franks, Jutes, and Angles pouring into the south and east of the country, totally obliterating Romano-British culture. Meanwhile the inhabitants of Ireland, unaffected by the Roman interlude and by the Germanic raiders, initiated folk movements of their own along the whole of the western seaboard of England and Wales, adding to the confusions of the age.

For the British Isles the fifth century was a time of far-reaching and often violent change. The Roman province of Britannia remained under nominal Roman control until 410, in which year the emperor Honorius formally relinquished control of the province in a famous letter telling the inhabitants of the cities to look after their own defense. What then happened is obscure in detail, but with the complete breakdown of central authority and the collapse of the economic system, it seems that the country split into a number of self-contained kingdoms each with its own ruler or protector.

The principal threat in these early years came from the Picts, who occupied much of Scotland and who a few years before (in 367) had been involved in the devastating raid on the Roman province. As a protection against Pictish raids the Britons held a council at which the decision was taken to admit Saxons, presumably as settlers, who would be required to repel the attackers from the north. In making this decision the Britons were simply adopting a widely accepted policy which had been general practice throughout the Roman Empire for at least a century. Gildas, a western Briton writing soon after these events, explains what happened: "The barbarians, admitted into the island, succeeded in having provisions supplied them, as if they were soldiers and about to encounter... great hardships for their kind entertainers." After a while they complained that "their monthly supplies were not copiously contributed to them... and declared that, if larger munificence was not piled upon them they would break the treaty and lay waste the whole of the island." The threat soon became reality, the rebellious Saxons devastating cities and countryside alike "until [they] burned nearly the whole surface of the island and licked the western ocean with red and savage tongues." Some Britons retreated to the hills and forests of the west, others escaped overseas to Brittany; but eventually the rebellion was over, and the Saxons returned to their homes in eastern England.

Then followed a period of British resistance culminating in a decisive victory at Mount Badon in about A.D. 500, after which an uneasy peace was maintained between the two communities. But urban life was now a thing of the past: The cities "deserted and dismantled, they lie neglected because, although wars with foreigners have ceased, domestic wars continue" (Gildas). It sounds very much as though British society had reverted to the state of tribal warfare which existed when the Romans arrived five hundred years before.

In 549 a plague of considerable severity depopulated the land. Then began the inexorable western advance of the English settlers. After the battle of Dyrham fought in 577 just north of Bath, the English captured the old Roman cities of Bath, Cirencester, and Gloucester. Thus they arrived at the very boundaries of Wales and Dumnonia (Cornwall) which still retained their British-Celtic culture.

While Britain was experiencing the expansion of the English along its eastern coasts, the west coasts were being settled by the Irish. Irish raids were well underway by the end of the fourth century and continued well into the fifth. The Irish Sea had never been fully controlled by the Romans, and now with the decline of Roman power on land it became the link between Ireland and the adjacent coasts of Scotland, Wales, and Cornwall which received the immigrants.

The most intensive of the Irish settlements took place in southwestern Wales, in Pembrokeshire (the region recently renamed Dyfed after its ancient name). The settlers came from the dynasty of Leinster in sufficient numbers to set up a kingdom of their own and firmly to implant the Irish

Irish moved into Anglesey and northwest Wales.

A third force of Irish, emanating from Ulster, crossed into Scotland (incidentally giving the name to the country; for Scotti was the general name applied to the Irish immigrants). Their settlement extended along the west coast, to the north of the Antonine Wall (now Argyll), and was of sufficient intensity to create a strong and unified kingdom known as the Kingdom of Dálriata, which was to play a significant part in the subsequent history of the area. Finally there was the Irish settlement of Cornwall, a peninsula which retained its predominantly Celtic culture until the English penetration began in the ninth century. Judging by the memorial stones, carved with ogham inscriptions, found in the southwest, the Irish settlers came from southwest Wales during the fifth century: several of the Cornish inscriptions record the same names as those found on memorials in Dyfed.

The story of the fifth century in the British Isles is both complex and, in many areas, obscure, but the principal re-formations in society are tolerably clear. While the east was being absorbed by Germanic settlers from the Continent, largely (but not entirely) replacing the Romano-Celtic pop-

The various cultural influences which impinged on the British Isles are shown on these pages.

Far left: The Celtic cross from Carew, Wales (ninth century A.D.), is an example of the hybrid style brought about as the result of the Christianization of Celtic art.

Above: The inside of a broch in Glen Beg near Glenely, Scotland. Brochs were stone-built towers built in the first century B.C. to first century A.D. which continued to be occupied for several centuries. They represent the culmination of a traditional style of Celtic architecture extensively distributed in the far north of Britain.

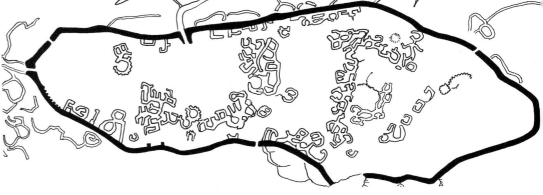

language. Smaller bands moved west along the Bristol Channel, raiding the Romano-British countryside and causing widespread disruption. One band penetrated the mountainous center of Wales to set up a kingdom in Brecknock. The distribution of these early Irish settlers is shown by discoveries of their ogham inscriptions which cluster in Pembrokeshire and Carmarthenshire, where the densest settlement took place, but are scattered widely in the southwest. At about the same time another band of

ulation, the western peninsulas were being settled by peoples of pure Celtic descent from Ireland. Elsewhere, between these two opposed cultures, the descendants of the Romano-British population were maintaining a precarious hold; while in Scotland, north of the Antonine Wall, the Picts, substantially Celtic in origin and largely untouched by Rome, maintained and developed a distinctive culture of their own.

Above: The Welsh hillfort of Tre'r Ceiri within which the native population continued to live throughout the Roman period.

Above left: Invaders from abroad: Anglo-Saxon warriors seen in combat on the Franks casket (around A.D. 700).

Opposite page, top: Another hybrid, a repoussé bronze from the hillfort of South Cadbury dating to the end of the Iron Age or the beginning of the Roman period: a classicized version of a Celtic head.

The Irish immigration from the west and the steady advance of the English settlement from the east caught the old Romano-Celtic population of western Britain in a kind of pincer movement. The result was inevitable: Large bodies of population moved south, across the Channel, to settle in the Armorican peninsula.

The principal causes of the migration is obscure. Gildas, however, implies that it was the revolt of the Saxon mercenaries, when, in describing the flight of the Britons, he describes how some refugees "with loud lamentations passed beyond the seas." He does not specifically mention Armorica, but movement in this direction seems a reasonable supposition. We should not, however, forget that Devon and Cornwall were also subject to immigration from Ireland in the fifth century, and there can be little reasonable doubt that the pressure on land caused by these incomings added to the flight of the Britons.

Most of the Veneti's
strongholds were
so situated on the ends
of spits or headlands
that it was impossible
to approach them
by land
when the tide rushed in
from the open sea...
and they were also
difficult to reach
by sea, because
at low tide the ships
would run aground
on the shoals.
For these reasons
the strongholds
were hard to attack.

Caesar

Traditional links between Armorica and western Britain can be traced back to the third millennium B.C. By the middle of the second millennium an extensive network of trade bound the two areas closely. It was during this period that the megalithic monuments in both countries developed a degree of similarity.

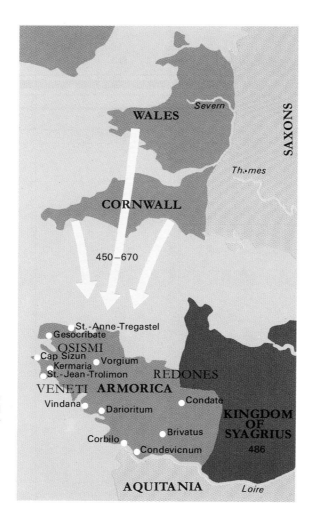

The migration southward appears to have been on a large scale. Substantial parts of Devon were stripped of their population, leaving the land open for the English settlers who moved in and imposed their own system of names on the empty countryside. The organization behind the exodus is indicated by the sixth-century writer Procopius of Caesarea, who describes how large numbers of Britons, ruled by their own kings, went annually to the land of the Franks where they were settled in thinly populated areas. It is very tempting to interpret this movement as the deliberate settlement of British mercenaries to serve the weakening Gallo-Roman state as confederates to drive off Saxon invaders. In other words, the initial British settlement of Armorica may well have been very

similar to the controlled settlement of Germanic peoples in the east of England to protect the land from the Picts.

Armorica at the time was in a state of almost constant rebellion against the central Roman authority. The first revolt took place in 409 when the local inhabitants, "encouraged by the example of the island Britons, had thrown off the Roman yoke" (Zosimus). A few decades later they were referred to as a "fickle and undisciplined people" prone to rebellion and in the throes of an active resistance movement. It was into this land, seething with discontent and lawlessness, threatened by the Saxons, and suffering from severe depopulation, that the British settlers moved in considerable numbers to create a new existence for themselves. The migration continued into the

sixth century, by the end of which Armorica (or Gallia Ulterior as it is referred to in the *Gaulish Chronicle*) became Brittany. The Gallo-Roman language was replaced by a type of Celtic very similar to Cornish, and the peninsula was drawn back once more into the Celtic world to remain aloof from the rest of France for centuries to come. It was as if the clock had been put back five hundred years to the decades before Caesar:

The Veneti are the most powerful tribe on the Brittany coast. They have the largest fleet of ships, in which they traffic with Britain...and as the coast lies exposed to the violence of the open sea and has but few harbors, which the Veneti control, they compel nearly all who sail the waters to pay toll. Caesar, *Gallic Wars*

In Caesar's time the tribes of the two peninsulas were in active contact, and in both areas "cliff castles"—specialized defended enclosures on clifftop promontories—were being built as places of refuge.

Above: The Breton cliff castle at Cap Sizun.

169

While Britain was undergoing the traumas first of Roman invasion and later of the Germanic migrations, Ireland remained largely isolated, able to maintain its own Celtic tradition without hindrance. The great prose saga *Táin Bó Cualnge* (Cattle-Raid of Cooley) gives some indication of how the island was organized in the first centuries of the first millennium A.D. Ireland was at this stage divided into four parts—*Ulaid* (Ulster), *Connachta* (Connacht), *Laigin* (Leinster), and *Mumu* (Munster)—each of which was a large kingdom. Ulster was ruled by Couchobar macNessa from the court at Emain Macha; while Connacht, its great rival, was ruled by Queen Medb, whose rath was on the hill of Cruachain. At this stage the two southern kingdoms were of comparatively little significance.

Society was closely similar to that of the pre-Roman Celts of Europe—the same raiding, head-hunting, chariot warfare, the same exuberant boastfulness, and the same inability to work in larger groups for the common good.

In the period following that represented by the *Táin*, a new dynasty makes its appearance in Meath, in the Irish midlands, using as its royal center the much revered hill of

Niall—called Uí Néill—rapidly extended their power over most of the rest of northern Ireland, the most far-reaching change being their annexation and subsequent dismemberment of the ancient kingdom of Ulaid (Ulster) which stretched from Antrim to Donegal. This process took place in the middle of the fifth century. First the Airgialla of the central part of Ulster were subdued and the ancient site of Emain Macha was taken. Soon afterward, about 428, Donegal was taken, the newly won territories being divided by the two sons of Niall who ruled from Ailech. Niall's third

The sheela-na-gig represents the Irish goddess of Creation. The age of the megalithic tombs is well represented by great ritual monuments like New Grange *(above)*, third millennium B.C.); while the Iron Age, both pagan and Christian, has left innumerable defended enclosures. Of the royal sites, the hill of Tara *(above right)* is the most evocative.

Tara. Traditionally the founder of the dynasty was Niall Noígiallach (379–ca. 428) whose mother, "Cairenn, curly black-haired daughter of Sachell Balb of the Saxons," had probably been acquired in a raid on Roman Britain. The descendants of

son remained in the south to succeed his father at Tara. Thus the north of Ireland was divided into the kingdom of northern Uí Néill, with its center at Ailech, and that of the southern Uí Néill who were based on Tara. From 506 to 1036 the position of head of the dynasty was shared alternately between these two centers.

While the conquest of Ulster was being undertaken in the north, there was continuous conflict in the south between the Uí Néill and the traditional rulers of Leinster who had occupied the midland plain before Niall's arrival. But by 513 local resistance had been overcome.

The southern half of Ireland was, at this time, more culturally advanced than the north, partly because contacts with Gaul, particularly with Aquitaine, had been maintained. The constant conflict between the Uí Néill of Tara and the people of Leinster greatly weakened the Leinster dynasty and enabled the Munster dynasty of Eóganacht (the descendants of Eógan) to emerge as leaders of the south, dominating the routes across Ireland from their royal capital established on the rock of Cashel in the plain of Tipperary. Although there were intermittent intertribal rivalries, the kingdom of Munster remained, by and large, peaceful, and it was here that the cultural life of Ireland flourished. The panegyric poetry of Munster was written down in the later sixth century, and by A.D. 600 vernacular writing had already begun. The density of ogham inscriptions in the area emphasize the development of its aristocratic culture. By the early Christian period, then, the old Ireland of the *Táin*, with its four kingdoms, had changed dramatically. Ireland was now divided into seven kingdoms: the recently established kingdom of the Uí Néill at Tara, together with Munster, Connacht, the remnants of Leinster, and the three separate kingdoms which emerged from the fragmentation of the old kingdom of Ulster. Each of these was composed of a number of tribes *(tuatha)*—about one hundred in all—whose chieftains owed allegiance to the regional king. Overall control of the south remained with the Eóganachta, while the north owed allegiance to the Uí Néill, who were accepted as the high kings of all Ireland throughout the rest of the first millennium.

Writing of the overlords in this way might give the impression of a sophisticated socio-political structure, yet the available evidence suggests that early Christian Ireland was still essentially a Celtic country organized in much the same way as the Celts of pre-Roman Europe.

⊓ Megalithic monuments

⋰ Celtic sanctuaries

◖ Hillforts

♛ Centers of royal power

☿ Important monastic sites

The art of Ireland in the first millennium is a mixture of pagan Celtic themes and Christian symbolism.

Left: The enamel inlaid figure of a man from Email sits cross-legged in a position highly reminiscent of the gods on the Gundestrup caldron.

Opposite top: The brilliant sculpture of the tenth century is represented by the martyrdom of a Christian bishop—one of the narrative panels on the cross of Nuiredach, Monasterboice, County Louth.

The first firm date in Irish history is A.D. 431—the year in which, according to the *Chronicle* of Prosper of Aquitaine, Pope Celestine I sent Palladius to minister to "those of the Irish who believed in Christ." It was in the following year, so the *Annals of Ulster* record, that Patrick arrived in Ireland. Herein lies a problem: if the dates can be accepted, then the conversion of Ireland had begun some while before Patrick arrived. The matter is further confused by the *Annals'* treatment of Patrick's death, for which three dates are given: 457, 461, and 492. Such evidence leaves ample scope for interpretation and speculation. Some scholars believe there were two

SAINT PATRICK AND THE IRISH MONKS

A multitude of Irish artworks attest to the maintenance of the Christian traditions throughout the centuries in the Celtic fringe lands. The carved stone from Boa Island, County Fermanagh *(above)*, is believed to be a work of the seventh century A.D.

Patricks: the elder, known as Palladius, who died in 461; the younger, Patrick the Briton, would have arrived at about this time and died in 492. An alternative view is that Patrick the Briton preceded Palladius and died about 430. There are of course other possibilities, and the controversy is likely to continue, not least because, for some, it is a highly emotive issue.

That Patrick existed, and played a prominent part in spreading Christianity in Ireland, is not in dispute, but the fact that the early genealogies and lives of the saints imply that Christianity was already practiced among some of the communities of the south before the advent of Patrick, lends strong support to those who accept the activities of earlier missionaries.

Of Patrick's exploits we have two reliable sources—two letters written in Latin in the mid-fifth century, claiming to be by the saint himself. One of the letters, the *Confessio*, provides many details of his early life. He was, he claims, brought up in the

civilized countryside of Roman Britain but was captured by Irish raiders while still a boy and carried off to Ireland as a slave where he was forced to herd the flocks of his master. Six years later, guided by a voice from heaven, he made a two-hundred-mile trek to the coast, where he found a merchant ship bound for Gaul with a cargo of dogs (presumably hunting dogs). After a voyage of three days' duration, he landed in France, finding the country to be in a state of terror and desolation as the result of the barbarian raids. Eventually he returned to his family in Britain, but after a while he was again approached by heavenly messengers and heard the voice of the Irish crying out, "We beseech thee, holy youth, to come hither and walk among us." Realizing his duty, he became ordained and set off for Ireland, despite opposition from the Church authorities, to convert the heathen Irish.

The simple story is of outstanding interest. Patrick was probably born at the end of the fourth century when the fast collapsing Roman province of Britain was being wracked by Irish raids. He was presumably an educated Romano-British youth for whom the Church was the obvious vocation, and he would thus have carried to Ireland the traditions, learning, and prejudices of a provincial Roman. It is hardly surprising therefore that the Church which he founded in Ireland, no doubt modeled on the Church in Britain, was purely Roman in origin and episcopal in organization.

That many of the Irish kings accepted Christianity means that the new faith spread with little aggression or bloodshed. There were "countless numbers" of converts, and land was readily given by the local kings for the establishment of churches. These early complexes were simple circular enclosures, rather like the secular ring forts, containing a church or oratory, a priest's house, and a kitchen. They were governed by bishops and were called "cities"—a reminder that the Irish Church was modeled on the Roman, where episcopal seats were established in the *civitates*. But even at this early stage it is possible to recognize the beginnings of monasticism, which from the sixth century was to give the Celtic Church its special character.

The Lord will be with thee:
go thou
but straight before thee;
take to thee
first my little bell,
which until thou
reach the well
that we have mentioned
shall be speechless;
but when thou
attainest to it
the little bell will
with a clear melodious voice
speak out:
so shalt thou know the well,
and at the end
of nine years and a score
I will follow thee
to that place.

St. Patrick, Irish traditional

The stone carvings at center depict, respectively, a priest holding a crook and a bell that symbolizes the Gospel message (found on White Island, Lough Erne, Fermanagh), and St. Patrick in bishop's vestments, with a snake at his feet as in the legends (from a fifteenth-century grave slab).

173

THE NEW CULTURE

Of all the early monasteries the most dramatic is the monastery of Skellig Michael, situated on a bare pyramid of rock sticking out of the Atlantic Ocean off the southwest coast of Ireland. It is difficult to find a more remote and austere spot.

Patrick attempted the impossible: to implant upon a dispersed community with a simple, tribally organized economy a complex episcopal administration which had evolved in the thoroughly urbanized context of the Roman Empire. He was after all a provincial Roman, and to him the Roman system seemed appropriate. What is perhaps the most remarkable aspect of the mission is that it succeeded so dramatically.

Gradually throughout the fifth and early sixth centuries, the ecclesiastical organization established by Patrick became transformed to suit Irish society. The diocese, the administrative unit of the Church, disappeared and bishops lost their organizational duties. Instead, monasteries, following the teachings of their individual founders, became the dominant religious force. The Irish Church evolved in relative isolation, cut off from the great Christian centers of mainland Europe. The western sea routes, however, remained open, linking the countries surrounding the Irish Sea with the Mediterranean world. The wine trade continued to flourish, introducing into the western parts of the British Isles fine pottery and wine amphorae from North Africa. But alongside these luxuries came the knowledge of the monastic life which had developed so intensely in Egypt. All along the Atlantic seaboard monastic

life took root: in Spain, Aquitaine, western Britain, and Ireland. Irish monks also traveled to the west of Britain to study in the monasteries of Whithorn in Galloway and at St. David's in southwest Wales. There they learned the value of asceticism and returned to Ireland to build their cells in isolated locations in order to spend their lives in fasting and prayer. St. Enda, returning from Whithorn, moved far into the west to establish a cell on the bleak Aran Islands where he and his companions lived a life of hardship and simplicity—it was to mark the beginning of the wave of asceticism which swept Ireland and transformed the country's religious life. Irish monks congregated around the cells of the founders in large communities, and the idea of the monastic family was readily absorbed. The primatial see at Armagh became a mon-

Above: This rough early relief from one of the pillars of Carndonagh, Ireland, shows a warrior with sword. It typifies the style of the most primitive Irish art.

astery at the end of the fifth century, while at Kildare a mixed community of monks and nuns was established by St. Brigid. At Clonard the church created by Patrick was transformed into a monastery by St. Finnian, who had been influenced by the monks of southern Wales. It soon became famous throughout Ireland.

It is easy to understand why the monastic system so rapidly replaced the episcopal system introduced by St. Patrick. Irish society was still organized in the Celtic manner, its basis being the tribe (tuáth) which was made up of a number of clans. The urban-derived episcopal system was both alien and inappropriate to Ireland; but the monastery was a concept which could readily be absorbed into the Celtic social organization. The monastery was, after all, a family governed by an abbot: it was little more than a religious version of the tuáth controlled by a chieftain. Thus the soil of Ireland, fertilized by St. Patrick's mission, provided a sympathetic environment for Mediterranean monasticism to take root. The ninth- or tenth-century Catalogus Sanctorum, looking back on the fifth and sixth centuries, divided the saints of Ireland into three "orders": the first was St. Patrick, the second were the saints who founded the great monasteries, the third "those who dwell in desert places and live on herbs, water, and alms and have nothing of their own." Although this threefold division should not be taken to imply a chronological evolution, the third order—the anchorites—do come comparatively late in the period. The life of the hermit, the ascetic who renounced everything, was a style of Christian behavior learned ultimately from Egypt via Spain and Gaul, but it became widespread in the Celtic west. To a Celt, membership of the family was an essential part of his well-being. It was logical, therefore, that in renouncing all

The tradition of erecting a simple engraved memorial stone over graves or a holy location was gradually transformed to give rise to the distinctive art of the High Cross. The inspiration for the style is quite clearly the work of the bronzesmith and the goldsmith whose intricate designs were copied in stone. Presumably these great crosses of the ninth and tenth centuries are copies of heavy wooden crosses whose arms were probably stabilized with cross braces at the angles—evolving into the highly distinctive form of the Irish High Cross.

One of the earliest groups, of which the Ahenny cross *(below, third from right)*, is a fine example, has a limited distribution in the south of Ireland. The bosses and interlace designs are a strong reminder of the metalwork tradition which they attempt to copy. This style dates to the eighth century.

A little later "Scripture Crosses" develop: the face of the cross was now divided into rectangular panels within each of which a different scene was depicted, some of which included nonreligious subjects. The tradition of the carved High Cross continues with some vigor into the twelfth century.

Crosses below, from left to right: Duvillaun, Kilnasaggart, Glendalough, Clonmacnoise, Clonmacnoise, Ahenny, Clonmacnoise, Monasterboice.

Early Christian architecture is widespread in Ireland. "St. Columba's House" (*right*), built of stone and mortar in 814 on the site of a wooden structure, is among the best preserved ruins of the St. Columba monastery at Kells.
The walls, more than a meter thick, surround a small cell-like room.

worldly possessions, he should also give up the luxury of community life. Thus many young men returning to Ireland from abroad shunned the comparative comfort of the well-established monasteries and made the ultimate sacrifice to be alone in the wilderness. Others made the same sacrifice—total divorce from family—by seeking solitude among strangers. Such men, in their quest of penance through exile, fueled the missionary movement which spread knowledge of the Celtic Church across the face of western Europe (pp. 186–189).

My hand is weary with writing; my sharp great point is not thick; my slender-beaked pen juts forth a beetle-hued draught of bright blue ink.
A steady stream of wisdom springs from my well-colored neat fair hand; on the page it pours its draught of ink of the green-skinned holly.
I send my little dripping pen unceasingly over an assemblage of books of great beauty, to enrich the possessions of men of art—whence my hand is weary with writing.

Irish traditional, eleventh century

Some monks spent much time in the scriptoria of the abbeys copying out the gospel books and transcribing other manuscripts thought useful. The twelfth-century miniature above shows the famous chronicler Bede at work.

Opposite: The circular tower developed late, partly as a response to Viking attack. Some towers were isolated, but sometimes they were attached to churches, as in this ninth-century example at Glendalough.

transcribed in Latin, they scribbled charming verses—influenced by Latin meter but redolent with a Celtic awareness of the natural world. That these great centers of learning could develop was in considerable part due to their Celtic heritage; for the tradition of druidic and bardic schools was strong in pagan Ireland, and the monasteries were their natural successors.

The early monasteries were modest structures, much like large homesteads, consisting of an enclosing wall and ditch within which were the principal buildings: the church or oratory, usually built of timber but sometimes of stone; the cells of the monks, which would often be simple circular structures of wattle and daub; the guest house; the refectory; and the school. Besides the buildings themselves, there might be various types of stone monuments. Memorial stones carved with ogham script were common, particularly in Munster, from the fourth to the seventh century. Simple roughly hewn slabs and pillars carved with the Christian symbol Chi-Rho and monograms in Greek and Latin also became popular to mark graves, and the grave slab of the founder frequently became the most revered spot in the monastic complex—the focus of the pilgrim's visit. These monuments were comparatively modest in execution: it was not until the eighth century that the elaborately carved high crosses began to be made to adorn the holy places. Together with fine metalwork and the magnificent manuscripts, they represent the artistic culmination of the Golden Age of early Christian Ireland.

In spite of the harsh austerity practiced by the anchorites in the wilds, the monastic communities rapidly developed as centers of letters and learning. The culture practiced and taught was hybrid—a mixture of Roman superimposed on Celtic. The monks could write Latin, and many had a reasonable knowledge of classical authors. But in their art the Celtic freedom dominates, and in the marginal notes to the manuscripts which they so laboriously

In the *scriptoria* of the monasteries the skilled scribes spent their lives copying and illuminating manuscripts. The range of their work varied enormously—religious tracts, the lives of the saints, natural history, astronomy, and, of prime importance, the gospel books used at the altar, on which the greatest care and love were lavished. The monks transcribed in Latin and in Irish, sometimes to relieve the monotony, adding marginal notes of their own or composing lively poems in the vernacular. It is to the monastic scribes that we owe the survival of the ancient oral traditions of pagan Ireland. Painstakingly they transcribed the sagas to written form, censoring them of the worst excesses of heathenism. In collecting these old oral traditions, to which enormous prestige still attached,

Guardians of Ancient Myths and Legends

One of the most complete manuscripts of the famous pagan saga, the *Táin Bó Cualnge*, is contained in the Book of Leinster which was compiled in the twelfth century. The Leinster text is a corrected version of the story which was originally written down several centuries earlier. Several other, less complete, editions survive.

the monks preserved a record of pagan Celtic times quite unique in the ancient world.

Their attitude to this archaic record is amusingly summed up by the twelfth-century scribe who, having copied the whole of the *Táin Bó Cualnge*, could not resist adding a personal view: "But I, who have written this history, or rather fable, am doubtful about many things in this history or fable. For some of them are the figments of demons, some of them poetic imaginings, some true, some not, some for the delight of fools."

THE PILLOW TALK

Once when the royal bed was laid out for Ailill and Medb in Cruachan fort in Connacht, they had this talk on the pillows:

"It is true what they say, love," Ailill said, "it is well for the wife of a wealthy man."

"True enough," the woman said. "What put that in your mind?"

"It struck me," Ailill said, "how much better off you are today than the day I married you."

"I was well enough off without you," Medb said.

"Then your wealth was something I didn't know or hear much about," Ailill said. "Except for your woman's things, and the neighboring enemies making off with loot and plunder."

"Not at all," Medb said, "but with the high king of Ireland for my father—Eochaid Feidlech the steadfast, the son of Finn, the son of Finnoman, the son of Finnen, the son of Finngoll, the son of Roth, the son of Rigéon, the son of Blathacht, the son of Beothacht, the son of Enna Agnech, the son of Aengus Turbech. He had six daughters: Derbriu, Ethne, Ele, Clothru, Muguin, and myself Medb, the highest and haughtiest of them. I outdid them in grace and giving and battle and warlike combat. I had fifteen hundred soldiers in my royal pay, all exiles' sons, and the same number of freeborn native men, and for every paid soldier I had ten more men, and nine more, and eight, and seven, and six, and five, and four, and three, and two, and one. And that was only our ordinary household.

"My father gave me a whole province of Ireland, this province ruled from Cruachan, which is why I am called 'Medb of Cruachan.' And they came from Finn the king of Leinster, Rus Ruad's son to woo me, and from Coirpre Niafer the king of Temair, another of Rus Ruad's sons. They came from Conchobor, king of Ulster, son of Fachtna, and they came from Eochaid Bec, and I wouldn't go. For I asked a harder wedding gift than any woman ever asked before from a man in Ireland—the absence of meanness and jealousy and fear.

"If I married a mean man our union would be wrong, because I'm so full of grace and giving. It would be an insult if I were more generous than my husband, but not if the two of us were equal in this. If my husband was a timid man our union would be just as wrong because I thrive, myself, on all kinds of trouble. It is an insult for a wife to be more spirited than her husband, but not if the two are equally spirited.

The *Táin*

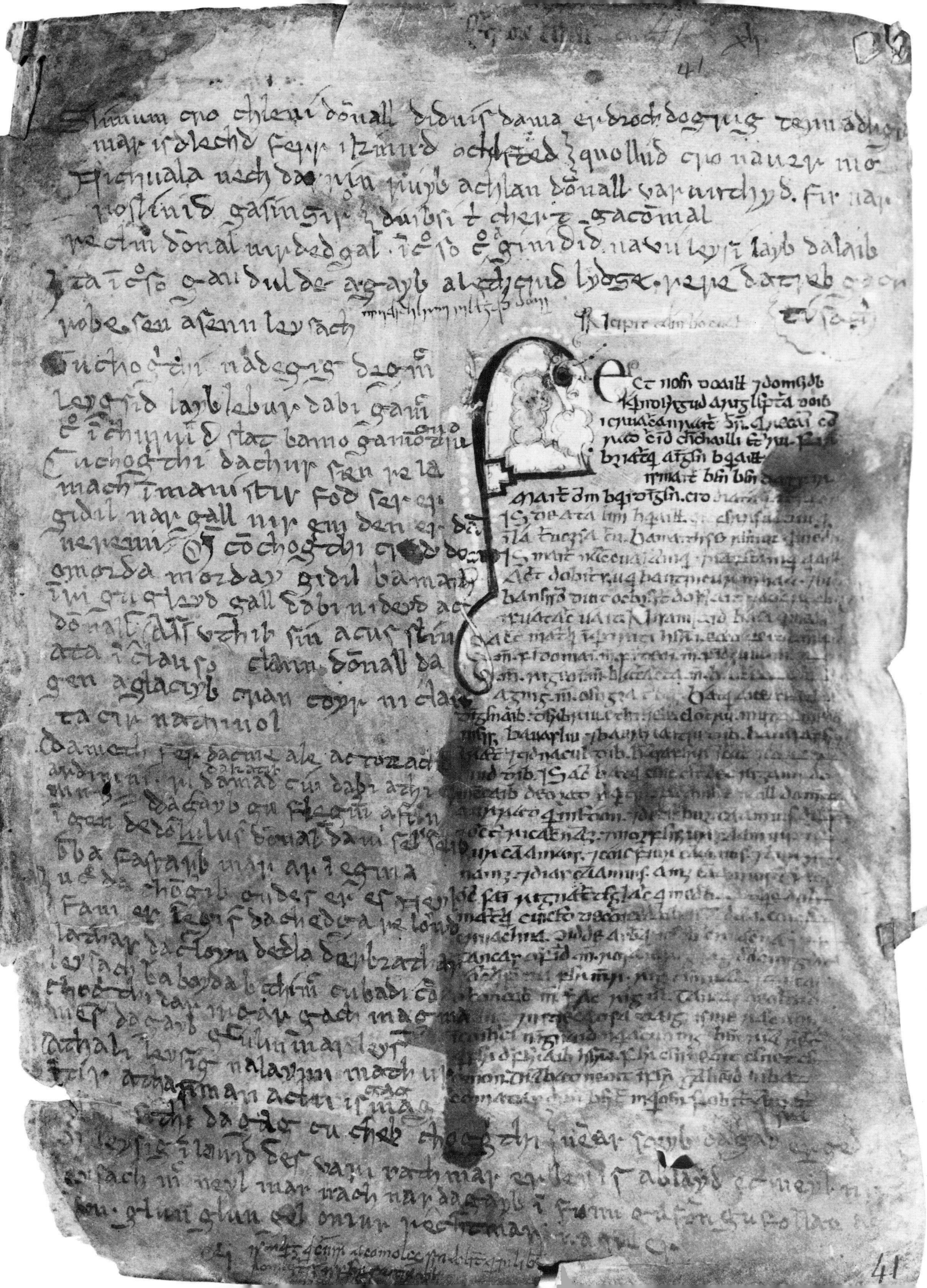

The Arthurian legends, which relate back to events in the fifth century, were much loved in later times and were taken over by the more propaganda-conscious kings of England. There were many medieval accretions to the legend. The Round Table, for example, was added in the early Middle Ages, in the age of chivalry when the knights were considered equal. But the complex myth of the Holy Grail may have developed from an early story in which a magic caldron is mentioned—perhaps a distant reflection of the caldron associated with the pagan god Dagda.

Above: Twelfth-century miniature of the Last Supper: the round table here may have inspired the adoption of the Round Table in later Arthurian stories.

In the early twelfth century, Geoffrey of Monmouth, a minor ecclesiastic of Welsh descent, published his *History of the Kings of Britain*—a strange and fanciful compilation that begins with the settlement of the island by Brutus, great grandson of Aeneas, and ends with the Age of King Arthur. His source, he claims, was an ancient document in the British language given to him by one Walter, archdeacon of Oxford. Whether such a document existed we shall never know, but what is clear is that beneath the colorful fantasy and invention, of which Geoffrey's work is largely compiled, there are threads drawn from Welsh monastic writing and from Breton sources.

Geoffrey's book formed the foundation for the rich Arthurian tradition which grew by accretion throughout the Middle Ages, championed by the Plantagenet kings. It presented a highly respectable pedigree for the ruling house to adopt, and once Arthur could be freed from close association with the Welsh by dexterous manipulation—which involved some highly dubious medieval excavations at Glastonbury—then the British monarch could boast of origins quite as illustrious as those of his French rival. Politically acceptable and appealing to the romantic age of chivalry, Arthur was assured of a wide and highly uncritical audience: his exploits expanded with their constant retelling.

Yet behind all the nonsense lay some traditions which originated in the sixth century, when, evidently, the name of Arthur was revered throughout western Britain. Belief in him as a folk hero can be traced back to a compilation called the *History of the Britons*—a ragbag of folklore and other scraps gleaned from Welsh documents, put together in the ninth century by a Welsh cleric, Nennius. Arthur emerges simply as a war leader who spearheaded the British resistance against the Saxons in the years around 500, fighting a series of highly successful battles. The memory of these deeds lived long in the early Welsh literature. He is mentioned briefly in the long poem, *Gododdin*, composed about 600. Other early poems mention his followers, his horse, his kinsfolk, and his bards. In the famous Welsh legend the *Mabinogion*, Arthur occurs many times. Perhaps the most interesting story in this legend tells how a young man, Culhwch, in order to win Olwen as his bride has to perform a series of fantastic

tasks and enlists the aid of Arthur. The story provides the medium for the skills of the hero to be displayed, but it has all the verve and energy of the Irish sagas. The close relationship is further emphasized by the inclusion of famous figures from Irish mythology and by the strong similarities between the arrival of Culhwch at the court of Arthur and Lug's arrival at the court of Nuada in the Irish *Battle of Moytura*. This part of the *Mabinogion* is clearly in the same broad tradition as the early Irish sagas, reflecting the fabulous world of the pagan Celtic period seen through later eyes.

What emerges from the confusing detail of the Arthurian legends is that a folk hero or heroes, singly or collectively called Arthur, led a resistance movement against the Germanic settlers in western Britain in the late fifth and early sixth centuries. So great were his exploits, that the name of the hero was quickly absorbed into the traditions of Wales and merged with the older sagas and legends of the pagan Celtic period in stories like that of Culhwch and Olwen. The name was also revered in later poetry. Thus when Geoffrey of Monmouth was searching for a basis for his mythical *History of the Kings of Britain*, there was ample material readily to hand. All he did was present Arthur in an updated guise which suited medieval susceptibilities. The Arthurian theme, then, bridges the gap between the Celtic saga tradition and medieval and modern romantic literature.

The developed myth—Round Table and Holy Grail—is shown in the fifteenth-century book illustration from *Les Chroniques de Hainaut (left)*. Many of the great literary works of the European Middle Ages are poetic elaborations of old Celtic legends. Marie de France and Chrétien de Troyes, writing in France in the twelfth century, acknowledged their debt to "Breton" or Celtic sources. Chrétien's *Parsifal*, in turn, with its retelling of the quest of the Grail, had a strong influence on medieval culture. The three miniature paintings here, from the fourteenth-century Manessa codex, are illustrations for works of three German poets.

Gottfried von Strassburg *(left)*, wrote the twelfth–thirteenth-century version of *Tristan and Isolde* that inspired Richard Wagner.

The minnesinger Wolfram von Eschenbach ca. 1170–1220, author of a Middle High German *Parsifal*, is shown in his armor.

Heinrich von Meissen, called Frauenlob, ca. 1250–1318 *(right)*, wrote courtly works in praise of women, partly inspired by old Celtic love poetry.

THE BARDS

The important role of the bard in early societies is very clearly shown in Ireland. Here the bardic tradition flourished, combining mythology, history, current events and poetry in a vast oral anthology. The poems,

often thousands of lines long, recited to music, were an important part of Celtic culture, and gave the bard the kind of semi-magical, semi-mythical status typified in Europe by the legend of Orpheus, shown here in a fifteenth century relief by Luca della Robbia.

In early Irish society there were two classes of men who were responsible for literary and musical composition: the bards, whose task it was to compose poems in praise of their masters, and the *filid*—a word which originally meant "seers"—who in addition to being poets were endowed with certain supernatural powers: they could, for example, hurt or even kill by satire. In the *Táin*, Medb sends "the druids and satirists and harsh bards" against Fer Diad to "make against him three satires to slay him and three lampoons, and that they might raise on his face three blisters, shame, blemish, and disgrace."

The *filid* and the bards were trained in specially organized schools. All teaching was oral and was accomplished by the simple procedure of the master intoning and the pupils repeating the matter in unison. Significantly the Old Irish verb "to teach" means "to sing over." Once quali-fied, the *filí* would be free to travel, uttering panegyrics wherever he went, in expectation of reward. At the top of the poetic hierarchy was the *ollam*, who traveled and behaved in the manner befitting a minor king with a retinue of twenty-four men. No one could safely deny hospitality to such a man.

With the coming of Christianity, the magical attributes of the *filid* withered away, but the bardic tradition and the schools continued to flourish. The trade of the poet was still one of honor which required long years of apprenticeship to perfect. The principal difference was that, with Christianity, knowledge of Latin with its formal meter influenced the vernacular compositions, creating a new kind of syllabic lyric poetry.

The traditional schools of the bards and the *filid* were still active in the tenth century. Certain metrical tracts survive from this time prescribing the different meters to be practiced and the range of heroic literature which had to be studied in each year of the twelve-year apprenticeship. The length of the period of study is an interesting reminder of the twenty years which Caesar recorded to be the time needed to train a druid.

The twelfth century saw the beginnings of a renewed vigor in the bardic schools in Ireland, and it is in this period that much of the best Welsh poetry was written. The poetic renaissance may well be attributed to the patronage of the Welsh king Gruffudd ap Cynan, who, having spent his youth in Ireland, returned to his native Gwynedd, probably bringing Irish poets and musicians back with him. In both countries the twelfth century saw the beginnings of a stricter form of composition which was carefully preserved by families of hereditary bards, eventually giving rise to stereotyped and rather dull work bound by rigid conventions. The principal themes remained much the same as before: the patron was praised, the glory of his ancestors was paraded, and his personal generosity and bravery in battle were eulogized. Careful craftsmanship soon replaced freshness and originality, and the bardic tradition lapsed into mechanical dullness. Even so, bardic schools still flourished in Ireland as late as the seventeenth century.

SENILITY

Before I was bent-backed, I was eloquent of speech, my wonderful deeds were admired; the men of Argoed always supported me.

Before I was bent-backed, I was bold; I was welcomed in the drinking-hall of Powys, the paradise of Wales.

Before I was bent-backed, I was handsome, my spear was in the van, it drew first blood—I am crooked, I am sad, I am wretched.

Wooden staff, it is Autumn, the bracken is red, the stubble is yellow; I have given up what I love.

Wooden staff, it is Winter, men are talkative over the drink; no one visits my bedside.

Wooden staff, it is Spring, the cuckoos are brown, there is light at the evening meal; no girl loves me.

Wooden staff, it is early Summer, the furrow is red, the young corn is curly; it grieves me to look at your crook.

Wooden staff, knotty stick, support the yearning old man, Llywarch, the perpetual babbler....

Boisterous is the wind, white is the hue of the edge of the wood; the stag is emboldened, the hill is bleak; feeble is the old man, slowly he moves.

This leaf, the wind drives it, alas for its fate! It is old—this year it was born.

What I have loved from boyhood I now hate—a girl, a stranger, and a gray horse; indeed I am not fit for them.

The four things I have most hated ever have met together in one place; coughing and old age, sickness and sorrow.

I am old, I am lonely, I am shapeless and cold after my honored couch; I am wretched, I am bent in three.

I am bent in three and old, I am peevish and giddy, I am silly, I am cantankerous; those who loved me love me not.

Girls do not love me, no one visits me, I cannot move about; ah, Death, why does it not come for me!

Neither sleep nor joy come to me after the slaying of Llawr and Gwen; I an irritable carcass, I am old.

Welsh; attributed to "Llywarch Hen; ninth century

THE HARP OF CNOC Í CHOSGAIR

Harp of Cnoc Í Chosgair; you who bring sleep to eyes long sleepless; sweet, subtle, plangent, glad, cooling, grave.

Excellent instrument with the smooth gentle curve, trilling under red fingers, musician that has charmed us, red, lion-like, of full melody.

You who lure the bird from the flock, you who refresh the mind, brown spotted one of sweet words, ardent, wondrous, passionate.

You who heal every wounded warrior, joy and allurement to women, familiar guide over the dark-blue water, mystic sweet-sounding music.

You who silence every instrument of music, yourself a pleasing plaintive instrument, dweller among the Race of Conn, instrument yellow-brown and firm.

The one darling of sages, restless, smooth, of sweet tune, crimson star above the fairy hills, breast-jewel of High Kings.

Sweet tender flowers, brown harp of Diarmaid, shape not unloved by hosts, voice of the cuckoos in May!

I have not heard of music ever such as your frame makes since the time of the fairy people, fair brown many-colored bough, gentle, powerful, glorious.

Sound of the calm wave on the beach, pure shadowing tree of true music, carousals are drunk in your company, voice of the swan over shining streams.

Cry of the fairy women from the Fairy Hill of Ler, no melody can match you, every house is sweet-stringed through your guidance, you the pinnacle of harp-music...

Irish, Gofraidh Fionn Ó Dálaigh, ca. 1385

WHERE ARE YOU GOING TO, MY PRETTY MAID?

"Where were you going, fair maid," said he, "with your pale face and your yellow hair?" "Going to the well, sweet sir," she said, "for strawberry leaves make maidens fair."

"Shall I go with you, fair maid," said he, "with your pale face and your yellow hair?" "Do if you wish, sweet sir," she said, "for strawberry leaves make maidens fair."

Cornish popular poem, seventeenth century

Overleaf (pp. 184–185): The Book ▶ of Kells is one of the great masterpieces of early Christian Ireland. It was probably written and illuminated in Iona early in the ninth century but carried from there, unfinished, to the new monastery of Kells, County Meath, where many of the monks fled from the Viking raiders. The book, comprising the four gospels, is elaborately ornamented. It is the culmination of Irish artistic development. Each gospel begins with a portrait page (St. John, on p. 185)—the frontal pose and wide-eyed face belying the ultimate Byzantine inspiration—but the Celtic spirit is everywhere to be seen in the intensely complex curvilinear style of the illumination.

The bards of the Irish royal houses composed countless songs which subsequently became part of the repertoire of the medieval troubadours (above). Celtic poetry dating back to the eighth century has survived by this means.

183

THE MISSIONARIES' FIRST STEP

The reconstruction shows a typical Irish monastery. Enclosed within a defensive wall or earthwork, it much resembled contemporary homesteads. The principal building was, naturally, the church or oratory; there could be more than one depending on the popularity of the establishment. Other buildings included the refectory and the guest house. The monks lived in individual cells of wickerwork or (in this case) corbeled stonework built around the perimeter wall. The round towers (of which

The desire for isolation through voluntary exile, which encouraged the Irish monks of the sixth century to seek solitude on remote islands or in the depths of the uninhabited countryside, led some men to cross the seas to Britain and mainland Europe, there to be alone among strangers. In this way the rigors of Celtic Christianity were introduced to a wider audience nearly a century after St. Patrick had first set foot in Ireland.

Among the first missionaries to leave Ireland was St. Columba, prince of the northern Uí Néill. In 563, with twelve companions, he set sail for Argyll, where one of the offshoots of his people, the Dálriata, had already settled, and there, on the remote offshore island of Iona, he founded a monastery. Iona was soon to become the ecclesiastical head of the Celtic Church in

political acts of this kind the prestige and patronage of the new establishment was firmly established.

Early in the seventh century Iona offered sanctuary to the exiled king Oswald of Northumbria, and when, in 634, he returned to his kingdom he invited the monks of Iona to settle among his people. Thus, the next year, Aidan, with twelve disciples, set out for Northumbria choosing as the site for their monastery the island of Lindisfarne, off the Northumberland coast in the North Sea. Lindisfarne and Iona were soon to become great cultural centers revered throughout the civilized world. Together they nurtured Celtic culture in the tranquillity and comparative safety of their island retreats.

Irish missionaries spread to all parts of Britain, some coming directly from Ireland,

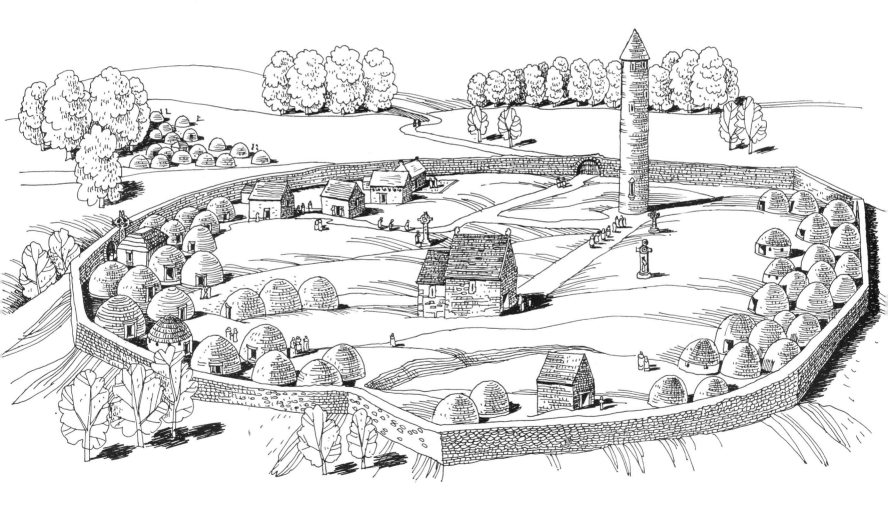

about eighty survive in Ireland) were bell towers from which the monks were summoned to prayer, but they also served as secure places for monks and the monasteries' treasures in times of danger during the Viking raids. Towers were probably first built in the early tenth century.

Ireland, Scotland, and England. But it was more than that: it was a political center. At Iona he inaugurated Aidan king of the new territory of Dálriata, while at the same time establishing a peaceful relationship with the king of the northern Picts. Through

others from Iona. In the north they penetrated the Hebrides and sailed north to Orkney and Shetland reaching as far as Iceland. By the seventh century the Irish Celtic Church was known in all parts of the British Isles.

St. Brigid's monastery in Kildare was one of the most famous establishments in Ireland; founded in the late fifth century, it served both monks and nuns. It was a place of pilgrimage and grew rich. A seventh-century description of the church describes it as a many-windowed building, divided into three parts by screens which were ornamented by paintings and linen hangings, and with an ornate door. The fine tower *(left)* was added to the establishment in the tenth century.

The comparative comfort and opulence of St. Brigid's is in striking contrast to the monastery on barren, sea-battered Skellig Rock far out in

the Atlantic off the southwest coast of Ireland. The buildings—a group of beehive cells and two little oratories—are terraced into the side of the rock five hundred feet above the sea. There is a tiny cemetery with roughly inscribed grave slabs and protected garden plots where a few herbs and vegetables were persuaded to grow.

187

ST. COLUMBANUS

ST. FRIDOLIN

ST. CILIAN

ST. BONIFACE

THE RETURN TO THE CONTINENT

The Irish missionary settlement in Britain was only part of a much wider phenomenon. In the sixth century great numbers of missionaries crossed to Gaul, the Rhineland, Switzerland, and Italy. Some of them, like St. Gall, were hermits who sought nothing but the solitude of the Swiss mountains. Others were intent upon converting the heathen and setting up monasteries—men like St. Columbanus, who in 590 landed in Gaul and founded the famous abbey of Luxeuil. Men of such missionary zeal inevitably came into conflict with the secular authorities. St. Columbanus made a lifelong enemy of Queen Brunhilde of Burgundy, who eventually drove him from the country. However, he remained undaunted and continued his travels, arriving in northern Italy in 614 where he founded another abbey at Bobbio.

The energy and conviction of these men who were prepared to travel vast distances through dangerous and politically unstable territory is remarkable; but their faith was such that they were sustained and through their rigorous example encouraged others, heathen and Christian alike, to adopt their own demanding standards and regimes.

St. Columbanus Born in Leinster, he was a member of the religious community of St. Comgall of Bangor in County Down. About 590 he and twelve disciples set out for the Continent, traveled through western Gaul, and settled in Burgundy, where he founded abbeys at Luxeuil and Fontaine. He was forced to move on, through the court of Austria to Switzerland, and stayed for a while near Bregenz. Finally he traveled south through the Alps to Lombardy, where he founded a monastery at Bobbio.

St. Fridolin In his missionary wanderings in the sixth century, Fridolin founded a monastery and church on the island of Säckingen in the Rhine. He is still honored as the patron saint of Glarus, Switzerland.

St. Cilian The Irish bishop Cilian came to be called the apostle of Franconia for his work in that area of Germany. He died a martyr's death at Würzburg in the year 697.

St. Columba As a member of the royal house of the Uí Néill, Columba might have become king. Instead he chose the Church. He crossed to Argyll (western Scotland) where a branch of his people had recently settled, and there, on the island of Iona, founded a monastery which soon acquired great prestige. He served there as priest and abbot until his death in 597.

St. Cuthbert Born in about 634, Cuthbert spent his early life in England as a shepherd. In ca. 651 he entered the monastery at Melrose in Scotland, which followed the rule of St. Columba, and later moved to the Columban community at Lindisfarne, where he became abbot. From here he spent much of his time traveling about Northumberland spreading the gospel and converting the heathen.

St. Boniface Boniface was a West Saxon born ca. 675. He studied in monasteries at Exeter and Nursling, where he came under the influence of the teaching emanating from Canterbury. His first short missionary visit abroad was in Frisia (716–717). For twenty years he worked among the Germans and Franks.

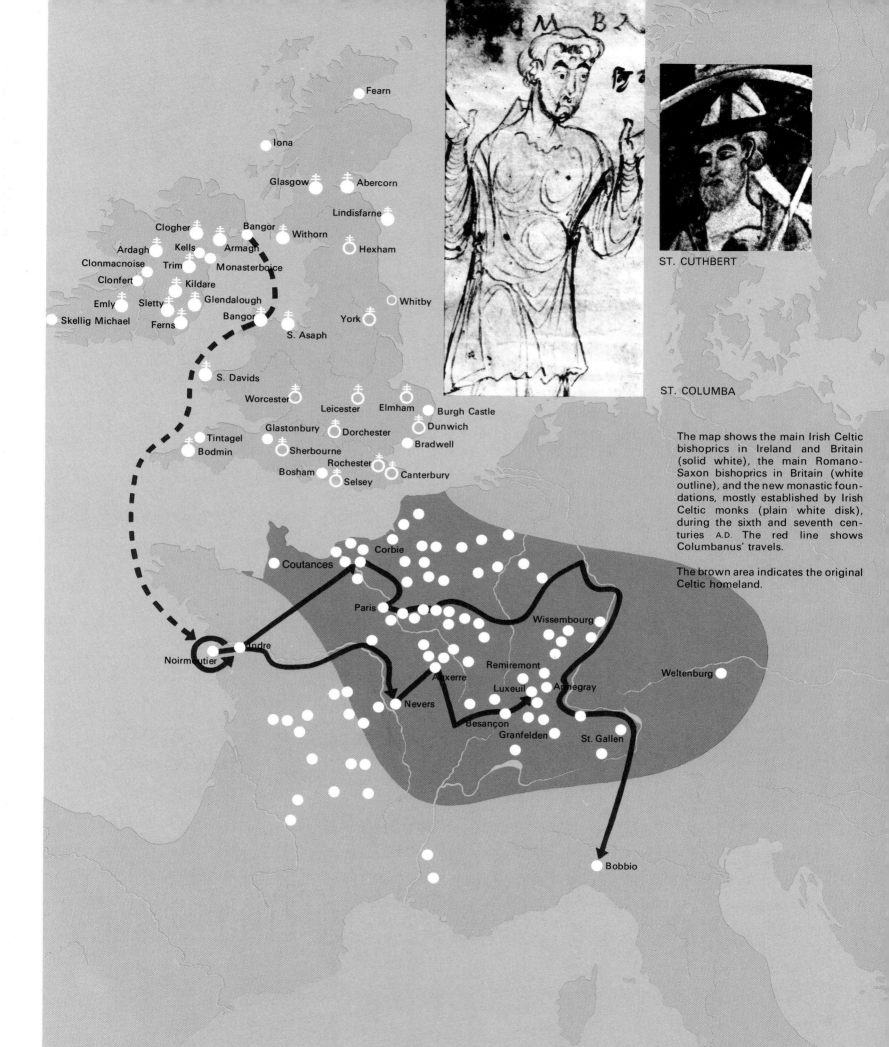

Fearn

Iona

Glasgow ⚲   Abercorn ⚲

Lindisfarne ⚲

Clogher ⚲   Bangor ⚲   Withorn

Ardagh   Kells ⚲   Armagh ⚲   Hexham ⚲

Clonmacnoise   Trim   Monasterboice

Clonfert   Kildare ⚲

Emly   Sletty   Glendalough ⚲   Whitby

Skellig Michael   Ferns   Bangor   York ⚲

S. Asaph ⚲

S. Davids ⚲

Worcester ⚲   Leicester ⚲   Elmham ⚲   Burgh Castle

Glastonbury ⚲   Dorchester ⚲   Dunwich ⚲

Tintagel   Bradwell

Bodmin   Sherbourne ⚲

Rochester ⚲   Canterbury ⚲

Bosham   Selsey ⚲

ST. CUTHBERT

ST. COLUMBA

The map shows the main Irish Celtic bishoprics in Ireland and Britain (solid white), the main Romano-Saxon bishoprics in Britain (white outline), and the new monastic foundations, mostly established by Irish Celtic monks (plain white disk), during the sixth and seventh centuries A.D. The red line shows Columbanus' travels.

The brown area indicates the original Celtic homeland.

Corbie

Coutances

Paris

Wissembourg

Indre

Noirmoutier   Remiremont   Weltenburg

Auxerre   Luxeuil   Annegray

Nevers

Besançon   Granfelden   St. Gallen

Bobbio

The Eastern Franks and the inhabitants of Thuringia were converted by the preaching of St. Cilian, who was subsequently martyred in Würzburg.

Below: Martyrdom of St. Cilian. ninth-century miniature, Landesbibliothek, Stuttgart.

Right: the twelfth-century miniature from Cîteau, France, recalls the felling of the Holy Oak of the Germans by St. Boniface, as a demonstration of the superior power of the Christian God.

In a Celtic society which so loved to hear stories of bravery and miraculous happenings, it was inevitable that the exploits of the early missionaries should come to be recorded for frequent retellings in the monasteries. Just as the daring of the chieftains had inspired the young men of the pagan Celtic world to deeds of valor, so the acts of the early saints edified their followers and reconfirmed them in their faith. Thus in the seventh century there came into existence a considerable body of literature describing the lives of the saints. It served many purposes: education and inspiration, certainly; but it was also an influential means of propaganda, particularly at a time when the Celtic Church was in conflict with the Church of Rome (pp. 192–193). Moreover, if a monastery wished to acquire popularity, it was essential for the exploits of its founding saint to be given wide publicity.

The early Lives derived ultimately from a literary form of which the Acts of the Apostles was the earliest example. Later the funeral oration formed the model. By the late fourth century the narrative style of presentation had evolved in Europe, and when in the seventh century Muirchu wrote the earliest surviving *Life of St. Patrick*, he noted in his introduction that he was composing in a new style which had been introduced into Ireland earlier that century. The classic Life is Adamnán's *Life of St. Columba*. It is divided into three parts: the saint's prophecies, his miracles, and his visions. Though composed about 685, it is already old-fashioned in its structure, the new narrative style of biography having by now gained widespread acceptance.

The Lives, then—mixtures of fable, fact, good sense, and wishful thinking—were avidly read for entertainment and inspiration. Today, while they provide only a skeletal history of the missionary movement, as a reflection of the aims and aspirations of the early Celtic Christian community they are of incomparable value.

ST. COLUMBA'S ISLAND HERMITAGE

Delightful I think it to be in the bosom of an isle, on the peak of a rock, that I might often see there the calm of the sea.

That I might see its heavy waves over the glittering ocean, as they chant a melody to their Father on their eternal course.

That I might see its smooth strand of clear headlands, no gloomy thing; that I might hear the voice of the wondrous birds, a joyful tune.

That I might hear the sound of the shallow waves against the rocks; that I might hear the cry by the graveyard, the noise of the sea.

That I might see its splendid flocks of birds over the fullwatered ocean; that I might see its mighty whales, greatest of wonders.

That I might see its ebb and its flood-tide in their flow; that this might be my name, a secret I tell, "He who turned his back on Ireland."

That contrition of heart should come upon me as I watch it; that I might bewail my many sins, difficult to declare.

That I might bless the Lord who has power over all, Heaven with its pure host of angels, earth, ebb, flood-tide.

That I might pore on one of my books, good for my soul; a while kneeling for beloved Heaven, a while at psalms.

A while gathering dulse from the rock, a while fishing, a while giving food to the poor, a while in my cell.

A while meditating upon the Kingdom of Heaven, holy is the redemption; a while at labor not too heavy; it would be delightful!

Irish; author unknown; twelfth century

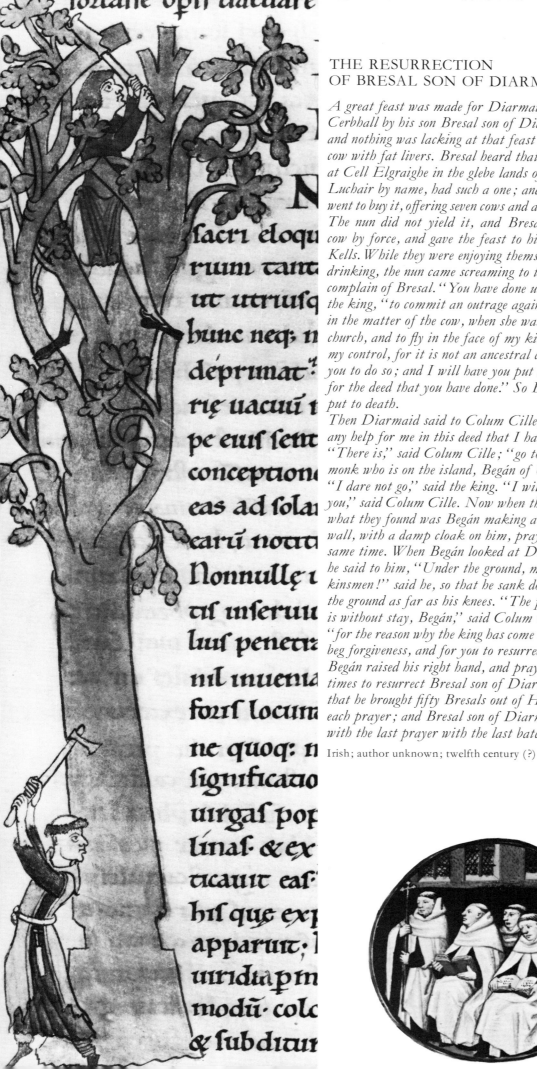

THE RESURRECTION OF BRESAL SON OF DIARMAID

A great feast was made for Diarmaid son of Cerbhall by his son Bresal son of Diarmaid; and nothing was lacking at that feast except a cow with fat livers. Bresal heard that a nun at Cell Elgraighe in the glebe lands of Kells, Luchair by name, had such a one; and Bresal went to buy it, offering seven cows and a bull for it. The nun did not yield it, and Bresal took the cow by force, and gave the feast to his father at Kells. While they were enjoying themselves drinking, the nun came screaming to the king to complain of Bresal. "You have done unjustly," said the king, "to commit an outrage against the nun in the matter of the cow, when she was in her church, and to fly in the face of my kingship and my control, for it is not an ancestral custom for you to do so; and I will have you put to death for the deed that you have done." So Bresal was put to death.

Then Diarmaid said to Colum Cille, "Is there any help for me in this deed that I have done?" "There is," said Colum Cille; "go to the old monk who is on the island, Begán of Ulster." "I dare not go," said the king. "I will go with you," said Colum Cille. Now when they arrived, what they found was Begán making a stone wall, with a damp cloak on him, praying at the same time. When Begán looked at Diarmaid, he said to him, "Under the ground, murderer of kinsmen!" said he, so that he sank down into the ground as far as his knees. "The protection is without stay, Begán," said Colum Cille, "for the reason why the king has come to you is to beg forgiveness, and for you to resurrect his son." Begán raised his right hand, and prayed three times to resurrect Bresal son of Diarmaid, so that he brought fifty Bresals out of Hell with each prayer; and Bresal son of Diarmaid came with the last prayer with the last batch of them.

Irish; author unknown; twelfth century (?)

I wish,
O son of the Living God,
ancient eternal King,
for a secret hut
in the wilderness
that it may be my dwelling.
A very blue shallow
well to be beside it,
a clear pool for washing away
sins through the grace
of the Holy Ghost.
A beautiful wood
close by around it
on every side, for the nurture
of many-voiced birds,
to shelter and hide it.

Irish, tenth century

The Celtic monastic tradition in Europe was eventually overshadowed by other styles of religious community which evolved in continental Europe—Benedictines, Cistercians, Carmelites, and Dominicans *illustrated in that order, left to right;* the roundels from the Book of Hours; the manuscript illumination is twelfth century.

The Benedictine order was instituted in Italy in the mid-sixth century following the rule of St. Benedict. It was introduced into the British Isles by St. Augustine. The Cistercians were a reformed order which took their name from the abbey of Cîteaux in Burgundy, founded 1098. The friars—Dominicans, Carmelites, and others—who became prominent in the medieval church believed that instead of isolating themselves in monasteries they should go out and preach to the world; their concept of religious life was therefore radically different from that of the earlier monks.

Behind the Easter controversy lay a split more fundamental than the simple calculation of a date. In the Celtic Church Easter was the time when man's quest for divine light came to the fore (symbolized by St. Christopher from Jerpoint Abbey, *top left*). In the Roman Church, however, it was firmly associated with the physical and metaphysical resurrection which was precisely dated to three days after the crucifixion (Resurrection by Verrocchio, *top right*). The Easter controversy was thus a battle of ideologies fought with symbols.

The individual
becomes a bearer of Christ,
that is, a bearer
of the spirit of the sun;
not a mere recipient
of the spirit, but one who
receives and radiates it,
as the full Moon reflects
the light of the sun.
Thus, the individual
becomes a bearer of Christ,
a Christoforus.

R. Steiner

The hermit cells on Skellig Michael *(above)* symbolize Celtic monasticism—small-scale, rigorous, and autonomous. Each monastery was self-contained and under the control of its own abbot. Although bishops existed in the Celtic Church, there was no episcopal administration. The Roman Church, on the other hand, reintroduced into Britain by St. Augustine at the end of the sixth century, was centrally organized and under the control of bishops who commanded substantial regional territories.

The settlement of the heathen Saxons in the east of Britain in the fifth century stifled the growth of Christianity, which had taken root during the Roman occupation. Only in the west of the island did it survive, where, as we have seen, having become firmly established in Ireland, the Celtic Church developed a distinctive character of its own. Meanwhile in the rest of Europe the Roman Church continued to flourish, largely out of touch with events in the west.

In 596 Pope Gregory decided to send a mission to the English. Augustine was chosen to head the group, and, after a show of reluctance, he landed in Kent in 597. There he was received by King Ethelbert (whose wife was a Christian) and was given permission to live and teach in Canterbury. Within a few months the king himself was converted. In 601 a second mission reached England with letters from the Pope confirming Augustine as archbishop, and within three years bishops were established in Rochester and in London following the conversion of the king of the East Saxons. Not long afterward, however, Augustine died, and the zeal of the early English Church began to lapse.

Elsewhere in England the Roman Church met with more success. Paulinus, based in York, established a strong presence in Yorkshire and Northumberland. Others followed, and within about forty years of Augustine's landing in Kent most of the

English, with the exception of a few enclaves in the south, had been introduced to Roman Christianity.

The two powerful Christian churches, the Celtic and the Roman, met in Northumberland. The Roman mission had achieved success under the sponsorship of King Edwin, but on his death much was lost. The new king, Oswald, decided to invite the monks of the Celtic monastery of Iona (where he had taken temporary refuge) to restore Christianity to his kingdom. It was in this context that the community on Lindisfarne was established, whence the monks, borne on by missionary fervor, spread Celtic Christianity far beyond the borders of Northumbria. With the Roman Church of Paulinus firmly established in York, it was inevitable that the two churches, with their very different traditions, should sooner or later come into conflict.

The strength of the Celtic Church had been very much underestimated by Rome. In reply to one of the questions Augustine addressed to Pope Gregory concerning his relations with the Celtic Church, Gregory replied, "We commit them all to your charge, that the unlearned may be taught, the weak strengthened by persuasion, and the perverse corrected by authority." If these really were Gregory's words, then he showed an abysmal lack of understanding of the true situation. Augustine did meet twice with the Celtic bishops, but nothing

came of it. The long isolation of the Celtic Church had bred an independent spirit, and its teaching had diverged far from that of Rome. Yet neither Church could afford to ignore the other: Rome's power lay in its centralization, with the pope at its head, while the strength of the Celtic Church stemmed from its missionary zeal.

When eventually the conflict surfaced, it was presented around comparatively trivial points: the method of calculating the date of Easter, the procedure to be adopted in baptism, and the correct style of tonsure. In choosing these matters to try their strengths, it was almost as if the churches had decided to fall back on the ancient Celtic tradition of fielding heroes in single combat to avert an all-out fight which neither side wanted. The analogy is fanciful but not inappropriate.

The Easter conflict had complex origins. In order to determine the date of Easter it was necessary to relate certain calculations based on the lunar calendar with those based on the solar year, adopting different time cycles of 8, 11, 19, and 84 years. The scheme used by the Celtic Church involved the 84-year cycle which had been approved in the council of Arles held in 314. The Alexandrians, however, preferred the more accurate 19-year cycle. After some debate this was adopted by Pope Leo in the middle of the fifth century, and all the Roman churches followed suit. Thus the Celtic Church, in adhering to the old system, found itself out of step. The problem was discussed widely in the 630s, as the result of which the southern Irish Church decided to conform to Rome. The northern Irish Church and Iona and its dependencies remained aloof. The situation led to inconvenient anomalies: in Northumberland King Oswald, who followed the Celtic Church, found himself celebrating Easter, while his queen, who had been taught by Paulinus, was still observing Lent!

The dispute was finally referred to a synod held at Whitby in the autumn of 663. Although only the Easter question was debated, other differences cannot have been far from people's minds. The Roman case, eloquently put by bishop Wilfrid, won the day, but it was to take many generations before the two churches approached each other in anything like unity.

The acceptance by the Irish Church of the Roman method of calculating Easter marked the beginning of the dominance of the Roman Church

and the gradual loss of identity by the Celtic. Easter was calculated according to the Roman system (as in the Easter chart of the monk Byrthferth, A.D. 1011, shown here), and gradually the two churches came closer together.

The pope, Gregory I, the head of the Roman hierarchy, now became the symbolic head of the Celtic Church as well.

Left: The twelfth-century cross at Dysert O'Dea is a dramatic visual reminder of the influence of Rome on indigenous Irish culture. While the cross is in the Irish tradition, the symbolism of Christ dominant over his earthly vicar (the Pope) is Roman. In the late eleventh century a group of Irish monks went to the Continent to settle near Ratisbon. To begin with, they lived in their traditional cells, but after the death of their abbot they established a new foundation adopting the rule of St. Benedict—the first Irish Benedictine abbey on the Continent.

THE HEART
OF MEDIEVAL CULTURE

One of the companions of St. Columbanus was St. Gall. Both men left the monastery of St. Comgall of Bangor in County Down, Ireland, in about 590 to begin their wanderings in western Europe. Outspoken in their stand on the Easter controversy and rigorous in their demands for stricter discipline, they made enemies in the Burgundian court and were forced to move on to the neighborhood of Bregenz, Austria, where they parted. St. Columbanus passed through the Alps into Lombardy to found the monastery at Bobbio, while St. Gall, in 612, settled in Switzerland, where he was eventually buried.

Such was the fame of St. Gall that the monastery which was established at his tomb, in 720, soon developed into one of the greatest seats of learning in Europe, with a library of unsurpassed magnificence. St.

Key to the parts of the ninth-century plan for the abbey of St. Gall:

1. Hostels for servitors, sheep, pigs, goats, horses, cows.
2. Kitchen for guests and guest house.
3. Towers: St. Gabriel's and St. Michael's.
4. Western and eastern paradise (or atrium).
5. Kitchen.
6. Shops (of coopers, potters, grain, brewery, bakery, mill, press).
7. Refectory.
8. Cloister.
9. Cellar.
10. Infirmary and physician.
11. Novitiate.

The famous library at St. Gall contains a plan, drawn about 820, of an idealized Benedictine monastery *(right)*. The illustration on the left, a copper plate engraving, is an eighteenth-century view of the St. Gall monastery. The arrangement was dominated by the main church with its many altars and great western towers. To the south lay the cloister, with refectory and dormitory close by. Farther south were the domestic buildings and workshop, while the monastic farm lay to the west.

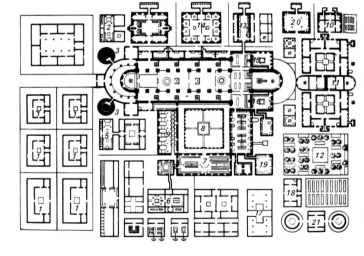

Gall, like Bobbio, lay close to the old road—the *via barbaresca* along which the Irish pilgrims passed en route to Rome. They were always eager to arrive at the monasteries along their way, to have access to the monastic libraries, while the monks, for their part, would have been glad to receive visitors to share their learning and hear news of the outside world. In this way, monasteries like St. Gall became the great cultural centers of Europe.

By the ninth century vast numbers of wandering Irish in organized bands were regularly crossing Europe—reflecting perhaps the innate love of migration which had so characterized their Celtic ancestors.

12. Cemetery.
13. Abbot's house.
14. School.
15. Scriptorium, Library.
16. Sacristy vestry.
17. Barn and threshing floor.
18. Gardener.
19. Baths.
20. Leeching.
21. Chickens, caretaker of fowl, geese, and latrina.

The world has laid low,
and the wind
blows away like ashes
Alexander, Caesar, and all who were
in their trust;

Irish fishermen set out for the catch: a scene that has changed little with the centuries.

Opposite page: The famous Calvary from St. Thégonnec, Brittany.

THE CELTS TODAY

Grass-grown is Tara,
and see Troy now how it is —
And the English themselves,
perhaps they too
will pass!

Anonymous Irish poem, seventeenth-eighteenth century

They constitute a minority in the late twentieth-century Western world—a series of minorities scattered in diverse nations. From antiquity to the present, they have been tossed this way and that in the stormwinds of international politics. And "Celtic fringe"—the term used to describe them today—bespeaks fractionalism and political insufficiency.

Is there more to the Celtic revival than nostalgia, more to their identity than rhetoric and wishful thinking? The Celts of today can point as evidence to the languages they spoke: to Celtic, Irish, Welsh, and Breton, revived by poets and scholars and now spoken daily by many as living languages.

Another sign of Celtic life today, again in the cultural realm, is the survival of custom: dress, music, folklore, old Celtic place-names, and family traditions that derive from the old clans. But the Celts do not base their identity on language and folklore alone. The Celts today may be a fringe group in France and Britain, and a scattered minority in the vast United States—in Ireland they constitute a nation. Whatever the fate of the separatist movements in various nations today, the twentieth century has seen one example of a Celtic revival that is a political reality.

The desire of a people to recognize their oneness and to distinguish themselves by name and custom from other groups is a deep-seated human need. The Greeks might have called the barbarians *Keltoi*, but the Celts were concerned to recognize their membership in smaller groups—each of which had a distinctive name. It is most unlikely that the individual tribes believed themselves to be part of a larger ethnic entity. The growth and spread of the Roman Empire, the turmoil of migration which followed its collapse, and the emergence of modern Europe destroyed the old order, creating new nations and new loyalties. Nations tended to grow by agglomeration. Thus France absorbed Brittany in the sixteenth century, while Britain became, nominally, one nation as the result of Acts of Union from 1536 to 1801.

But these conflations, while in the spirit of postmedieval European development, were essentially political unions. The ethnic minorities of Ireland, Scotland, Wales, Brittany, the Isle of Man, and Cornwall still recognized their own uniqueness, and from the late eighteenth century they have sought, and sometimes fought, to preserve their individuality, first by saving their languages and customs from extinction and more recently by their increasingly loud calls for political independence. To what extent independence is economically practicable is highly debatable. A unified Ireland could, clearly, function efficiently if religious differences among its peoples could be overcome, but few would suggest that a free Cornwall could exist in isolation except as a tourist curiosity.

Devolution, self-determination, and local autonomy have become a significant political issue in the last decade. Sometimes it is confused by the excesses of revolutionary extremism; more often it is made to look irrelevant and ridiculous by the theatrical nostalgia encouraged by the tourist industry. But below these superficial excrescences there lies the simple human desire for identity—identity with a group of acceptable size distinguished by common culture, language, and history. It is in the Celtic fringes of Europe that these roots are most deeply embedded, unmoved by nearly two thousand years of political upheaval. Hardly surprising, therefore, that the call for devolution is a Celtic cry.

197

THE TRADITIONAL HOMELAND

In the Highlands and Islands of Scotland, Ireland, Wales, Cornwall, and Brittany, Celtic culture remains strong, despite centuries of attempted acculturation by the Vikings, the Normans, and more recently by the English and the French. Why these islands and peninsulas should retain so much of their indigenous culture is explained largely by their geography: they are remote, difficult of access, rugged, and comparatively easy to defend. Over much of the area the bedrock is old, extensively of igneous origin, and lacks the fertility of more easterly areas. Moreover, the comparatively high altitude of this fringe of Europe and its exposed position in relation to the Atlantic Ocean ensure an unusually

high rainfall. This in turn has affected soil and landscape.

Although there have been slight changes in climate over the last three thousand years, which have rendered some of the areas once farmed by man no longer desirable, and in the Highlands of Scotland the deliberate harassment of peasants has driven them from the land, the Celtic fringes were never densely populated nor were they highly productive of food. It was for this reason that the Romans cared little for them. Some roads were built and small provincial towns developed in the more accessible parts of those territories which were conquered; but so long as the scattered populations behaved and a constant supply of minerals was produced, the indigenous communities were left to themselves. The land was not productive enough to interest the speculators, who, in the more fertile areas, were developing large farming estates. Much the same was true for the post-Roman centuries, and it was not until union with England and France, in the last five hundred years, that real attempts to colonize the land from the east began.

Considerable areas of the "Celtic" lands are remote from centers of civilization. Large farming estates are still comparatively rare; more usually the land is farmed by family units living amidst their fields in the numerous farmsteads which pepper the landscape. The scene in parts of Wales or in Cornwall is strongly reminiscent of the pre-Roman Iron Age settlement pattern.

Those areas which retain something of their Celtic character are the western extremities of Europe: peninsulas and islands thrust into the Atlantic Ocean. The remoteness of these lands has preserved them from much of the turmoil of folk movement of the medieval period.

IRELAND

In 1801 Ireland was formally joined to the rest of the British Isles, but in 1921 after a serious uprising Southern Ireland (Eire) gained its independence. Northern Ireland still remains part of the United Kingdom. Population: N. Ireland, 1.54 million; Eire, 2.98 million. Gaelic is widely spoken, especially in the west.

SCOTLAND

Scotland was joined to England and Wales by the Act of Union, 1707. The Scottish National Party (SNP) is working towards the separation of Scotland from the rest of the British Isles but lacks majority support. Population: 5.18 million, of whom only 1.8 percent can speak Gaelic. (In 1971 there were 338 people who could speak only Gaelic.)

ISLE OF MAN

Though part of the British Isles, the Isle of Man is administered according to its own laws by the Court of Tynwald. The Island is not bound by British law unless it opts to be. Population: 0.05 million, of whom only 165 (in 1961) spoke Manx.

WALES

Wales was united with England in 1543 and has remained in the United Kingdom since then. The Welsh Nationalist Party (Plaid Cymru) seeks separation, but in 1979 the people voted overwhelmingly against de-volution. Population: 2.64 million, of which 0.51 million can speak Welsh. In 1971 there were 32,725 people who were able to speak only Welsh.

CORNWALL

One of the counties of England largely untouched by the English emigrations of the period A.D. 400–1000. Some sporadic nationalist noises but no serious suggestion of separation. Population: 0.38 million. Cornish is a dead language, but there are signs of its academic revival.

BRITTANY

Brittany became part of France in 1532. Separatist movements, in particular the FLB (Front pour la Libé-ration de la Bretagne), are working towards self-government though with little success. Population (Basse-Bretagne): 1.5 million, of which less than 50 percent can speak Breton.

The "Celtic lands" of western Europe have a tiny population (less than 14 percent of the population of France and Britain) and of this number probably less than half are indigenous. The Celtic languages are spoken by less than four million people.

WHO ARE THE CELTS OF TODAY?

The Celtic lands still show some continuity with long ago. The stone walls and houses of the bare, lonely Aran Islands (*right*) are centuries old; and the parceling up of the land, like the atmosphere of the place, appears to have changed very little since the early Middle Ages.

Traditional aspects of life in the Celtic fringes can still be found, but they are fast dying out except where nationalist movements or the tourist industry are working to maintain them. It is often difficult to distinguish between the genuine survival of traditions and their revival for emotional or political ends.

The traditional costumes of these Breton women are a survival. So too are the Breton bagpipes, but "traditional" music has become a political weapon.

The populations of the Celtic fringes are of course very mixed. Wales, Cornwall, and Brittany were subjected to a degree of Romanization. The Viking settlement in eastern Ireland introduced a new ethnic element, while in all regions an Anglo-Norman or Norman-French veneer can be traced. Yet in spite of this, indigenous Celtic traditions remain strong, and the great mass of the population is of Celtic origin.

The Celtic fringes can boast a strength of 13 to 14 million people—a not inconsiderable number when compared with 46 million for England and 50 million for the rest of France.

The individual characteristics of each Celtic region not only give it an identity but also serve as a reminder of the inheritance of the past. With the growth of nationalism in all areas, folk customs have been rescued from extinction and carefully nurtured to provide a new awareness of nationhood. In Wales, for example, interest in Welsh culture grew dramatically during the eighteenth century, frequently encouraged by the anglicized gentry. The Society of the Gwyneddigion, founded in 1771, was set up to foster an interest in Welsh literature and published much that was in danger of disappearing. Unfortunately, romantic fabrications were interspersed with genuine material. Much the same problem arose when the Eisteddfod (an annual gathering of bards) was revived in 1789. To give the proceedings a greater picturesqueness, a spurious neo-druidic charade was incorporated which still, sadly, is allowed to detract from the authenticity of the occa-

Economy is not easy to manipulate for nationalistic ends. Breton fishermen supply the markets today as they have always done.

sion. The contestants and audience are never allowed to forget their Celtic heritage; indeed, one of the subjects set in the Eisteddfod of 1858 was the capture of Rome by the Celtic chieftain Brennus.

In the Highlands and Islands of Scotland, echoes of the Celtic social structure can still be recognized, particularly in the clan system, which is avidly adhered to by a significant percentage of the community. The organization of the clan under a laird (chieftain) has much in common with the organization of the Celtic tribe, while the fierce loyalties and vicious blood feuds between clans, which so characterized the seventeenth and eighteenth centuries, are a direct reflection of the earlier Celtic way of life. So too are the Highland games—traditional gatherings of Highland peo-

ples—which feature contests of strength such as throwing the hammer and tossing the caber, together with piping and dancing competitions. The need for a dispersed and tribally organized community to come together annually for competitive entertainments is very deep-rooted. On such occasions the gods would have been worshiped and political decisions taken. Now only the spectacle remains, for the amusement of tourists and nostalgic expatriates.

Each part of the Celtic fringe has its own very distinctive characteristics: the deep religious sensitivity of the Irish, the Welsh love of music and poetry, the austere aloofness of the Highlanders—characteristics which have become caricatures in the jokes of musical hall comedians but are not entirely mythical.

Irish villagers stand idly in typical pose, a sign of the times: many parts of Ireland today have a shortage of women.

Cattle rearing is still a vital part of the Irish economy. A form of wealth and status in the Celtic period, cattle now provide produce for export.

Contests of strength figure in the Highland games of Scotland. Much loved by tourists is tossing the caber.

Llanfairpwllgwyngyllgogerychwyrndrobwllllantysiliogogogoch

The Welsh are proud of what they claim to be the longest place name in the world, seen here in the railway station sign.

Above: The handwriting of a Gallo-Roman scratched on the base of a pottery vessel of the first century A.D.

Ogham was a type of script developed for ease of writing on stone or wood in the lands around the Irish Sea. It consisted simply of groups of lines inscribed on either side of the corner of a block, each group representing a letter. This example *(right)* comes from Balla-queeney in the Isle of Man.

The languages spoken by Celtic peoples today belong to two groups: Brythonic (or P-Celtic) and Goidelic (or Q-Celtic). Brythonic is called P-Celtic because *qu* appears as a *p* sound, whereas in Goidelic it remains *q*. The Goidelic dialects include Irish, Gaelic (spoken in the west coasts of Scotland), and Manx; while Welsh, Cornish, and Breton belong to the Brythonic branch. This distribution is the result of the migrations of the fifth and sixth centuries A.D. Before that the position was simpler: Brythonic was spoken in Britain and Goidelic in Ireland. The migration of the Irish westward introduced the Goidelic dialect into the western parts of Scotland, where it became known as Gaelic, and into the Isle of Man; while Brythonic remained in use in Wales and Cornwall and was carried to Brittany by the folk movements from Devon and Cornwall in the fifth and sixth centuries.

The Irish form of Celtic remained dominant in Ireland—in spite of the inroads of the Vikings, French, and English—until the sixteenth century, when English began to take over. But in Scotland the Celtic language had begun to be replaced by English somewhat earlier. In the Isle of Man, Manx was spoken extensively in the seventeenth century but has died out, apart from its use on ceremonial occasions. In Cornwall, too, Celtic expired in the eighteenth century, but in Brittany it has remained. Today about half of the population can speak Breton. Celtic can be heard widely throughout western Ireland though hardly at all in Ulster, while in Scotland only fifteen percent of the population are Gaelic speaking, but they are concentrated in the Hebrides.

In Wales, however, twenty-six percent of the population speak Welsh, and the Welsh Language Act of 1967, affirming the equal validity of Welsh and English, has ensured that in at least one area of the Celtic world the Celtic tongue will survive the inroads of alien languages.

Article 2

The national territory consists of the whole island of Ireland, its islands and the territorial seas.

Article 3

Pending the re-integration of the national territory, and without prejudice to the right of the Parliament and Government established by this Constitution to exercise jurisdiction over the whole of that territory, the laws enacted by that Parliament shall have the like area and extent of application as the laws of Saorstát Éireann and the like extra-territorial effect.

The writing of the Picts, living in Scotland, is uncommon. This inscription *(left)* appears on the base of the memorial stone from St. Vigeans, Angus, Scotland. The minuscule Pictish inscription contains the names Drosten Voret Forcus but cannot otherwise be read.

Text opposite: The first three articles of the Constitution of Ireland *(Bunreacht na hEireann).* The Constitution was enacted by the people on 1 July 1937 and came into operation at the end of that year.

Below: A page from a late thirteenth-century Welsh manuscript, the White Book of Rhyddech.

AN NÁISIÚN

Airteagal 1

Deimhníonn náisiún na hÉireann leis seo a gceart do-shannta, do-chlaoite, ceannasach chun cibé cineál Rialtais is rogha leo féin do bhunú, chun a gcaidreamh le náisiúnaibh eile do chinneadh, agus chun a saol polaitíochta is geilleagair is saíochta do chur ar aghaidh do réir dhúchais is gnás a sinsear.

Airteagal 2

Is é oileán na hÉireann go hiomlán, maille lena oileáin agus a fharraigí teorann, na críocha náisiúnta.

Airteagal 3

Go dtí go ndéantar athchomhlánú ar na críochaibh náisiúnta, agus gan dochar do cheart na Párlaiminte is an Rialtais a bunaítear leis an mBunreacht so chun dlínse d'oibriú insna críochaibh náisiúnta uile, bainfidh na dlithe achtófar ag an bPárlaimint sin leis an límistéir céanna lenar bhain dlithe Shaorstát Éireann, agus beidh an éifeacht chéanna acu taobh amuigh den límistéir sin a bhí ag dlithibh Shaorstát Éireann.

THE NATION

Article 1

The Irish nation hereby affirms its inalienable, indefeasible, and sovereign right to choose its own form of Government, to determine its relations with other nations, and to develop its life, political, economic, and cultural, in accordance with its own genius and traditions.

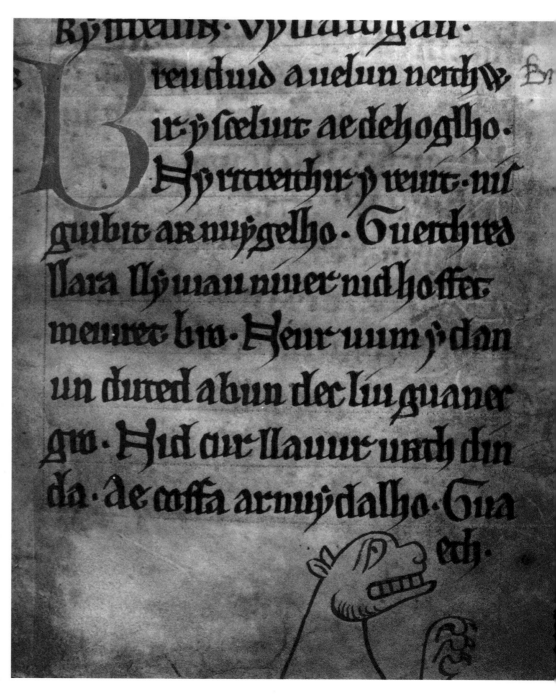

LITERATURE

The great literary traditions of Ireland and Wales could not have failed to make a profound impression on writers of the last three centuries. Patrick Kavanagh's poem (quoted far right) distills the essential truth: without a myth the poet is starved; his work becomes sterile. The Celtic west, with its enormously rich mythology, has sustained generations of exceptional writers, all of whom, knowingly or not, have derived strength from their native past.

In Scotland literary revival went hand in hand with fierce patriotism, but the leading men—Macpherson, Burns, Scott—remained dedicated Unionists. For them the noble Highlander, clinging desperately to the last remnants of his Celtic way of life, provided the literary stimulus. But swathed in nostalgia, the image was romantic rather than overtly political. Scotland had little ancient literature (in spite of Macpherson's dubious attempts to provide it with some), and this, combined with the rapid demise of Gaelic, goes some way towards explain-

Compared to the brilliant literary tradition of Ireland (and to a lesser extent Wales), Scotland and Brittany have contributed little to the modern literary scene. One reason may be that their mythologies had died before the age of enlightenment could give a new impetus to European culture. The thread with the past had been broken and could only be mourned.

In Ireland and in Wales the conscious nourishing of cultural traditions in the

The link between true Celtic literature and the literature of the more recent Celts is tenuous. In the conscious revival of the eighteenth century genuine Celtic literature was rescued from obscurity, but much that was spurious was mixed with it. James Macpherson's *Poems of Ossian* (1765), which he claimed were translations of the Gaelic poems of Ossian, a legendary warrior and bard, son of Finn, were substantially

JAMES MACPHERSON

F.R. CHATEAUBRIAND

LADY
AUGUSTA GREGORY

J.M. SYNGE

W.B. YEATS

composed by Macpherson himself. The spurious *Ossian* became famous internationally: it was well-known by Châteaubriand, republished by Goethe, and inspired the great Hungarian poet Sándor Petofi, who used the image of the Celt to symbolize freedom. Irish literature was more responsibly served (in the late nineteenth century) by Lady Gregory's fine translation *Cuchulain of Muirthemne*.

ing why the development of Scottish nationalism has not provided the stimulus for a reinvigorated literary tradition. Scotland has failed to produce modern writers of internationally recognized stature.

Much the same is true of Brittany. The savage repression of the Breton language by the French killed what little of the Celtic spirit may have survived the Middle Ages. Thus Chateaubriand was left to brood in melancholy on the past, inspired by Macpherson's "translations" of Celtic poetry and Rousseau's myth of the noble savage. He was alone, inspiring few, initiating no tradition.

seventeenth and eighteenth centuries ensured a continuity. The foundation of the Society of Gwyneddigion in 1771, dedicated to the study of Welsh literature, may have encouraged much revivalist nonsense, but it provided a real focus for the preservation of the Welsh language and the development of its literature.

If in Wales literary revival became enmeshed in a nostalgic antiquarianism, in Ireland it took a different course. From the time of Swift it was biting, political, and relevant, but it was not until the foundation of the Gaelic League in 1893—dedicated to keep the Irish language alive and to preserve Irish customs—that Irish literature came of age. In 1899 Lady Augusta Gregory, W. B. Yeats, and Edward Martyn founded the Irish Literary Theater and soon after, with Yeats and Synge, Lady Gregory set up the Abbey Theater in Dublin.

The atmosphere of innovation at the turn of the century encouraged many young writers, but it could not exert sufficient hold over James Joyce, for whom Paris, Trieste, and Zurich offered a more congenial home away from the claustrophobic censorship of the Irish Catholic Church. It is a sad comment on modern Ireland that until recently its most original writers have felt forced to flee to find freedom in which their creative abilities might develop.

Standing back from the great volume of literature produced by these writers, it is fair to ask what, if anything, the Celtic tradition has contributed to their work. There are three separate threads which we can distinguish: satire, saga, and language.

There could hardly be a more damning indictment of English attitudes to Ireland at the time and of the pseudoeconomic nonsense that was being put forward as policies. It was satire of a most powerful and dangerous kind, which would have done credit to a Celtic bard. The satirical tradition was to some extent continued by Shaw but his targets, the morals and manners of the London literary scene, were easy game.

The love of saga can most readily be seen in the works of Joyce and in particular in *Finnegans Wake*, published in 1939—an epic in all senses of the word. It is perhaps not too fanciful to see in its two principal characters—the Dublin publican, who is everyman, and his wife, the quintessential woman, or sometimes the River Liffey—something of the abstraction with which the Celt, listening to his sagas, would have been very much at home.

....I grew
Uncultivated and now the soil
turns sour,
Needs to be revived by a power
not my own.
Heroes enormous who
do astounding deeds—
Out of this world.

Patrick Kavanagh, "A Personal Problem"

G.B. SHAW

DOUGLAS HYDE

DYLAN THOMAS

JAMES JOYCE

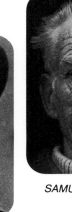

SAMUEL BECKETT

Satire was perfected at an early date by Jonathan Swift—Anglican priest and essayist—whose vitriolic ink flowed against the bigotry of his times. To give one example, in a brilliantly cutting essay entitled "A Modest Proposal," he wrote,

I have been assured...that a healthy child well nursed is at a year old a most delicious nourishing and wholesome food whether steamed, roasted, baked, or boiled....I do therefore humbly offer it to public consideration that of the hundred and twenty thousand children already computed...[one] hundred thousand may at a year old be offered in sale to the persons of quality and fortune.

Finally, we can note language and the Celtic love of alliteration. Compare the sound of this eleventh-century Welsh verse,

*Ar gad gad grendde, ar gryd
gryd graendde
Ac am Dâl Maelfre mil fanieri*

with this description published in 1954:
It is spring, moonless night in the small town, starless and bible-black, the cobblestreets silent and the hunched courters-and-rabbits' wood limping invisible down to the sloe-black, slow, black, crowblack, fishing boat-bobbing sea.

The writer, Dylan Thomas, could not speak the Welsh language, but his spirit was Welsh.

No migration
has occurred in the world
at all similar to that
which is now
pouring itself
upon the shores
of the United States....
In a single week
we have again and again
received into
the bosom of our society
numbers as great
as a Gothic army.

Democratic Review, 1852

THE LAST MIGRATION

The setting of the sun in the west must have had the emotional appeal among primitive peoples that it still has today. The feeling that beyond the Atlantic Ocean there lay a miraculous land encouraged St. Brendan to make his voyage into the unknown. It also inspired hundreds of thousands of Celts to leave their homes to seek their fortunes in America.

St. Brendan's ancient voyage westward from Ireland, out into the Atlantic, was in many ways symbolic of what was to come. It achieved nothing, but then nothing was expected: the Atlantic coast was the limit of the real world.

The discovery of America at the end of the fifteenth century introduced a totally new dimension. For persons forced into a corner by political or religious persecution or by hunger, there was now another solution: to take ship for the new lands beyond the ocean. It was a way out which in the next four centuries was to be adopted by thousands of Celts in their last migration. Among the earliest causes of the Celtic exodus was religious persecution. The Civil War in Britain had brought the Puritans to power, but with the Restoration of the monarchy in 1660 their position became increasingly untenable, particularly in Wales where Presbyterians, who acted as a mediating influence in England, were few.

In two years (1660–1661) ninety-three Puritan clergymen were ejected from their parishes. John Miles, for example, simply gathered his congregation around him and left for America to found a town of his own called Swanzey in Massachusetts. Other sects soon suffered from the displeasure of the crown. In 1677 it was the turn of the Quakers, who were imprisoned and even threatened with burning alive. So severe was the persecution that when William Penn acquired the grant of Pennsylvania from the King in 1681, the Welsh Quakers bought forty thousand acres of land from him and the next year set sail for their new land. In 1683 Arminian Baptists fled from Radnorshire to the outskirts of Philadelphia, and later, in 1701, Calvinistic Baptists joined them but soon moved to a new territory lower down the Delaware. The result of the exodus was twofold: at home the religious communities were so depleted of their active young men that they withered and died; while in Pennsylvania the Welsh community had grown to such proportions that in the early eighteenth century it was even commercially viable to publish books in the Welsh language.

Religious persecution of the late seventeenth century was replaced in the nineteenth century by agrarian poverty as the prime cause of migration. Nowhere is this better demonstrated than by Ireland in the 1840s and 1850s. In the forty years from the Act of Union in 1801 to the census of 1841, the population of Ireland had increased from five million to over eight million—an increase of exponential proportions. The holding capacity of the land could barely contain them, and as the population increased, so the lot of the agrarian poor became increasingly more wretched. Then in three successive years, 1845, 1846, and 1847, the potato crop, which had provided the staple diet of the Irish, failed. The result was misery and starvation, which could be alleviated only by mass migration. In the Great Famine alone, about a million people died, and an equivalent number migrated—most of them to America—cutting the population by twenty-five percent. While the British government can justly be accused of failing to take a sufficiently firm hold on the grossly inefficient Irish economy, no action could have prevented the famine and its consequences.

The Irish exodus to America was not confined to the famine years. Emigrants had left in the preceding decades and in the twenty years from 1841 to 1860 about 1.75 million people fled the country. The next forty years (1861–1900) saw the loss of about half a million a decade. Thereafter, until about 1940, the number gradually declined. In all, America received nearly 5 million Irish Celts in barely 120 years.

The situation in Scotland was somewhat different. Until about 1680 Scotland's prosperity had increased, but thereafter a decline set in, intensified by a series of poor harvests. Viewing the general economic situation, it seemed to many Scots that one way out of their troubles was to emulate the English and, by founding colonies abroad, procure protected trading rights. Many Scotsmen had been included in English trading ventures earlier in the century; now it was Scotland's turn to look after her own interests. Thus, inspired by William Paterson, they decided to found a colony at Darien in middle America, close to the present day mouth of the Panama Canal. In the face of Spanish resistance and totally without the support of the English government, the venture was doomed to disaster. The difficulty of the excessively long sea journey and the fever-ridden landscape claimed several thousand

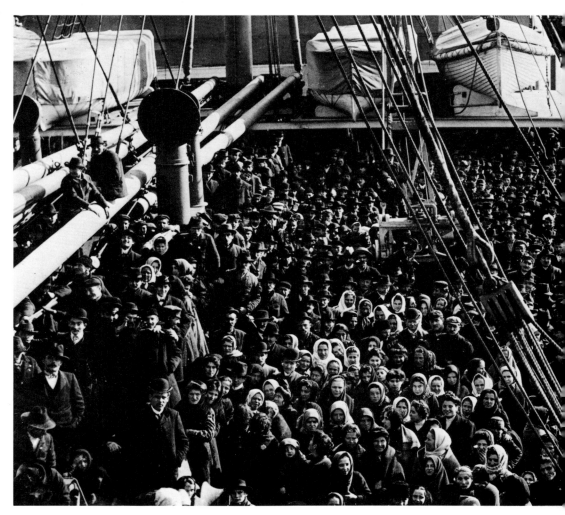

lives, and the venture collapsed in bankruptcy, leaving the country severely shaken and demoralized.

In 1707, within a few years of the end of the Darien fiasco, the Act of Union was passed binding Scotland with England and Wales. In the discontent which followed, culminating in the two great rebellions of 1715 and 1745, the Celtic social system of the Highlands came under increasing

The majority of the immigrants to America were from the lower levels of Old World society. They offered themselves as farm workers and laborers. Most of them were fleeing from religious persecution or from famine. Many came under some form of servitude, having sold themselves to ships' captains in exchange for the ocean passage. Migration was a hazardous business; in the eighteenth century, as many as one-third died at sea from the overcrowding and squalor of the ships. On arrival, the contracts which each of the "servants" had signed, binding himself to a period of four to seven years of work, were auctioned to the highest bidder. In the nineteenth century conditions for the migrants improved.

attack. The clan chieftains were stripped of their rights of "hereditary jurisdiction" and their followers disarmed, while the wearing of the kilt—the symbol of clanship—was forbidden. Even more insidious was the work of the Society for the Propagation of Christian Knowledge whose enthusiasm for setting up schools in the Highlands dealt a death blow to the Gaelic language. The dislocation caused by these sweeping social changes and the effects of the Highland clearances added to the grow-

Orkneymen serving in Canada, but that they constituted four-fifths of the company's employees gives some idea of the cultural impact. Thereafter about seventy men a year were enlisted to serve contracts of five or ten years. Although some returned home, many stayed, creating colonies in Manitoba, Saskatchewan, and Alberta. In these Canadian provinces familiar Orcadian place names—Scapa, Stromness, Kirkwall—can still be found. Although the company's ships ceased to call at the Islands in 1891 the century from 1850 to 1950 saw a constant migration westward to swell the already sizable Orcadian communities of Canada.

Many of the men who sailed from Stromness in the company's ships were craftsmen and specialists—bricklayers, boat builders, and sailors—the kind of men necessary for the well-being of the trading stations. Elsewhere in America in the industrial areas of the eastcoast a different kind of expertise was required which could not be supplied by the sailors of the Orkneys or the peasants of agrarian Ireland but which was fast developing in the coal fields of south Wales. The greatest advance was the development of a technique for using anthracite to smelt iron ore—a method pioneered by George Crane and David Thomas in the years following 1837. The new process at once attracted the attention of the American company that owned the great anthracite beds of Pennsylvania, and in 1839 Thomas

The eviction of Irish peasants which gained momentum after the great famine of 1845–1847 contributed to the tide of emigrants fleeing Ireland. In 1878–1879 the Land League was founded by Michael Davitt to counter the extortions of the landlords. By mass meetings and social ostracism the League attempted to focus adverse publicity on landlords, agents, or those who rented land from which the previous tenant had been evicted. (The word "boycott" derives from one such agent, Captain Boycott, who became the focus of attention in 1880.) The Land League's success can in part be attributed to money sent home by Irish Americans.

Right: A family on the ferry to Ellis Island, the United States Bureau of Immigration's receiving station, about 1900. Migrating Celts, Welsh, Scots, and most of all Irish—arrived in rapidly growing numbers from the 1840's onwards.

ing number of Scots who saw salvation only in migration.

Farther north, in the Orkney Islands, remote from the political traumas which engulfed Scotland, emigration of a different kind was underway. In 1670 the Hudson Bay Company received its charter from Charles II giving it exclusive trading rights and administrative responsibilities for the vast area of Rupert's Land—the territory drained by the rivers flowing into Hudson Bay. The company's need for immigrant workers was met by the population of Orkney, since Stromness on Mainland (the largest of the Orkney Islands) was frequently the last port of call before the trading vessels faced the Atlantic. In 1702 Captain Grimmington was instructed to call at Orkney to enlist a dozen suitable men. Numbers were never great, and by 1800 there were only 416

For many immigrants, the ocean passage to reach the New World was not the last journey. Although the Irish and other Celtic groups tended to settle in the cities of the eastern American seaboard, thousands of others pushed on westward across the continent in the now legendary wagon trains.

Migrants of Celtic origin made an impressive contribution to America's rise to industrial pre-eminence. The Scottish-born inventor Alexander Graham Bell made possible the transmission of verbal messages by electricity with his perfection of the tele-

A.G. BELL

S.M. JONES

A. CARNEGIE

H. LAUDER

J.M. CURLEY

J.F. KENNEDY

was persuaded to settle in Pennsylvania to develop the American anthracite iron industry. It was inevitable that large numbers of miners took the opportunity to escape from the south Welsh valleys to try their skills in the New World. In the later decades of the nineteenth century other skilled workers, including the tin platers from the Swansea area, followed.

Seen from an American point of view, the assimilation of huge numbers of immigrants posed serious problems. In 1840, 84,000 immigrants arrived, mostly from Ireland and Germany, but by 1854 the number had risen to 428,000. The problems of integration of so vast a number of aliens were enormous. Residents feared that they would be swamped, and since the majority of the immigrants were Catholic, anti-Catholicism began to take root. The influence of the Pope was seen as a threat to civil institutions and to republican government. But more pressing were the problems caused in the already overcrowded cities where employment was in short supply. Opposition soon became focused in a political association: the Know-Nothing, or Native America, movement. Few men of stature were attracted to such reactionary ideals—America was, after all, the place where the poor and oppressed of Europe could find freedom—and inevitably the movement failed, many of its supporters transferring to the Republican party.

By far the most numerous of the American Celtic minorities were the Irish. Loyalty borne of ethnic origins and a common religion, and intensified by the force of reaction against it, cemented the Irish-American population and created a powerful political lobby which no government could (or can) afford to overlook. When, in the 1880s, a British Home Secretary was heard to complain that the rebellious Irish were now out of reach of the British government, he was showing an awareness of

The period 1840–1925 saw the maximum influx of British and Irish to the United States. Less than half a million entered America in the period 1820–1840, but in the next twenty years the number had reached 2.4 million. The influx remained steady at about one million a decade until about 1900. The map shows the main centers of immigration from Scotland, Wales and Cornwall (regions shown in brown, cities as squares) and Ireland (regions outlined in white, cities shown as circles).

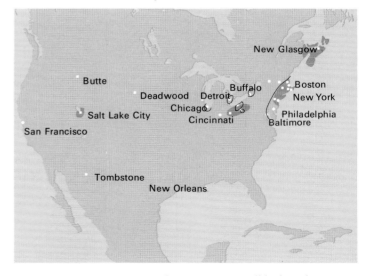

phone. Samuel Milton Jones devoted the fortune he made in the oil business to the reform of industrial practices. In the 1890s he introduced an eight-hour day and a minimum wage for his employees. Andrew Carnegie, of Scottish extraction, was the key figure in the American steel industry from 1873 to 1901. He used his great wealth to support many cultural and scientific institutions. Harry Lauder exemplifies the "Celtic" contribution to American show-business, and through it, to the entertainment business worldwide. J.M. Curley became a symbol of the emergence of the Irish from their

the new political reality. Forty years later Lloyd George could not fail to take note of the opinions of the New York Irish when formulating his policy on Ireland.

proletarian status to political eminence. The 35th President of the United States, John Fitzgerald Kennedy, himself of Irish descent, was also the first Roman Catholic to hold the office.

Each of our Celtic countries has had a distinctive history which has fashioned its political climate and its aspirations, but all are now on the threshold of some degree of independence.

Brittany was first to be integrated with its larger neighbor, France, at the Treaty of Vannes in 1532; Wales followed soon after and became part of Britain as the result

THE CRY FOR FREEDOM

In Northern Ireland thirty-three percent of the population is Catholic. As a minority they have suffered economically from the policies of the Protestant majority, which have, over the years, encouraged the Catholics to emigrate. The Civil Rights movement of the 1960s attempted to right the wrongs by securing civil rights for all. In August 1969 the Catholic quarter of Derry refused entry to the police; the sectarian fighting which ensued marked the beginning of a new era of violence.

of a series of acts of parliament passed between 1536 and 1543. Scotland was added following the Act of Union in 1707, and on the first of January 1801 the United Kingdom of Great Britain and Ireland came into being.

In Ireland pro- and anti-British feeling polarized—Catholics demanded repeal of the Act and "Home Rule," while the Protestants favored "Unionism." By 1913 a Home Rule Bill looked likely to pass through the British parliament. The Protestant majority of Ulster reacted by setting up a paramilitary Ulster Volunteer Force to counteract the Citizen Army of the Catholics. Matters came to a head on Easter Sunday 1916 when the Irish Republican Brotherhood rose up to declare the Irish Republic, but the movement was smashed with ill-considered ferocity by the British troops. All fifteen leaders, having surrendered, were court martialed and executed.

The rising was a turning point: appalled by the severity of the British action, moderate opinion swung behind the Republicans, while Irish-American attitudes hardened against Britain.

In the General Election of December 1918 the reorganized Sinn Fein won 73 of the 105 Irish seats, but instead of sending its representatives to Westminster, it set up its own Republican party in Ireland—the Dail Eireann—whose first step was to ratify the Republic proclaimed in 1916. "The evacuation of our country by the English garrison" was its first objective, and for the next two and a half years it pursued this end by guerrilla warfare with the aid of its own Irish Republican Army (IRA). Repression and counter measures instituted by Britain brought widespread revolt. It was clear to most observers that the only solution was partition, since the Protestant north steadfastly refused to be separated from the rest of Britain. After protracted negotiation held in 1921, the Anglo-Irish Treaty was signed setting up an Irish Free State in the south. Many Irish could not tolerate the compromise: the IRA removed its support, and a period of civil war ensued which lasted until May 1923. It was a confused period in which the different factions maneuvered for power, but out of the massacres and reprisals a mature nation —Eire—emerged. There the situation was to remain until 1969—Eire, a free nation, overwhelmingly Catholic, committed to the unification of Ireland, and Ulster, predominantly Protestant, wishing to remain in the United Kingdom: the tensions and instability of the situation were all too evident.

Compared with Ireland, the rise of nationalism in Scotland and Wales has been a subdued and stately affair. The Welshness of Wales focused, in the eighteenth and nineteenth centuries, on the revival of Welsh culture from which emerged the National Library, the National Museum, and the University of Wales, together with emotional trappings such as the Eisteddfod, larded with its spurious druidic nostalgia. But in 1886 events began to take a political turn with the formation of the Young Wales movement (Cymru Fydd) dedicated to ensuring that the Liberal Party pay greater attention to Welsh affairs. However, lack of leadership and the absence of a well-defined political philosophy led to the rapid collapse of the party. It was not until 1925 that nationalism once again

The Celtic regions underline their desire for independence by the use of their own flags and emblems. *Above:* The flag of Cornwall, the Irish Harp, and the Breton flag, carried by Bretons in a demonstration.

assumed a political image with the foundation of the Welsh Nationalist party (Plaid Cymru), whose avowed aim was to make Wales a self-governing domain within the Commonwealth. As agitation for Home Rule mounted, so the British government responded. A Ministry of Welsh Affairs had been created in 1951, and in 1964 a Secretary of State for Wales was appointed; thus by constitutional methods the Welsh nation was beginning to gain recognition. Meanwhile cultural nationalism gained strength particularly after the foundation of the Welsh Language Society in 1963,

which aimed at giving the Welsh language equal status with English. The election of 1967, in which Plaid Cymru gained seats in Westminster for the first time, marked the beginning of a new era.

In Scotland the many small nationalist groups which had emerged out of nineteenth-century unrest came together in 1928 to create the National Party for Scotland, whose aim it was to press for Home Rule. Further amalgamation led to the formation of the Scottish National Party in 1934, but it was not until the 1960s that the party emerged from political obscurity:

But it would be
a great mistake to believe
that peace
can be achieved
simply by the
elimination of violence.
Those who hold that view
are condemned
to repeat the past.
The sort of trouble
we have seen in
Northern Ireland
has occurred there now
in almost every decade
for the past sixty years.
Can we not learn
from this?
The damage to
Northern Ireland
is great. It is not
measured simply in terms
of lives and suffering
though there
the tragedy has been
on an appalling scale.
It is not simply in the
damage to property
and the bitterness
which follows
from communal strife.
It is also in the entire
fabric of
Northern society.

John Lynch, TD,
Fianna Fail Annual Conference,
18 February 1978

In the last decade separatist movements have been more active in all the Celtic countries. To the earlier concern with cultural identity has been added a move towards political action, ranging from protest to terrorism.
In Northern Ireland, 1,889 people have been killed (1,396 civilians, the rest military or constabulary), while Provisional IRA bombings in England have killed 61 civilians. Financial support from American Irish is a significant factor in maintaining the state of aggression.
Opposite: The burial of an IRA volunteer.

in 1962 it had less than 2,000 members; in 1968 there were over 100,000.

Nationalism in Brittany is strongly linked with the desire to preserve the language. *Hep Brezhoney, Breizh ebet*—"Without Breton, no Brittany"—sums up the spirit precisely; but enforced *francisation* in the eighteenth and nineteenth centuries has so permeated Brittany with French language and culture that separation seems highly unrealistic. The FLB *(Front pour la Libération de la Bretagne)* is, however, active particularly in the university, while the PDG *(Le Poing dans la Gueule)*, an extreme group with close links with the IRA, takes a more anarchistic line, demanding "a fight to the death against the French state." Neither is yet a significant political force. The last decade has seen the intensification of separatist ideals. In Northern Ireland the Civil Rights movement of the 1960s, encouraged by the IRA and by left-wing activists, has developed a revolutionary fervor which has stimulated an equally violent opposition among the Protestant majority. In August 1969 sectarian fighting in the Bogside—the Catholic quarter of Derry—led to the intervention of the British government. Since then British troops have been stationed in Northern Ireland in an attempt to control sectarian strife, but the battle between Protestant and Catholic continues amid demands that the British troops be withdrawn and Ireland be united as a nation wholly separate from the rest of Britain.

In Scotland calls for independence have gained an impetus from the discovery of North Sea oil. Believing themselves now to be economically self-sufficient, some nationalists have pushed for complete separation from England. However, since the inhabitants of Orkney and Shetland, off whose coasts most of the oil lies, wish to remain part of Great Britain, the economic viability of a Free Scotland is debatable. The Welsh are under no delusions about their economic dependence on a united Britain. It is in this light that we must interpret the results of the referenda held in March 1979 offering a degree of political autonomy to Wales and Scotland. The Welsh overwhelmingly rejected the idea, while only about one-third of the Scottish voters were in favor. It remains to be seen what the next steps towards the re-creation of separate Celtic nations will be.

THE CELTS IN RETROSPECT

The Celts succeeded,
under the stimulus
which came to them
from Etruria and Macedon
and Marseilles,
in developing a style
of their own
which is
sufficiently distinctive
to enable our modern
Western archaeologists
to plot out the course
and extent of
these Celtic migrations
on the basis
of the remains
of the Celtic culture
which have come
to light.

Arnold J. Toynbee

The two things, according to Cato the Elder, which the Gauls valued, were glory and wit. The Celts shook the foundations of all the states of Antiquity, but they founded none of lasting importance. The superficial way in which they settled their newly-won territories, no less than their avoidance of water travel and mastery of the sea... demonstrates that this was not their historical destiny. They were bad citizens, but good mercenaries and excellent subjects; they submitted to the Romans with as little difficulty as they conquered in Asia Minor. The national history of the Gauls comes to an end with the death of Vercingetorix, just as that of the Galatians does with the death of Mithridates.

Theodor Mommsen

The Celtic culture as a whole, developing very early on, about 1000 B.C., and reaching its finest expression around 500 B.C., is a fundamental part of Europe's past. This is not to underrate the subsequent influence of the Latin and Germanic peoples on this part of Europe. But the Celtic foundation was already present.

Thus, European culture is inconceivable without the Celtic contribution. Even when the presence of the Celts in their original territory is no longer obvious, we must acknowledge the fact: they are at the root of the Western European peoples who have made history.

Hermann Noelle

The Celts have contributed something that we find nowhere else in the art of Antiquity: translation to, and development in, the third dimension of very largely non-representational decoration, based on a calculated play with curves. It is the finest achievement of their period of maturity. This relief art which, for want of a better name, we describe as plastic, displays the characteristics of molding as well as those of carving and chasing. It has, particularly in the Islands, a softness which suggests polishing; slopes which evoke sand dunes, with their shadows and their sinuous ridges; imperceptible changes of plane, which facilitate the creation and transformation of mass. This

intermediate zone between the linear and the dimensional, between "geometric" curves and the relief figure or motif, is the exclusive property of the Celts.

J. M. Duval

The most striking quality about the early medieval Celtic literatures, the more striking when one compares other contemporary literatures of Europe, is their power of vivid imagination and freshness of approach; as if every poet, gifted with a high degree of imaginative insight, rediscovered the world for himself. Where other medieval literatures are conventional and even hackneyed, early Celtic literature is capable of being highly original. This is not true of that genre which was most esteemed by the Celtic peoples themselves, the official "bardic" poetry, though even there the irrepressible vividness of Celtic thought breaks through. Fortunately other kinds of poetry were composed apart from the bardic, and it is there that the qualities referred to are mainly found.

K. H. Jackson

The ancient Celts bequeathed more than language, literature, and works of art to European civilization: They gave it the heritage of a sensitivity and an intellectual disposition which, down the centuries, remains the protagonist in a continuing dialogue with the various manifestations of the classical tradition. These two intellectual concepts only appear to oppose each other: two systems of thought and expression of differing nature, they are to some extent complementary. A study of the relationship between the Celtic art of the second Iron Age and contemporary Mediterranean art demonstrates this with particular clarity.

Not to recognize the validity of the specific characteristics of the historic Celts is to deny the existence of a deep-rooted dialectic system which has, with remarkable energy over the ages, given form to a European culture, which is an integral part of our inheritance.

M. Szabo

Right: High Cross of the Scripturer, 10th century Cloumalnoise, Ireland.

Overleaf: The Dolmen Pentre Ifan near Nevern, Pembroke, Wales.

What remains from the military campaigns which periodically
shook ancient Europe, and which brought the Celts
to the conquest of part of Europe,
which, by the workings of their own particular destiny,
they had to relinquish under pressure
from the Romans and the Germanic tribes?
Only one of their states was to be reestablished:
namely Ireland.
All their other efforts to establish political entities
belong among the greatest failures
in the history of ancient Europe.
Their adventure,
made up of bloody defeat and glorious
but transitory revival,
and continuous wrangling dispute, reflects the nature of a people,
born rebels against any rigid order,
who could never manage to attain the concept of a state.
And yet the Celts played a great part in history.
Their opponents themselves were fully aware of their importance....

In the course of their turbulent history,
made up of short-lived successes and crushing reversals,
the Celts effectively worked like yeast on European culture,
despite the shortcomings
which prevented them establishing a state of their own.
The rich variety of their artistic achievement, highly developed
both in conception and execution—rational,
but also, as antithesis to the classical, irrational—is a substantial contribution
to the genesis of European art.
Of what survives of the Celts,
their sculptures and decorative art are still today
the most eloquent
and vivid evidence of the culture which united this restless people.

R. Lantier, *The Celts*, from vol. 3 of *Historia Mundi* (Berne, 1954)

So time in its passing
draws each thing forth, with benefit
to men, and Reason
bears each thing
into the realms of light.
For, seeing in their mind how
one thing illuminates
another, men reached the summit
of perfection in the arts.

Lucretius

Caesar, *De bello gallico* (quoted on pages 29, 126, 144, 146, 152, 168, 169). From Julius Caesar, *The Conquest of Gaul*, ⓒ 1951 by S.A. Handford. Quoted by permission of Penguin Books Ltd.
— *De bello gallico* (quoted on pages 48, 75, 108, 110). From B. Tierney, ''The Celtic Ethnography of Posidonius: Translation of the Texts by Athenaeus, Diodorus Siculus, Strabo, Caesar'', *Proceedings of the Royal Irish Academy* 60 (1960): 247 ff. Quoted by permission.
Diodorus Siculus, *Bibliotheca historica* (quoted on pages 5, 38, 50, 57, 82, 83, 96). From B. Tierney, ''The Celtic Ethnography of Posidonius'' (see above). Quoted by permission.
Livy, *Historae* (quoted on pages 83, 128, 131, 132). From Livy, *The Early History of Rome*, ⓒ 1960 by the Estate of Aubrey de Sélincourt. Quoted by permission of Penguin Books Ltd.
Strabo, *Geographica* (quoted on pages 28, 29, 56, 67, 94, 108). From B. Tierney, ''The Celtic Ethnography of Posidonius'' (see under Caesar, above).
Tacitus, *Historae* (quoted on pages 29, 155, 156, 157). From *The Histories*, ⓒ 1976 by Kenneth Wellesley. Quoted by permission of Penguin Books Ltd.
Táin Bó Cuailnge (quoted on pages 70, 77, 178). From *The Tain, Translated from the Irish Epic*, ⓒ 1969 by Thomas Kinsella. Reprinted by permission of the Dolmen Press and Oxford University Press.
Additional Celtic literature (quoted on pages 98, 183, 188, 190, 191, 196). From *A Celtic Miscellany: Translations from the Celtic Literatures*, ⓒ 1951, 1971 by Kenneth Hurlstone Jackson. Reprinted by permission of Penguin Books Ltd.

GENERAL

Allen, Derek. *An Introduction to Celtic Coins*. London, 1978.
Cunliffe, B. *Iron Age Communities in Britain*. 2d ed. London, 1978
Daicoviciu, C., and Condurachi, E. *Rumänien*. (*Archaeologia Mundi* series.) Geneva, 1972.
Dillon, Myles, and Chadwick, Nora K. *The Celtic Realms*. London, 1967.
Duval, Paul-Marie. *Les Celtes*. Paris, 1977.
— *Paris Antique des origines au 3e siècle*. Paris, 1961.
— and Kruta, V., eds. *Les mouvements celtiques du 5e au 1er siècle avant notre ère*. Paris, 1978.
Filip, Jan. *Celtic Civilization and Its Heritage*. 2d ed. Prague, 1977.
— ed. *The Celts in Central Europe*. Scékesfehérvar, Czechoslovakia, 1975.
— *Enzyklopädisches Handbuch zur Ur- und Frühgeschichte Europas*. 2 vols. Stuttgart, 1966, 1969.
Forrer, Robert. *Keltische Numismaten der Rhein- und Donaulande*. Strasbourg, 1908.
Hatt, Jean-Jacques. *Kelten und Gallo-Romanen*. (*Archaeologica Mundi* series.) Geneva, 1970.
Herm, Gerhard. *Die Kelten: Das Volk, das aus dem Dunkel kam*. Düsseldorf, 1975.
Hubert, Henri. *Les Celtes depuis l'époque de La Tène et la civilisation celtique*. Paris, 1974.
Kraft, Georg. *Beiträge zur Kenntnis der Urnenfelderkultur in Süddeutschland*. Bonn, 1927.
Kruta, Venceslas, and Lessing, Erich. *Les Celtes*. Paris, 1978.
Moreau, Jacques. *Die Welt der Kelten*. Paris, 1978.
Nash, D. *Settlement and Coinage in Central Gaul, ca. 200–50 B.C.* Oxford, 1978.
Pobe, Marcel, and Roubier, Jean. *Kelten – Römer*. Olten, Switzerland, 1974.
Powell, T.G.E. *The Celts*. London, 1958.
Raftery, Joseph, ed. *The Celts*. Cork, 1967.
Ross, Anne. *Everyday Life of the Pagan Celts*. London, 1970.
Szabo, M. *The Celtic Heritage in Hungary*. Budapest, 1971.
Todorović, J. *Kelti u Jugoistočno j Europi*. Belgrade, 1974.
— *Skordisci: Istorija i Kultura*. Belgrade, 1974.
Wyss, René. *Der Schatzfund von Erstfeld*. Zurich, 1975.

CELTIC SOCIETY

Cunliffe, B., and Rowley, T. *Lowland Iron Age Communities in Europe*. Oxford, 1978.
— *Oppida: The Beginnings of Urbanization in Barbarian Europe*. Oxford, 1976.
Duval, P.M., and Kruta, V. *L'Habitat et la nécropole à l'âge du fer en Europe occidentale et centrale*. Paris, 1975.
Hallstatt Archaeological Society. *Hallstatt: Kultur und Natur einer 4000jährigen Salzstätte*. 2 vols. Hallstatt, Austria, 1953–1954.
Jacobi, Gerhard. *Werkzeug und Gerät aus dem Oppidum von Manching*. Wiesbaden, Germany, 1974.
Jacobsthal, Paul. *Early Celtic Art*. 2 vols. Oxford, 1944.
Joffroy, René. *La tombe princière de Vix*. In *Monuments et Mémoires de la fondation Eugène Piot*, vol. 47. Paris, 1968.
Kimmig, Wolfgang. *Die Heuneburg an der oberen Donau*. Stuttgart, 1968.
Kraemer, Werner, and Schubert, Franz. *Die Ausgrabung in Manching, 1955–1961*. Wiesbaden, Germany, 1974.
Markale, Jean. *Les Celtes et la civilisation celtique*. Paris, 1970.
— *La Femme celte: Mythe et sociologie*. Paris, 1973.

Megaw, John V.S. *Art of the European Iron Age*. Bath, England, 1970.
Noelle, Hermann. *Die Kelten und ihre Stadt Manching*. Pfaffenhofen, Germany, 1974.
Normand, B. *L'âge du fer en Basse Alsace*. Strasbourg, 1973.
Norton-Taylor, Duncan. *The Celts*. Amsterdam, 1975.
Penninger, Ernst. *Der Dürnnberg bei Hallein*. 2 vols. Munich, 1972.
Piggott, Stuart. *Ancient Europe from the Beginnings of Agriculture to Classical Antiquity*. Edinburgh, 1965.
Spindler, Konrad. *Der Magdalenenberg bei Villingen*. Stuttgart, 1976.
Vasic, R. *The Chronology of the Early Iron Age in Serbia*. Oxford, 1977.
von Reden, Sibylle. *Die Megalith-Kulturen: Zeugnisse einer verschollenen Urkultur*. Cologne, 1978.
Wheeler, R.E.M., and Richardson, K.M. *Hill-forts of Northern France*. London, 1957.

RELIGION AND MYSTERY

de Vries, Jan. *Keltische Religion*. Stuttgart, 1961.
Duval, P.M. *Les Dieux de la Gaule*. Paris, 1976.
Le Roux-Guyonvarc'h, Francoise. *Keltische Religion*. In *Handbuch der Religionsgeschichte*, vol. 1. Göttingen, Germany, 1971.
MacCana, P. *Celtic Mythology*. London, 1970.
Ross, Anne. *Pagan Celtic Britain*. London, 1967.
Sharkey, John. *Celtic Mysteries: The Ancient Religion*. London, 1975.
Sjoestedt, Marie-Louise. *Dieux et héros des Celtes*. Paris, 1940.

THE GENIUS OF THE CELTS

Chadwick, Nora K. *The Druids*. Cardiff, 1966.
Duval, P.M., and Hawkes, C. *Celtic Art in Ancient Europe*. London, 1976.
Jacobsthal, J. *Early Celtic Art*. Oxford, 1944.
Piggott, Stuart. *The Druids*. London, 1968.
Szabo, Miklos, and Petres, E. *Eastern Celtic Art*. Szekesfehérvar, 1974.
Varagnac, André, and Fabre, Gabrielle. *L'art gaulois*. Paris, 1964.

THE DESTINY OF THE CELTS

Birley, Anthony. *Life in Roman Britain*. London, 1968.
de Beer, Gavin. *Hannibal: The Struggle for Power in the Mediterranean*. London, 1969.
Ebel, C. *Transalpine Gaul: The Emergence of a Roman Province*. Leiden, 1976.
Grant, Michael. *Julius Caesar*. London, 1969.
Le Gall, Joël. *Alésia, archéologie et histoire*. Paris, Fayard, 1963.
Schlette, F. *Kelten zwischen Alesia und Pergamon*. Leipzig, 1976.
Todorovic, J. *Skordisci*. Novi Sad and Belgrade, 1974.

THE ISLAND CELTS

Alcock, Leslie. *By South Cadbury, Is That Camelot...* London, 1972.
Bieler, Ludwig. *Irland. Wegbereiter des Mittelalters*. Olten, Switzerland, 1961.
Bowen, G.G. *The Settlements of the Celtic Saints in Wales*. Cardiff, 1954.
Chadwick, N. *Early Brittany*. Cardiff, 1969.
de Paor, M., and de Paor, L. *Early Christian Ireland*. London, 1960.

Dillon, Myles. *Early Irish Literature*. Chicago, 1948.
— *Early Irish Society*. Dublin, 1954.
— *Irish Sagas*. Cork, 1970.
Gsaenger, Hans. *Irland, Insel des Abels*. 2 vols. Freiburg Br., Germany, 1969–1970.
Hibert, Christopher. *The Search for King Arthur*. New York, 1977.
Jackson, K.J. *A Celtic Miscellany*. London, 1951.
— *The Oldest Irish Tradition: A Window on the Iron Age*. Cambridge, 1964.
Kinsella, T. *The Tain*. London, 1970.
Laing, L. *Late Celtic Britain and Ireland. ca. 400–1200 A.D.* London, 1975.
Markale, Jean. *L'épopée celtique en Bretagne*. Paris, 1975.
— *La tradition celtique en Bretagne armoricaine*. Paris, 1975.
O'Rahilly, T.F. *Early Irish History and Mythology*. Dublin, 1946.
Rhys, John. *Celtic Folklore, Welsh and Manx*. Vol. 1. Oxford, 1901.
Severin, Tim. *The Brendan Voyage*. London, 1978.
Thomas, Charles. *Britain and Ireland in Early Christian Times, A.D. 400–800*. New York, 1975.
Thurneysen, R. *Die irische Helden- und Königssage*. Halle, Germany, 1921.

THE CELTS TODAY

Greene, David. *The Irish Language*. Reprinted. Cork, 1977.
Howarth, Herbert. *The Irish Writers, 1880–1940*. New York, 1959.
Hyde, Douglas. *A Literary History of Ireland from Earliest Time to the Present Day*. London, 1899.
Jones, Maldwyn A. *Destination America*. New York, 1976.
MacLiammoir, Michael. *Ireland*. London, 1977.
Marzio, Peter C., ed. *A Nation of Nations: The People Who Came to America* (Smithsonian Institution). New York, 1976.
Merian (monthly publication). Issue on Ireland. Vol. 29, No. 5. Hamburg, 1976.
— Issue on Wales. Vol. 27, No. 6. Hamburg, 1974.
Rother, Frank, and Rother, A. *Die Bretagne: im Land der Dolmen, Menhire und Calvaires*. Cologne, 1978.
Smith, Edwin, and Cook, Olive. *Scotland*. London, 1967.
Uris, Leon, and Uris, Jill. *Ireland: A Terrible Beauty*. New York, 1976.

PICTURE CREDITS

Abbreviations

P: Photo
c.: Century
mill.: Millennium
Ms.: Manuscript
fol.: Folio
v.: Verso
r.: Recto

2 Helmeted goddess. Bronze. Kerguilly en Dinéault (Finistère, France). 1st c. A.D. Musée de Bretagne, Rennes.
4 Detail of bronze flask. Dürrnberg (Austria). Late 5th–early 4th c. B.C. Salzburger Museum Carolino-Augusteum, Salzburg.
6 Celtic warrior in battle. Bronze. Rome (Italy). Late 3rd c. B.C. Staatliche Museen, Berlin.
7 Celtic warrior. Relief. Detail of silver plated caldron. Gundestrup (Himmerland, Denmark). Mid–1st c. B.C.–3rd c. A.D. (date controversial). Nationalmuseet, Copenhagen.
9 Statuette of goddess. Clay. Cirna (Romania). ca. 1500 B.C. Muzeul de Istorie al R.S.R., Bucharest. P: Erich Lessing/Magnum.
10–11 Landscape. P: Hanspeter Renner.
12 Cattle. Detail of a seal stamp. Mesopotamia (Iraq). Late 5th mill. B.C. Musée du Louvre, Paris. P: Hirmer Fotoarchiv.
13 Dairy. Frieze. Tell al'Ubaid, Mesopotamia (Iraq). 4th mill. B.C. Museum of Baghdad. P: Georg Gerster.
14 *Top*: Stonehenge. Megalithic ceremonial ruin. Wiltshire (England). ca. 2500 B.C. P: Aerial Photography, University of Cambridge.
Middle left: Cremation urn from Singen (Germany). ca. 1200 B.C. Badisches Landesmuseum, Karlsruhe.
Middle right: Cremation urn from Ihringen (Baden-Württemberg, Germany). ca. 1200 B.C. Museum für Urgeschichte, Freiburg im Breisgau.
Bottom left: Bell-shaped beaker. Goodmanham (Humberside, England). ca. 2000 B.C. British Museum.
15 *Top right:* Belt boss. Bronze. Langstrup (Zealand, Denmark). 15th–14th c. B.C. Nationalmuseet, Copenhagen.
Middle right: Neolithic axe-blades. Auvernier (Switzerland). Schweizerisches Landesmuseum, Zurich.
16 *Left:* Horse rider on bronze axe. Hallstatt (Austria). 600 B.C. Prähistorische Abteilung, Naturhistorisches Museum, Vienna.
Center: Bronze pail. Hallstatt (Austria). 7th–6th c. B.C. British Museum.
Right: Bronze figure. Idrija (Yugoslavia). 8th–5th c. B.C. Prähistorische Abteilung, Naturhistorisches Museum, Vienna.
17 *Top:* Hallstatt site (Austria). Painting by Isidor Engl. Prähistorische Abteilung, Naturhistorisches Museum, Vienna.
Bottom, left to right:
Detail of bracelet. Gold. Reinheim (Germany). Late 5th–early 4th c. B.C. Landesmuseum für Vor- und Frühgeschichte, Saarbrücken. P: Staatliches Konservatoramt.
Iron spearhead. La Tène, Marin-Epagnier (Switzerland). ca. 250–120 B.C. Schweizerisches Landesmuseum, Zurich. P: From René Wyss, *Funde der jüngeren Eisenzeit, Aus dem Schweizerischen Landesmuseum*, Bern, 1957.
Detail from cart handle. Bronze and enamel. Thames, Brentford (England). Late 3rd c. B.C. Museum of London.
Brooch terminal in shape of human head. Bronze. Oberwittighausen (Baden-Württemberg, Germany). Late 5th–early 4th c. B.C. Badisches Landesmuseum, Karlsruhe.
20–21 Hill fort Old Oswestry (England). P: Aerial Photography, University of Cambridge.
22 Burial practices, Hallstatt cemetery (Austria). Painting by Isidor Engl. Prähistorische Abteilung, Naturhistorisches Museum, Vienna.
23 *Top, left to right:*
(All from Musée des Antiquités Nationales, St. Germain-en-Laye.)
Shell-shaped vessel. Terra-cotta. Thuisy (Marne, France).
Pottery vessel. Bergères-les-Vertuses (Marne, France).
Vessel with engraved ornaments. Prunay (Marne, France).
Vessel with painted decoration. Tourbe (Somme, France).
Right, top to bottom:
Ring from Edingen (Germany). Drawing by Franz Coray after G. Kraft.
Clasp and needle. From a grave near Egg (Switzerland). 1200–800 B.C. Schweizerisches Landesmuseum, Zurich.
Ring from Edingen (Germany). Drawing by Franz Coray after G. Kraft.
24 *Above:* Animal ornament. Detail of bronze situla. Este (Italy). 4th c. B.C. Museo Nazionale Atestino, Este.
25 *Top left:* Horse rider. Detail of Gundestrup caldron. See page 7.
Right, top to bottom:
Iron spearhead with short socket. La Tène, Marin-Epagnier (Switzerland). 250–120 B.C. Schweizerisches Landesmuseum, Zurich. P: From René Wyss, *Funde der jüngeren Eisenzeit, Aus dem Schweizerischen Landesmuseum*, Bern, 1957.
Iron spearhead with long socket. La Tène. See above.
Iron slashing sword. Grandson (Switzerland). 8th c. B.C. Schweizerisches Landesmuseum, Zurich.
Redrawing of military scenes on Hallstatt sword. (Damaged original in Naturhistorisches Museum, Vienna.) P: Römisch-Germanisches Zentralmuseum.
Iron spearhead with long blade. La Tène, Marin-Epagnier. 250–120 B.C. See above (iron spearhead).
Iron spearhead with narrow blade. La Tène, Marin-Epagnier. 250–120 B.C. See above (iron spearhead).
26 *Top left:* Gallic coin with lion. Silver. ca. 2nd c. B.C. Bibliothèque Nationale, Cabinet des Médailles, Paris.
Top right: Gallic coin of Redones tribe with rider. Gold. ca. 1st c. B.C. See above (*top left*).
Bottom left: Musician. Bronze statuette. Neuvy-en-Sullias (Loiret, France). 1st–3rd c. A.D. Musée Historique et Archéologique de l'Orléanais, Orléans. P: Jaques.
Bottom right: Druid. Bronze statuette. Neuvy-en-Sullias (Loiret, France). 1st–3rd c. A.D. See above (*bottom left*).
27 *Left:* Carved pillar. Sandstone. Pfalzfeld (Germany). 5th–4th c. B.C. Rheinisches Landesmuseum, Bonn. P: SCALA.
Top left: Roman coin with Gallic battle equipment. Denarius. ca. 48 B.C. British Museum, Department of Coins & Medals.
Top right: Gallic coin of Aulerci Cenomani with wreathed head. Gold. ca. 1st c. B.C. Bibliothèque Nationale, Cabinet des Médailles, Paris.
Bottom right: Dancing female figurine. Bronze. Neuvy-en-Sullias (Loiret, France). 1st c. A.D. Musée Historique et Archéologique de l'Orléanais, Orléans. P: Jaques.
28 *Top right:* Medieval scribe. Miniature. Bibliothèque Nationale, Paris, P: Giraudon.
Middle left: Virgil between two muses. Mosaic. Sousse (Tunesia). Museum Tunis. P: Giraudon.
Bottom center: Herodotus. Marble bust. Benha (Egypt). 2nd c. A.D. The Metropolitan Museum of Art, Gift of George F. Baker, 1891, New York.
29 *Top to bottom:*
Strabo. From Theret's *Les Vrais Portraits et Vies des Hommes Illustres*, 1584. P: Radio Times Hulton Picture Library.
Julius Caesar. Marble bust. Museo Nazionale, Naples. P: Alinari.
Pliny the Elder. Engraving. Bibliothèque Nationale, Paris. P: Lauros-Giraudon.
Posidonius. Bust. Museo Nazionale, Naples. P: Alinari.
30 *Top right:* Queen Medb (?). Detail of Gundestrup caldron. See page 7.
Middle: Colophon to Saint Matthew. Detail. The Durham Gospel Fragment I. Ms. A.II.10, fol. 3v. Durham Dean and Chapter Library. P: Courtesy of the Dean and Chapter of Durham Cathedral.
31 The Book of Durrow. Ms. fol. 3v. 7th c. A.D. Trinity College, Dublin. P: Courtesy of the Board of Trinity College, The Green Studio.
32 Rosmerta and Mercury. Gallo-Roman sculpture. Musée des Antiquités Nationales, St. Germain-en-Laye.
33 *Middle above:* Celtic coin with lancer. Silver. Hungary. ca. 1st c. B.C. National Museum, Budapest. P: Erich Lessing/Magnum.
Bottom: Ornate sword handle. Bronze. Châtillon-sur-Indre (Indre, France). 1st c. B.C. Musée Archéologique Thomas Dobrée, Nantes.
34 *Middle right:* Scythian horseman. Detail of collar. Gold. Kul Oba (Ukraine, Russia). 4th c. B.C. The Hermitage, Leningrad.
Bottom left: Bronze hydria. Grächwil (Switzerland). 6th c. B.C. Historisches Museum, Bern. P: Schweizerisches Landesmuseum.
35 *Middle above:* Burial chamber of *Hohmichele*, Heuneburg. Hundersingen (Baden-Württemberg, Germany). Reconstruction sketch. P: Courtesy Institut für Vor- und Frühgeschichte der Universität Tübingen.
Bottom, left to right:
– Dagger in sheath.
– Dagger. Iron and bronze.
– Sheath, back.
Magdalenenberg near Villingen (Baden-Württemberg, Germany). ca. 6th c. B.C. P: Institut für Ur- und Frühgeschichte der Universität Erlangen-Nürnberg.
36 *Top right:* Floor plan of tomb at Vix. Châtillon-sur-Seine (Côte-d'Or, France). From *Monuments et Mémoires* publié par l'Académie des Inscriptions et Belles-Lettres. Fondation Eugène Piot. Presses Universitaires de France, Paris, 1954. Tome 48ᵉ. Fascicule 1.
Middle left: Bronze krater of Vix (Côte-d'Or, France). Late 6th c. B.C. Musée Archéologique, Châtillon-sur-Seine. P: Lauros-Giraudon.
Middle right: Detail of Vix krater. See above.
37 *Middle above:* Heuneburg. Hundersingen (Baden-Württemberg, Germany). P: Institut für Vor- und Frühgeschichte der Universität Tübingen.
Below right: Reconstruction sketch of the Heuneburg. Franz Coray after W. Kimmig.
38 Wine transport. Relief from Cabrières-d'Aygues (Vaucluse, France). Musée Calvet, Avignon.
41 St. Gotthard pass (Switzerland). P: Erich Lessing/Magnum.
42 Celtic fireplace. La Tène period. Reconstruction. Open-air museum Asparn a.d. Zaya (Austria). P: Courtesy Niederösterreichisches Landesmuseum, Museum für Urgeschichte Asparn a.d. Zaya.
43 Celtic feast. Reconstruction drawing by Mark Adrian. From Arnold Jaggi, *Helvetier, Römer, Alamannen...*, Paul Haupt Verlag, Bern, 1962.
44 *Top:* Small silver disk. Villa Vecchia, Manerbio sul Mella (Italy). 3rd–2nd c. B.C. Museo Civico Romano, Brescia. P: Rapuzzi.
Middle left: Head of woman. Detail of a statue. 1st c. B.C. or A.D. Musée de Bourges. P: G. Franceschi-Zodiaque.
45 Head of young man. Bronze. Prilly (Switzerland). 1st c. A.D. Historisches Museum, Bern.
46 *Top left:* Small man's mask. Bronze. Welwyn (Hertfordshire, England). 1st c. B.C. British Museum.
Middle left: Bronze belt-hook. Hölzelsau (Kufstein, Austria). Early 4th c. B.C. Prähistorische Staatssammlung, Museum für Vor- und Frühgeschichte, Munich.
Bottom left: Textile fragment. *Hohmichele*, Heuneburg. Hundersingen (Baden-Württemberg, Germany). Early 6th c. B.C. Römisch-Germanisches Zentralmuseum, Mainz.
Right: Celtic clothing. Reconstruction sketch by Franz Coray.
47 *Top left:* Gold bracelet. Waldalgesheim (Rheinland-Pfalz, Germany). 4th c. B.C. Rheinisches Landesmuseum, Bonn.
Top right: Silver torque with iron core. Trichtingen (Germany). 2nd c. B.C. Württembergisches Landesmuseum, Stuttgart.
Middle, left to right:
Silver brooch. Schosshalde, Bern (Switzerland). 4th c. B.C. Historisches Museum, Bern.
Bronze brooch. Oberwittighausen (Baden-Württemberg, Germany). Late 5th–early 4th c. B.C. Badisches Landesmuseum, Karlsruhe.
Bronze brooch. Conflans (Aube, France). 3rd c. A.D. Musée des Beaux-Arts et d'Archéologie, Troyes. P: Jean Bienaimé.
Two gold bracelets. Erstfeld (Switzerland). 4th c. B.C. Schweizerisches Landesmuseum, Zurich.
Middle, below right: Short sword from Hallstatt (Austria). Drawing by Friedrich Simony. From *Die Altertümer vom Hallstätter Salzberg und dessen Umgebung* by Friedrich Simony. Aus der Kaiserlichen-Königlichen Hof- und Staatsdruckerei, Vienna, 1851.
Bottom, left to right:
Scottish cloth. P: Publisher's Archives.
Gaul. Limestone figure. Auxerre (Yonne, France). 2nd–3rd c. A.D. Musée Archéologique, Auxerre.
Helvetian. Tile antefix. Vindonissa (Switzerland). Late 1st c. A.D. Vindonissa-Museum, Brugg. P: C. Holliger.
Female head with torque. Tile antefix. Vindonissa (Switzerland). Late 1st c. A.D. Vindonissa-Museum, Brugg. P: C. Holliger.
48 *Top right:* Three mother-goddesses. Relief. Vertillum (Côte-d'Or, France). Musée Archéologique, Châtillon-sur-Seine. P: Jean Roubier.
Bottom left: Coin of the Andecavi. Gold stater. Bibliothèque Nationale, Cabinet des Médailles, Paris.
Bottom right: Mother-goddess. Detail. See *top right.*
49 Cloaked figures. Relief. Housesteads (Northumberland, England). 3rd c. A.D. P: Department of the Environment, Crown Copyright.
50 *White Horse.* Uffington (Berkshire, England). ca. 1st c. A.D. P: A. Howarth, Daily Telegraph Colour Library.
51 Gallo-roman sculpture from Portieux (Vosges, France). Mid–3rd c. A.D. Musée Départemental des Vosges, Epinal. P: J.-C. Voegtlé, © 1979 Copyright by SPADEM, Paris and Cosmopress, Geneva.
52 *Top left:* Epona. Relief. Limestone. Altbachtal (Rhineland, Germany). Early 3rd c. A.D. Rheinisches Landesmuseum, Trier.
Top right: Rider god. Relief. Whitecombe Farm (Dorset, England). P: National Monuments Record.
Middle left: Gallic horse trader. Relief from tombstone. Musée Archéologique, Dijon.
Bottom left: Foal. Bronze. Catalaunum, Châlons-sur-Marne (France). Musée Municipal, Châlons-sur-Marne. P: Jean Roubier.
Bottom right: Foal. Bronze. Aventicum (Switzerland). Kunsthistorisches Museum, Geneva. P: Jean Roubier.
53 *Coins, left to right and top to bottom:*
Coin of the Unelli. Gold. Cotentin (Normandie, France). Early 2nd c. A.D.
Coin of the Parisii. Gold. Early 1st c. A.D.
Coin of the Atrebates. Gold. 1st c. A.D.
Coin of the Jura area. Gold. 1st c. A.D.
These four from Bibliothèque Nationale, Cabinet des Médailles, Paris.
Coin from Transylvania (Romania). Silver. Mid–3rd c. B.C. British Museum.
Bottom: Cult wagon. Bronze. Mérida (Spain). 2nd–1st c. B.C. Musée des Antiquités Nationales, St. Germain-en-Laye.
54 *Above right:* Coin with chariot driver.

museum, Zurich.
115 *Left:* Salt mining. Reconstruction sketch by Mark Adrian.
Right: Copper mining by fire-setting at Mühlbach-Bischofhofen (Austria). Diagram by Franz Coray after J.G.D. Clark.
116 Wheelwright at work. 17th–c. engraving by J.F. Bénard. P: Publisher's Archives.
117 *Top right:* Cast bronze wheels from ritual wagon from Trebnitz (Germany). Lithography by M.A. Meyn. From *Zeitschrift für Ethnologie*, vol. V, Verlag von Wiegandt, Hempel & Parey, Berlin 1873.
Far left: Genius with wheel, altar and cornucopia. Relief. Carlisle (England). P: Robert Hogg.
Center: Reconstruction of cult-chariot. Dejbjerg (Denmark). Nationalmuseet, Copenhagen.
Bottom right: Barrels. Detail of wine transport relief. See page 38.
118 *Top left:* Funerary cart from Ohnenheim (Alsace, France). Reconstruction sketch.
Below: Bronze hub from cart of Vix (Burgundy, France). ca. 500 B.C. Both from *Monuments et Mémoires*, Fondation Eugène Piot, Tome 48e. Presses Universitaires de France, Paris 1954.
119 Cult chariot. Bronze. Glasinac (Bosnia, Yugoslavia). Hallstatt period, ca. 700–500 B.C. Prähistorische Abteilung, Naturhistorisches Museum, Vienna.
120 *Far left:* Plowing scene after the rock engraving of Bedolina, Val Camonica (Italy). Drawing by R. Lunz.
120–121 Plowstone of late La Tène period. Sketches by Franz Coray after G. Jacobi.
Left to right:
– from Dornburg (Germany)
– from Unterach am Attersee (Austria)
– from Dünsberg (Germany)
– from Unterach am Attersee (Austria)
– from Idrija (Yugoslavia)
– from Mukachëvo (Russia)
121 *Top left:* Scottish crotter using foot plow. P: C. Curwen.
Middle right: Modern plow. P: Gebrüder Ott AG Maschinenfabrik.
122 *Top right:* Plaque in shape of a horse's head. Bronze. Stanwick (Yorkshire, England). 1st c. A.D. British Museum.
Middle row, left to right:
Linchpin from a chariot. Enameled iron and bronze. King's Langley (Hertfordshire, England). Early 1st c. A.D. British Museum.
Detail from a bridle. Bronze. Attymon (Galway, Ireland). National Museum of Ireland, Dublin.
Chariot mount. Bronze. Waldalgesheim (Rheinland-Pfalz, Germany). Late 4th c. B.C. Rheinisches Landesmuseum, Bonn.
Phalera. Bronze on iron. Horovicky (Bohemia, Czechoslovakia). Late 5th–early 4th c. B.C. Nàrodní Muzeum v Praze, Prague.
Detail from a bronze shield. Thames, Wandsworth (England). 3rd–2nd c. B.C. British Museum. P: Erich Lessing/Magnum.
Bottom right: Harness of Hallstatt period. Reconstruction drawing by Franz Coray after D.D.A. Simpson and Stuart Piggott.
123 *Far left:* Silver phalera. Villa Vecchia, Manerbio sul Mella (Italy). 3rd–2nd c. B.C. Museo Civico Romano, Brescia. P: Rapuzzi.
Top right: Reconstructed harness after fragments from La Tène, Marin-Epagnier (Switzerland). Reconstruction by Prof. Dr. E. Vogt. Schweizerisches Landesmuseum, Zurich.
Middle right: Detail of harness mount. Enameled bronze. Santon (Norfolk, England). 1st c. A.D. Cambridge Museum of Archaeology and Ethnology, Cambridge.
Bottom right: Detail of harness plaque. Bronze and enamel. Polden Hill (Somersetshire, England). 1st c. A.D. British Museum.
124 *Top:* Tools from La Tène period. Reconstructions. Museum für Urgeschichte, Asparn a.d. Zaya. P: Erich Lessing/Magnum.
124–125 *Bottom row, left to right:*
(Unless indicated otherwise, all are from Schweizerisches Landesmuseum, Zurich.)
Tweezers. La Tène, Marin-Epagnier (Switzerland). Musée Cantonal d'Archéologie, Neuchâtel.
Shears. La Tène, Marin-Epagnier. Musée Cantonal d'Archéologie, Neuchâtel.
Fishing trident. La Tène, Marin-Epagnier.
Two knives. La Tène, Marin-Epagnier.
Two edge-tools. La Tène, Marin-Epagnier.
File. La Tène, Marin-Epagnier.
Awl for leather manufacturing. La Tène, Marin-Epagnier.
Needle for leather manufacturing. La Tène, Marin-Epagnier.
Cutter for leather manufacturing. La Tène, Marin-Epagnier.
Pick. La Tène, Marin-Epagnier. Musée Cantonal d'Archéologie, Neuchâtel.
Saw. La Tène, Marin-Epagnier.
Edge-tool. La Tène, Marin-Epagnier.
Pointed hook. Port, near Bern.
Pruning-knife. La Tène, Marin-Epagnier.
Pruning-knife. Port, near Bern.
Sickle. Port, near Bern.
Two mattocks. Giubiasco (Switzerland).
125 *Top:* Representations of women, incised on pottery from Sopron (Hungary). 6th c. B.C. Drawing by Franz Coray after a copy in the Museum für Urgeschichte, Asparn a.d. Zaya.
Above center: Snaffle bit. La Tène, Marin-Epagnier (Switzerland). Musée Cantonal d'Archéologie, Neuchâtel.
Above right: Modern snaffle bit. P: Ursula Perret.
126 Rider and two men fighting. Clasp from St. Margarethen (Austria). Hallstatt period. Prähistorische Abteilung, Naturhistorisches Museum, Vienna.
127 *Above:* Head of a Gaul. Denarius. Rome, ca. 48 B.C. Collection ESR, Zurich. P: Leonard von Matt.
Bottom: Praetorian guard. Detail of a relief. Early 2nd c. A.D. Musée du Louvre, Paris. P: Réunion des Musées Nationaux.
128 Horsemen fighting. Belt clasp from Vace (Yugoslavia). Hallstatt period. Prähistorische Abteilung, Naturhistorisches Museum, Vienna.
129 *Top right:* Warrior. Stone stele from Hirschlanden (Germany). Early 5th c. B.C. Wurttembergisches Landesmuseum, Stuttgart.
Below right: Grave mound at Hirschlanden (Germany). P: Landesdenkmalamt Baden-Württemberg.
131 Celt-Iberian warrior. Relief from Osuna (Spain). 1st c. B.C. Museo de Arqueología Nacional, Madrid.
132 *Left:* Warrior. Limestone bust. Grézan (Gard, France). Musée Archéologique, Nîmes.
Right: Etruscan warrior. Bronze. Cagli (Italy). 2nd c. B.C. Museo Nazionale di Villa Giulia, Rome. P: Leonard von Matt.
133 Servian Wall. Rome, section near the Central Station. 6th c. B.C., rebuilt 4th c. B.C. P: Fototeca Unione.
134–135 Etruscan and Celtic warrior fighting. Limestone relief. Detail of tombstone from Bologna (Italy). 5th–4th c. B.C. Museum Bologna. P: Leonard von Matt.
136 *Left:* Head of Alexander. Tetradrachma from Pergamum (Asia Minor). ca. 297–281 B.C. British Museum.
Center: Macedonian shield with head of Pan. Coin of Antigonos Gonatas. Tetradrachma. 277–239. B.C. British Museum.
137 Tholos of the Athena temple. Delphi (Greece). ca. 370–360 B.C. P: Erich Lessing/Magnum.
138 Coin of Eumenes II. of Pergamum. Tetradrachma. 197–159 B.C. British Museum.
139 Fight of the giants. Detail of the great altar of Zeus from Pergamum (Asia Minor). 180–160 B.C. Staatliche Museen, Berlin. P: Bildarchiv Preussischer Kulturbesitz.
140 *Top to bottom:*
Scipio Aemilianus. Bronze bust. Musée du Louvre, Paris. P: Giraudon.
Hannibal. Silver coin from Carthage (Tunisia). 220 B.C. British Museum.
Gaius Marius. Bust. Museo Pio Clementino, Vatican. P: Alinari.
141 Woden. Relief. Detail of tombstone from Hornhausen (Germany). 7th–8th c. A.D. Landesmuseum für Vorgeschichte, Halle. P: Bildarchiv Foto Marburg.
142 Bronze boar. Bata (Hungary). 1st c. B.C. or A.D. Magyar Nemezeti Muzeum, Budapest. P: Erich Lessing/Magnum.
143 *Left:* Lesser sanctuaries inside the fortress at Sarmizegetusa (Romania). P: Roger Wilson.
Right, top to bottom:
Celtic silver coin. Tetradrachma from Dacia (Romania).
Celtic copy of a silver tetradrachma of Philippe II. of Macedonia. Lower Danube.
Celtic billon coin. Tetradrachma from Dacia (Romania). All three from Scnweizerisches Landesmuseum, Zurich.
144–145 Defeat of Roman army. Painting by Charles Gleyre. 19th c. Musée des Beaux-Arts, Lausanne. P: André Held.
146 Julius Caesar. Denarius from Rome (Italy). 44 B.C. Collection ESR, Zurich. P: Leonard von Matt.
147 Julius Casear. Marble statue. Palazzo Senatorio, Rome. P: Leonard von Matt.
148 Migration of the Helvetii. Drawing by Mark Adrian. From Arnold Jaggi, *Helvetier, Römer, Alamannen...*, Verlag Paul Haupt, Bern, 1962.
149 Defensive tactic by Cotta. Engraving from an 18th–c. edition of Caesar's *Commentaries*. P: Radio Times Hulton Picture Library.
150 Statue of Ambiorix. Tongres (Belgium). P: Studio Christiaens.
150–151 Vercingetorix. Coin of the Arverni. Gold stater. Bibiliothèque Nationale, Cabinet des Médailles, Paris.
152 *Far left:* Gallic warrior. Limestone statue. Vachères (Basses-Alpes, France). Late 1st c. B.C. Musée Calvet, Avignon. P: Roger-Viollet.
Center: Outline of siege works of Alesia (France). From Barry Cunliffe, *Rome and Her Empire*, McGraw-Hill Book Co., 1978.
Above right: Coin. See page 127.
153 *Top:* Roman fortification of Caesar's siege at Alesia. Full-scale reconstruction located at the Beaune *Archéodrome* on the Paris-Lyon expressway, France. P: Philippe Katz, Musée Archéologique de Dijon.
Center: Aerial view of Alesia (France). P: Photothèque française.
Bottom: See above (*top*).
154 *Top to bottom:*
Claudius I. Roman emperor. Aureus. Rome (Italy). A.D. 41–42. Collection ESR, Zurich. P: Leonard von Matt.
Hadrian's Wall. England. P: Brian Brake.
Hadrian. Roman emperor. Sesterce. Rome (Italy). A.D. 119–138. Collection ESR, Zurich. P: Leondard von Matt.
155 *Top left:* Defeated Britons. Stone relief on distanceslab from Bridgeness on the Antonine Wall (Scotland). Mid–2nd c. A.D. P: National Museum of Antiquities of Scotland.
Bottom right: *Britannia.* Sesterce. Rome (Italy) ca. A.D. 143–144. British Museum.
156 *Left to right:*
Armorer. Tombstone relief. Original in Musée de Sens, molding in Musée des Antiquités Nationales, St. Germain-en-Laye. P: G. Franceschi, exclusive Editions Arthaud, Paris.
Domestic scene. Tombstone relief. Neumagen (Rheinland-Pfalz, Germany). 2nd–3rd c. A.D. Rheinisches Landesmuseum; Trier.
Tavern scene. Tombstone relief. See above.
157 *Top left:* Hermes. Welschbillig (Rheinland-Pfalz, Germany). Late 4th c. A.D. Rheinisches Landesmuseum, Trier.
Top right: Boy. Marble bust. Musée Lapidaire, Arles. P: Jean Roubier.
Bottom left: Tribute payment. Relief. Neumagen (Rheinland-Pfalz, Germany). 2nd–3rd c. A.D. Rheinisches Landesmuseum, Trier.
Bottom right: Fuller at work. Tombstone relief. Original in Musée de Sens, molding in Musée des Antiquités Nationales, St. Germain-en-Laye. P: G. Franceschi, exclusive Editions Arthaud, Paris.
158 Celtic armor. Limestone relief on arch of Narbonne (Aude, France). Musée Régional de l'Histoire de l'Homme, Narbonne.
159 Head of Gorgon. From the pediment of the Sulis Minerva temple. Bath (Somerset, England). Roman Baths Museum, Bath.
160 Monastery of Skellig Michael (Kerry, Ireland). P: Ludwig Wüchner.
161 High-cross of Moone (Kildare, Ireland). 8th–9th c. P: P. Belzeaux/Zodiaque.
162 *Top right:* St. Brendan. Detail from 16th–c. engraving. P: Mansell Collection.
Bottom left: Dolmen from Ballina (Mayo, Ireland). P: Wolfgang Fritz.
Bottom right: Saxon shore-forts. From *Notitia Dignitatum*, 1436, after a Carolingian copy of a 5th–c. original. Ms. Canon Misc. 378, fol. 153v. Bodleian Library, Oxford.
163 God with horned headdress. Detail of helmet from Sutton Hoo (England). Early 7th c. British Museum.
164–165 Cliffs of Moher (Clare, Ireland). P: Wolfgang Fritz.
166 *Top:* Bronze face plaque. Cadbury Castle (England). P: Courtesy of Prof. Leslie Alcock.
Bottom left: High-cross near Carew (Wales, England). 9th c. P: Werner Neumeister.
167 *Top right:* Inside of a broch. Glen Beg (Wicklow, Ireland). P: Werner Neumeister.
Bottom left: Anglo-Saxon warriors in combat. From a whalebone casket. ca. A.D. 700. British Museum.
Bottom right: Diagram of hillfort of Tre'r Ceiri (Wales, England). Franz Coray after R.C.A.M.
168–169 Breton cliff castle. Cap Sizun, Finistère (France). P: Erich Lessing/Magnum.
170 *Top right:* Martyrdom of Christian bishop. Relief panel from Muiredach cross. Monasterboice (Louth, Ireland). Early 10th c. P: Wolfgang Fritz.
Above left: Sheela-na-gig. Relief from Errigal (Keeroge, Ireland). Ulster Museum, Belfast.
Bottom left: Spiral design on stone grave covering. New Grange (Meath, Ireland). 3rd mill. B.C. P: Edwin Smith.
Bottom right: Hill of Tara, near Dublin (Meath, Ireland). P: Aerial Photography, University of Cambridge.
171 Enameled bucket handle in shape of squatting figure. Oseberg (Norway). University Museum of National Antiquities, Oslo.
172 *Left:* Carved stone from Boa Island, Lough Erne (Fermanagh, Ireland). ca. 7th c. A.D. P: Edwin Smith.
Right: Priest holding crock and bell. Stone carving. White Island, Lough Erne (Fermanagh, Ireland). 9th c. P: Impartial Reporter.
173 St. Patrick. Grave slab carving. 15th c. Louth (Ireland). P: National Museum of Ireland, Dublin.
174 *Top right:* Monastery of Skellig Michael (Kerry, Ireland). P: Picture Archives of the Archaeological Department of University College Dublin, photo F. Henry.
Bottom left to right:
Warrior. Relief from pillar of Carndonagh (Donegal, Ireland). P: National Monuments, Commissioners for Public Works in Ireland.
Stele of Duvillaun (Mayo, Ireland). P: Picture Archives of the Archaeological Department of University College Dublin, photo F. Henry.
Stele of Kilnasaggart (Armagh, Ireland). P: Edwin Smith.
Stele of Glendalough (Wicklow, Ireland). P: Wolfgang Fritz.
Cross of Clonmacnoise (Offaly, Ireland). P: P. Belzeaux/Zodiaque.
175 *Left to right:*
High-cross of the Scriptures. Clonmacnoise (Offaly, Ireland). 10th c. P: Werner Neumeister.
Cross of Ahenny (Tipperary, Ireland). 8th c. P: P. Belzeaux/Zodiaque.
Flan's Cross. Clonmacnoise (Offaly, Ireland). 9th c. P: Werner Neumeister.
High-cross of Muiredach. Monasterboice (Louth, Ireland). Early 10th c. P: Werner Neumeister.
176 *Top right:* St. Columba's House. Kells (Meath, Ireland). Early 9th c. P: Werner Neumeister.
Left: Beda Venerabilis. From a 12th–c. edition of Beda's *Vita Sancti Cuthberti*. Ms. Add. 39943 fol. 2r. British Library, London.
177 St. Kevin's Kitchen. Glendalough (Wicklow, Ireland). 9th c. P: Wolfgang Fritz.
179 The Book of Leinster. 12th–c. Ms. Trinity College, Dublin.
180 *Left:* Last Supper of Jesus and his disciples. Miniature from a 12th–c. Syriac codex. Ms. Add. 7169 fol. 2r. British Library, London.
Right: Vision of the Holy Grail appearing at Arthur's court. French Ms. 112 fol. 5. 1470. Bibliothèque Nationale, Paris. P: Courtesy of Robert Hardinq Assoc.
181 *Left to right:*
Illuminations from the Manessa Codex. 14th c. Ms. 848. Universitätsbibliothek, Heidelberg.
– Gottfried von Strassburg. Fol. 364r.
– Minnesinger Wolfram von Eschenbach. Fol. 149b.
– Meister Heinrich Frauenlob. Fol. 399r.
182 Orpheus playing the lute. Marble relief by Luca della Robbia. 1437–1439. Museo dell'Opera del Duomo, Florence. P: SCALA.
183 Medieval troubadours. Drawing by Franz Coray.
184 The Incarnation Initial. The Book of Kells. Fol. 34. Early 9th c. Trinity College, Dublin. P: Courtesy of the Board of Trinity College, The Green Studio.
185 Portrait of St. John. The Book of Kells. Fol. 291v. See page 184.
186 Typical Irish monastery. Reconstruction sketch by Franz Coray after B. O'Hattrian.
187 *Left:* Tower in the cemetary of St. Brigid's Cathedral. Kildare (Ireland). 10th c. P: Edwin Smith.
Right: Skellig Rock in the Atlantic Ocean (Kerry, Ireland). P. Ludwig Wüchner.
188 *Left to right:*
St. Columban. Engraving. P: Publisher's Archives.
St. Fridolin. Detail on Glarus national banner (Switzerland). 15th c. Freulerpalast, Näfels. P: Foto Schönwetter.
St. Cilian. See page 190.
St. Boniface. From *Liber pontificarum* of Bishop Gundekar. 1071–1072. Gundekarianum, Eichstätt. P: Bildarchiv Foto Marburg.
189 *Left:* St. Columba. Pen-and-ink drawing. From Adamnans' Ms. *Vita Sancti Columbae*. 9th c. Ms. 555 fol. 166. Stiftsbibliothek, St. Gallen.
Right: St. Cuthberg shown as a bishop. Detail of a 12th–c. fresco in the Cathedral of Durham (England).

P: Courtesy of the Dean and Chapter of the Cathedral of Durham.
190 *Left:* St. Cilian. Miniature of the Codex bil. fol. 56. Landesbibliothek, Stuttgart. P: Bildarchiv Foto Marburg. *Right:* Benedictine friars. Marginal roundel from the *Book of Hours.* French, ca. 1470. Ms. lat. 1176 fol. 132r. Bibliothèque Nationale, Paris.
191 *Left to right:*
Felling of the Holy Oak. Initial from *Moralia in Job* by Gregory the Great. French, ca. 1111. Ms. 173 fol. 41r. Bibliothèque de Dijon. P: Minirel Création.
Carmelite friars. Roundel from the *Book of Hours.* See page 190.
Franciscan friars. Roundel from the *Book of Hours.* See page 190.
192 *Top left:* St. Christopher. Relief from Jerpoint Abbey (Kilkenny, Ireland). 15th c. P: Arnold Hintze.
Top right: The Resurrection. Terra-cotta by Andrea del Verrocchio. 1465–1475. Museo Nazionale, Florence. P: Alinari-Brogi.
Middle left: Hermit cells on Skellig Michael (Kerry, Ireland). P: Franco Cianetti.
193 *Left:* High-cross of Dysert O'Dea (Clare, Ireland). 12th c. P: Franco Cianetti.
Right, above: Easter chart. From Byrhtferth's *Compendium of Science.* 1011. Bodleian Library, Oxford.
Right, below: Pope Gregory I. Fresco in the Monastery of Sacro Speco, Subiaco (Italy). Early 13th c. P: Leonard von Matt.
194–195 Copper engraving of the Abbey of St. Gall (Switzerland). From *Idea Sacra Congregationis Helveto Benedictinae anno jubilei saeculares...,* 1702. Stiftsarchiv St. Gallen.
195 Simplified plan of the Abbey of St. Gall (Switzerland). Stiftsarchiv St. Gallen.
196 Irish fishermen. P: Anita Volland-Niesz.
197 Calvary from St. Thégonnec (Brittany, France). P: Josef Jeiter.
198–199 Landscape. From *Ireland, A Terrible Beauty,* by Jill and Leon Uris. P: Jill Uris.
200 *Bottom, left to right:*
Breton women. P: Elliott Erwitt/Magnum.
Breton bagpipers. P: Léo Pélissier.
Breton fishermen. P: Leni Iselin.
200–201 *Top:* Aran Islands (Ireland). P: Anita Volland-Niesz.
201 *Bottom, left to right:*
Irish villagers. P: Anita Volland-Niesz.
Cattle-market at Cahir (Tipperary, Ireland). P: Theo Frey.
Tossing the caber. Scottish Highland game. P: Publisher's Archives.
202 *Top right:* Longest place name. Wales (England). P: Werner Neumeister.
Middle left: Handwriting on a Gallo-Roman pottery vessel. La Granfesenque (France). 1st c. A.D. Musée de Rodez.
Bottom right: Ogham inscribed stone. Ballaqueeney, Isle of Man (Ireland). The Manx Museum and National Trust, Douglas.
203 *Top:* Stone from St. Vigeans, Angus (Scotland, England). P: Scottish Development Department.
Bottom: Page from the White Book of Rhyddech. ca. 1275–1300. National Library of Wales, Cardiff. P: Werner Neumeister.
204 *Top right:* Cattle-raid of Cooley. Illustration by John P. Campbell from a modern English translation of the

Táin bó Cuailnge. From Bernhard Fehr, *Die englische Literatur des 19. und 20. Jahrhunderts,* Berlin, 1923.
Middle, left to right:
James Macpherson (1736–1796). After a picture by Sir Joshua Reynolds. From Fehr, *Die englische Literatur...,* (see above).
René de Chateaubriand (1768–1848). Lithography by Achille Devéria. P: Roger-Viollet.
Lady Augusta Gregory (1852–1932). From Fehr, *Die englische Literatur....,* (see above).
John Millington Synge (1871–1909). After a drawing by Robert Gregory. From Fehr, *Die englische Literatur...,* (see above).
William Butler Yeats (1865–1939). 1932 photograph by Pirie MacDonald. P: The New York Historical Society.
205 *Left to right:*
George Bernard Shaw (1856–1950). P: Camera Press.
Douglas Hyde (1860–1949). P: Radio Times Hulton Picture Library.
Dylan Thomas (1914-1953). P: Camera Press.
James Joyce (1882–1941). 1928 photograph by Berenice Abbott. P: Collection, The Museum of Modern Art, New York. Stephen R. Currier Memorial Fund.
Samuel Beckett (born 1906). P: Camera Press.
206 Sunset at Land's End (Cornwall, England). P: Fritz Prenzel.
207 Crowded deck of the immigrant liner *Patricia* arriving in New York harbor, 1906. P: Edwin Levick, Courtesy of Library of Congress.
208 *Middle left:* Eviction of Irish peasants, 1848. Engraving. P: Mary Evans Picture Library.
Bottom right: Woman with child on the ferry to Ellis Island (USA), ca. 1900. P: Lewis Hine, Courtesy of International Museum of Photography, George Eastman House.
209 *Top:* Migrant wagon train P: Courtesy of the Smithsonian Institution.
Below, left to right:
Alexander Graham Bell (1847–1922). P: Radio Times Hulton Picture Library.
Samuel Milton Jones (1846–1904). P: City of Toledo Public Information Department.
Andrew Carnegie (1835–1919). P: Brown Brothers.
Harry Lauder (1870–1950). P: Courtesy of Library of Congress.
James Michael Curley (1874–1958). P: Courtesy of Library of Congress.
John F. Kennedy (1917–1963). P: Votava.
210 *Top:* Castle of Versaille (France). Engraving. P: Réunion des Musées Nationaux.
Bottom left: Catholic quarter of Derry (Ireland). From *Ireland, A Terrible Beauty,* by Jill and Leon Uris. P: Jill Uris.
211 *Left:* Slag heap at Ffestiniog (Wales, England). P: Werner Neumeister.
Right, top to bottom:
Cornish flag. P: Publisher's Archives.
Irish Harp. Artwork Franz Coray.
Breton demonstration in Rennes (France). P: Agence de Press SYGMA.
212–213 Burial of an IRA volunteer. From *Ireland, A Terrible Beauty,* by Jill and Leon Uris. P: Jill Uris.
215 High-cross of the Scriptures. Clonmacnoise (Offaly, Ireland). 10th c. P: Werner Neumeister.
216–217 Dolmen at Pentre Ifan, near Nevern, Pembroke (Wales, England). P: Werner Neumeister.

INDEX